RIDING THE WIND

Writing for Children and Young Adults

'*Riding the Wind* is a thoroughly researched how-to-write book, well-informed by the author's long career as a writer and teacher, full of practical advice, and written with humility and grace. Novice writer-readers, particularly those interested in writing for children and YA, will find it an accessible clear guide; more experienced writers will be refreshed and provoked into rethinking their own work and process. Unashamedly Christian in its approach, it encourages all writers to pursue excellence and to ride the Wind.'

Anne Bartlett, *author of Knitting*

'*Riding the Wind* is a book to be loved, to have page corners folded, passages underlined, notes scribbled in the margins. Carry it with you on your writing journey; there is no guide as gracious as its author Rosanne Hawke.'

Saskia Capon, tutor and post graduate student

RIDING THE WIND

Writing for Children and Young Adults

Rosanne Hawke

Published by Acorn Press
An imprint of Bible Society Australia
ACN 148 058 306 | Charity licence 19 000 528
GPO Box 4161
Sydney NSW 2001
Australia
www.acornpress.net.au | www.biblesociety.org.au

© Rosanne Hawke, 2024. All rights reserved.

ISBN 978-0-647-53347-5

First published by Morning Star Publishing in 2019,
ISBN 978-0-648-45376-5

Rosanne Hawke asserts his right under section 193 of the *Copyright Act 1968* (Cth) to be identified as the author of this work.

Apart from any fair dealing for the purposes of private study, research, criticism or review, no part of this work may be reproduced by electronic or other means without the permission of the publisher.

 A catalogue record for this work is available from the National Library of Australia

Cover and text design and layout by John Healy

For Mark Worthing
& all my students at Tabor Adelaide

Acknowledgements

Firstly, I want to thank Abba God for helping me write this book. My thanks then go to my colleagues Claire Bell (MA), Dr James Cooper, Dr Juhani Tuovinen, Dr Phil Daughtry, Dr Joh Wurst, and many of my students who helped me formalise this project. Thank you, Rev Dr Mark Worthing, for asking for this book and always challenging me to ride the wind and fly higher.

Thank you to those who have enriched my career including Eleanor Nilsson, Madeleine L'Engle, Katherine Paterson, Leland Ryken, Frederick Buechner, Ken Packer, the eKidnas (SA writers and illustrators), my agent Jacinta di Mase, and all my editors and the hundreds of authors whose work I've read who inspired me and still do.

Thank you also to Dr James Cooper and Saskia Capon for reading drafts and your helpful comments; thank you so much, Claire Bell, for your excellent editing and suggestions for Riding the Wind, to Amanda McKenna and the team at Morning Star Publishing, to Eleanor Nilsson, Saskia Capon and Anne Bartlett for your generous endorsements, and Professor Emeritus Leland Ryken for being so kind and gracious to write the preface.

I acknowledge and thank the following authors for their kind permission to quote their inspiring words: Kathryn Apel, Claire Belberg, Christina Booth, Janeen Brian, Susan J Bruce, James Cooper, DM Cornish, PH Court, Joy Cowley, Phil Cummings, Sally Dixon, Elizabeth Fensham,

Christina Booth, Janeen Brian, Susan J Bruce, James Cooper, DM Cornish, PH Court, Joy Cowley, Phil Cummings, Sally Dixon, Elizabeth Fensham, Sally Heinrich, Penny Jaye, Andrew Lansdown, May-Kuan Lim, Alison Lloyd, Lorraine Marwood, Glenda Millard, Scott Monk, Wendy Noble, Lisa Shanahan, Elizabeth Snow, Catch Tilly, Colleen Tuovinen, Jade Wyatt and Claire Zorn. If what they have contributed here has inspired you, do check out their details in the chapter notes and read their books/websites.

Contents

Acknowledgements..5

Preface..8

Introduction – Riding the Wind...11

1. A Writing Life..16
2. Children's Literature..39
3. Keeping Fit: Writing and Storytelling..48
4. Characters Can Write Your Story..58
5. Character and Plot..74
6. Writing Short Stories..89
7. Writing Picture Books..100
8. Writing Chapter Books...130
9. Writing Novels for Middle Grade, 9-12 years.........................143
10. Crossing Borders: Writing for Middle School and YA..........188
11. Rewriting and Editing as Writers...224
12. Reflecting On Our Writing...251
13. Writing for Children Matters..262
14. Preparing to Publish...286
15. A Publishing Story...296
16. Being an Author...308

Reading Lists..334

Chapter Notes...345

Preface

My brief commendation of *Riding the Wind* is that I like everything about it! Since more than that is expected in a preface, I will proceed to name the particular virtues of the book. Novelist EM Forster famously said that a story can have only one merit – that of making a reader want to know what happens next. Rosanne Hawke's book about writing makes the grade, being what is commonly called a page turner. Every page puts new material and fresh insights before its readers, and I found myself eager to see what the author would say about the next topic.

The primary beneficiary of this book is literary authors, who naturally want to know how to write in various genres and how to manage the publication process. I cannot imagine a better instruction book than this one for writers who are early in their careers. As a professor and reader of literature, I found myself equally interested in what Hawke says. People who love literature are naturally interested in the process by which literature is created, and additionally our theory of literature is based partly on what we know about the writing of it.

An obvious virtue of the book is its practical orientation. Hawke wants to make a difference in the lives of writers, so she sets about telling them how to do it. The advice has authority because Hawke is a professional writer and teacher of writing who has both the fund of information and the record of success to command a hearing. The continuous appeals to personal experience, buttressed by statements of other writers, lend a narrative quality to the book, as we listen to the story of how to be a writer.

Another virtue of the book is its scope. It covers all of the important topics. I was continually delighted by how the author speaks to every aspect of writing of interest to me, and then I was even more entertained by answers to questions that I would never have thought to ask. I do not hesitate to call this a 'no stone unturned' book on the subject of writing. Variety of content is a leading merit of the book, leading me to add the label 'never a dull moment.'

While it would have been a treat just to know what Rosanne Hawke has to impart about writing, her book also draws upon the insights of the whole guild of authors. The breadth of reading and research that feeds into the book is one of its greatest achievements.

A final genre into which I would place the book is that of a behind-the-scenes book. We all know the appeal of being taken behind the scenes of an event or performance. As a reader rather than writer of literature, I felt that this book showed me what the writing life is really like. This 'backstage visit' is both informative and entertaining.

This book has something for everyone. For aspiring writers, it is a practical 'how-to-do-it' manual of the highest quality. For people who read rather than write literature, it is a book of literary theory, imparting viewpoints on what literature is and how the thing we love is produced. For everyone who is curious about the writing life, here is a chance to find out. By the time I had finished, I felt that I had read the literary autobiography of someone I had come to admire very much.

Leland Ryken, Professor Emeritus of English,
Wheaton College, Illinois, 2019.

*He makes the clouds his chariot and
rides on the wings of the wind.* Psalms 104:3

Introduction – Riding the Wind

Writing for children is what I imagine riding the wind would be like; that rush of exhilaration, the soaring of ideas and creativity, the hanging on for dear life in case I fall off, but also the total satisfaction of doing what I was born to do, however hard it may be. In this book I want to share what that ride has been like. When I began writing for children, some people didn't take it seriously. When an early novel was launched a man asked me a question that most children's authors have heard at least once: 'When are you going to write a real book? Haven't you practised enough on kids' books?' He wanted an adult book, one he thought he would enjoy reading. He didn't know what an art form children's and young adult (YA) literature can be and how many adults read it for their own pleasure. May we never grow up if it means we cannot enjoy children's literature.

My students asked if I could treat this writing book as a memoir, keeping it personal by sharing how I became a writer and the writing practice that I've developed over the past twenty-five years to secure a younger reader's approval. They wanted anecdotes and tips from my writing life and practice, but I've also added comments from other writers since no two writers' processes are the same. I'll cover the tools that help me, including my worldview and faith, creative journals, reading logs, work environment, attitude, as well as what I've learned about character development and the writing of different forms of children's and YA books in the market. To quote one of John Marsden's titles, there's so much to tell you, but I'll aim to be brief. A book like this is never finished; by the time this goes to print I'll think of more to add or change. There are reading lists of resources at the back for more research. I also acknowledge that everything I know which isn't personal experience has developed through what I've learned from reading and sharing with other writers and students. We don't create in a vacuum, but from the stimuli that affect us every day.

When discussing the different types of writing for children (novels, picture books and so on) I give each form a section of its own, including the elements that need to be considered. This is in case some readers only want to read about novels or picture books. In this book I start with short stories as I find these are what most people I teach have attempted before taking a class. Picture books and chapter books are difficult to write, so I discuss them next, once a new writer becomes more used to writing for the younger age group.

However, I give character development an early chapter as it is my belief that character is the scaffold upon which all else in the story builds, and all forms of writing need to construct it strongly for the story to work. Although this book deals mainly with writing for children, I include a chapter on young adult writing as legally many YA characters are still children. This is probably why writers like me, who write for both

Introduction – Riding the Wind

children and YA, are still referred to as children's authors.

In the chapter called 'Keeping Fit' I show how quick/free writing and writing exercises help us to practise our craft. The 'Workout' suggestions in other chapters are more considered tasks that may have bearing on works in progress. Chapters are also included on some of the issues I have dealt with as a children's author as well as the ethics of working in this industry that have helped me along the way.

In Tabor Adelaide, the tertiary institution where I've taught part-time since 2006, students are required to study Introduction to Creative Writing before attempting Writing for Children; that is, the subject Writing for Children is considered a second-year subject and for good reason. Writing for children is harder than people think, but not impossible.

My students also suggested making this book accessible so that not only students will read it, but also new writers, or even those who enjoy reading about the journeys of other writers. It's good to remember that, whatever stage we are at in our writing career, we are always learning and becoming better writers.

I have a passion for encouraging people to write well. When we write and create (or co-create) we are doing what God loves doing: creating. Also, learning our craft well gives him glory. For me, writing is like prayer, as if I am writing in the presence of God, much like riding the wind. In this way our work becomes worship.

Can creative writing be taught?

Gifts, talents, perhaps even passion or vision cannot be taught, although they can be encouraged. But if I said teaching creative writing is a waste of time then I'd be lacking integrity writing this book. I wrote my first novel because my daughter wanted a book of her own. It was rejected. I gave it to a journalist friend, Ken Packer, to look at it for me. He taught me about point of view. When I re-wrote it, with the point of view changed, it read much better.

Each time an editor writes her suggestions on my manuscript I learn new techniques and I try not to make those mistakes again. So I believe the craft of writing, or the technical side of writing, can be learned. Because of this I think of myself as a facilitator of learning. A facilitator/teacher can discuss with others all she's learnt on her journey, and a critique group can also become a support that can guide and sustain us. If we are serious about writing we'll find others who are too, and be able to safely share our work with them. Thus we learn from each other.

Taking writing workshops inspired and taught me as well. When I studied for a PhD in Creative Writing, I realised I could write better than I knew. The manuscript of *Zenna Dare* was in my portfolio to enter the BA Honours program, and the *Wolfchild* manuscript became my Honours thesis which gained me entry into the PhD program. Studying with clever young BA graduates, and supervisors like Dr Eva Hornung (then Sallis), Kerryn Goldsworthy and Emeritus Professor Thomas Shapcott, helped me to write better and I learned much more about rewriting. It's been said by many that we are not writers but rewriters. Not everyone thinks of that perfect image in the first draft. We all improve as we practise our craft, but I found a course of study did fast track my progress.

However, the time when I learned the most about writing was when I was lecturing, helping others to understand how to hone their skills. It became a two-way street where we gained knowledge from each other.

1

A Writing Life

Dreams, goals and writerly thinking

Now we feel like jumping in feet first to begin this fabulous journey of writing for children, but I've found that we need to develop a writing life with a writerly mindset to make sure we make it out to the ocean.

First, it's important to know the difference between goals and dreams. Do you have the dream of having a children's book published? So did I, but what makes that dream happen, besides prayer or wishing? Can we control a dream? Dreams are good to have because they force us to make goals. To get a book published we can make a goal of writing 1000 words a day. Or we can make a goal of taking a class or joining a writing group to learn more. We need to set goals to bring us closer to the dream. When we've done all we can and submitted our story to a magazine or publisher, then it is out of our hands. We cannot control what the professional reader or editor will think of our work. That's when I start a new project to take my mind elsewhere.

So what is your long term goal? What smaller goals will you set to achieve it?

There's power in writing out a goal. I often plan my goals for a project or a life decision with a mind map (these are explained more in Chapter 4). The goals focus my mind so I'm clear about what to achieve. In the beginning of my writing career I prayed to discover what really mattered to me. I wanted to write to glorify God. And this is another important thing: what is your worldview? What are your values? Your beliefs about life and your place in it? These will affect your writing habit and also what you write. They will also affect what you think about yourself and your abilities.

Keep positive. It helps to write a list of things you can do well in your writing, and then a list of things you want to learn, and will learn. Value yourself as God values you. You are unique, with special skills. You are a writer. You have something to offer. Your brain acts on what your mind tells it. I've believed this for quite a while, so it's exciting to hear that neuroscientists are proving this is true. So tell your brain you're a writer and that you can finish the book you are working on. Take the focus from your weaknesses. Don't forget to make your goals achievable and bite-sized at first, then to reward yourself when a goal is achieved.

When my first book was released a wise lady prayed for me and my new career. She had a vision that I was happy, standing with a rose bowl in my hands; she presumed something good would happen, but she didn't know when that would be. It was a confirmation for me to keep on with my writing career. A call to write kept me focussed and positive in writing. Having a belief that writing is what God wanted me to do to glorify him kept me going through the rejections, publishing houses folding and the lean times. Madeleine L'Engle talked about the artist as being a servant who is willing to be a birthgiver.[1] Like Mary, who was called to give birth, so I felt called to write.

To keep on task I often make mission statements for a project I am working on: what is the goal that I am achieving? I keep it in the present tense. This helps me keep a positive mental attitude. An overall mission statement about our goals can help us with what we want to be and want to achieve in our lives. A book won't usually be written by someone who doesn't care whether they do it or not. Nor will it be written by a person who has little confidence in her creative abilities.

Once I wrote in a journal: *I am an author writing affirming books for children.* Another time I wrote this from Micah 6:8 as my career mission statement: *And what does the Lord require of you? To act justly and to love mercy and to walk humbly with your God.*

Are you creative?

At the beginning of each semester I tell my new students that they are all creative. Some drop eye contact. They are in a writing class, so they either know they are creative, or they think the class will make them so. 'I don't think I'm creative,' one will venture. Then I tell them how I know they are creative. 'We are all individual children of a creator God who loves creating things. We are made in his image. Do you think he'd miss out something as important as our creativity? A few visibly brighten. I ask them to write in their journal these words from the classic book, *If You Want to Write* (1938, 1987) by writer and teacher Brenda Ueland:

> Everybody is talented because everybody who is human has something to express.
>
> ...
>
> Everybody is original, if he tells the truth, if he speaks from himself.[2]

A Writing Life

There are many books written about developing creativity. Some explain how the right side of your brain is creative like Tony Buzan's work[3] with mind maps or that of Henrietta Anne Klauser.[4]

Readers often ask me about that first idea, the first spark of creativity that begins a book. This is how my YA novel *The Messenger Bird* (2013) was conceived:

> 'Play some more.' It's what I always call from my room when my father plays the piano late at night after coming in from the paddock, especially 'The Maiden's Prayer'. It is my favourite – maybe it is his too, for he plays it again until I fall asleep.
>
> Imagine forty years later finding that same piece of music, yellowed and curled at the edges, in a box of your father's effects. You can play it yourself now, and you almost hear the echo of a little voice, 'Play some more.' So you play it again, and you realise with a start that the voice is not an echo after all, but a warm sense of your father's closeness.
>
> When that happened to me, I decided music has the power to do almost anything – instigate a story, make something magical happen, be a link of communication between people, even bring someone from the past. In that moment [*The Messenger Bird*] was conceived – that first spark of creativity that has been described by Krauss as 'a burst of an instantaneous and originary act'.[5]

When NZ author Sherryl Jordan was asked how she thought up her ideas, she said this:

> I don't. Books 'appear' to me like movies in my head, all in the space of a few seconds. However, I may think about the book, and do research for many months before I begin writing.[6]

Recently I've found a problem keeping my equilibrium with my creativity since I've started walking in the mornings. On hot days I have to walk as soon as I wake and I miss that early time where creativity rises to the surface after sleep. This is my morning reflection time when I write spontaneously and catch ideas to fix my plots. This flows into prayer, which leads to writing. I've realised I still have to let that happen before I walk. When I don't, I can end up cleaning the house!

Pastor and blogger, Alison Sampson, writes about creativity and faith in her article, 'Prayer as the birthplace of Creativity'. She says the way she writes is no secret. 'Listening to the quiet voice, or the silence, is also the way I write. My experience of this [meditative] form of prayer is inseparable from my writing practice.'[7] Nor could I write a book from a single idea without prayer and the presence of God. Some artists speak of being like an aerial tuned into a muse or the universe. For me, the aerial is the presence of God and his Spirit is the source I'm tapping into for ideas and creativity.

Author Madeleine L'Engle believes creativity opens us up to revelation. 'In the act of creativity, the artist lets go of the self-control which he normally clings to, and is open to riding the wind.'[8]

The Creative Call by Janice Elsheimer (2001) is a helpful book reminiscent of *The Artist's Way* by Julia Cameron (1992). Elsheimer shows how to recognise and develop our creativity and to practise one's art in order to discover a deeper relationship with God. As Elsheimer points out, most artists see that creativity and spiritual growth are related, but she goes a step further: she understands the need to reconnect our talents back to God who created us and who calls us to be a co-creator with him.[9]

Tip
Find out when you do your best spontaneous writing where ideas flow, and guard it.

Guest Author — PH Court[10]
Three Creative Things

There are three things about highly creative people that stand out, but aren't what you might expect.

It's no mystical, magical thing. Isn't being truly creative all about being free, ethereal or just committed to letting it flow? Sure, inspiration is pretty wonderful but creativity, inspiration, the making of something unique, requires direction. Without a purpose, without a direction, creativity shrivels up and dies. It needs somewhere to go. So, first, creativity needs a purpose.

Second, creativity requires discipline. Again, not what we expect. We love the idea of sleeping late, maybe doing some stuff, then sitting back and being applauded for our amazing creativity. But it doesn't work like that. Successful, highly creative people have incredible discipline. Setting aside regular time to deliberately hone and shape their art is vital. Sure, inspiration will strike at 4 am or in the bath, but turning inspiration into a creative product that you can share with others, that takes discipline. Deliberately set aside time to create.

Finally, and most counter-intuitive of all, creativity needs rest. The most energy hungry part of your body is your brain. When you are in that time of disciplined creation, your brain is chewing through energy like an elite athlete. So, seriously, you need to be physically fit. But also, just like an athlete after a heavy training session, when you reach the end of your creative time, when a comedian steps off stage, when the musician stops composing or the writer pauses, you need to rest. Just rest. Do something totally mentally untaxing. Some very creative people refer to their 'post performance depression'. This is why that happens. It's not a bad thing, it's expected and is part of your creative life. Enjoy the rest, knowing that because you are disciplined, you can soon return to your passion, refreshed.

A writer's values

What are your values? These will be different for each person depending on worldview. A major part of our worldview is what we believe. Even when a person is an atheist, that person has a belief that God does not exist.

If you know what you stand for, you are on the road to reaching your goal. So decide what your major purpose is. What really matters to you? What is important enough to write about?

- What do you think of failure? Choose not to fear it. Each step, each critique, each rejection from a publisher is teaching you how to be a better writer. Also, knowing what you are trying to accomplish and why will help you sustain passion. Psalm 62 says there is no risk of failure with God, so why should we worry?
- Are you a perfectionist? Some writers won't start for they believe they won't do it well enough. We need to be sensible: new writers do not immediately write like Jane Austen or Wendy Orr. Maybe you will never write like an award-winning writer, but you will write the stories you are meant to. Unrealistic expectations like this lead to disappointment. Stop negative self-talk and be kind to the writer in you as you would be to another writer. Aim for excellence, not perfection. We can give God our best, be original and creative like him.
- Do you compare yourself or your writing to others in a negative way? Apparently, Mark

Twain said that comparison is the death of joy. As artists, we can never compare our work to another's in a way that could lead to jealousy, or even depression. When a book wins an award for which mine had also been a runner up, I need to thank God for that author's gift and God's blessing to him or her. And learn more about the craft from them. Let's not be threatened by another writer's talent, but rather be grateful for it. It is difficult being jealous of others when you are thankful for them. Rory Noland (1999) has excellent tips for having peace as an artist in his book *The Heart of the Artist*.[11]

- Star or servant? Our attitude can be one of humility as Lisa Shanahan's piece below shows, or we can act the part of the star and expect everything to happen for us. Fortunately, I haven't seen children's authors act like this in twenty–five years of working in the industry. Be sensitive if you suspect another writer is jealous of you. The people who truly have talent or success in publishing never need to flaunt it.

What does success mean to you?

I've seen a lot of complicated answers to this question, but success is actually achieving a goal. Therefore, affirming we have achieved a goal is important to our concept of success. Don't fear success either. I was so nervous before my first book was released that I wrote a poem about being a tiny animal in a shell and the tide washes me out into the public eye. That first book coming out, and subsequent ones, was scary. I have found it best to leave my personal success in God's hands.

Lisa Shanahan's response to having two of her books shortlisted in the 2018 Children's Book Council Awards shows the humility of a great writer when faced with success:

> I was astounded to discover that *Hark, It's Me, Ruby Lee!* and *The Grand, Genius Summer of Henry Hoobler* were both short-listed in the Children's Book Council Book of the Year Awards yesterday. I'm very grateful and quite undone. Even though writing is so solitary at times, I'm aware that writing a book is always done in community; that every book is in conversation in some way with other books, both past, present and future. It's a beautiful thing to be part of the children's book community in Australia. It's hard to articulate the debt I owe. I know for certain that all the good things I've ever learnt and am still learning about writing (because the apprenticeship never ends) have always come from the grand, genius goodness of sitting at the feet of the many brilliant writers and illustrators from this community.[12]

US literary agent, Steve Laube, says the secret to defining success for yourself is not in comparing numbers of sales and awards but being obedient to the task. When you focus on yourself, it goes back to 'me, myself, and I,' and you get wrapped up in yourself – in self-doubt, self-criticism – and you begin to worry, and worry eats away at your soul.[13] We need to focus on doing our best for God's glory, while praying and trusting that God's glory will be magnified in the work that we do.

Workspace

My writing life began on my bed in Pakistan. As I was writing the first draft of *Jihad* (1996) I became sick. I soon grew better, but while I was in bed people left me alone, so I kept writing that draft in bed. When we moved back to Australia to a house with three bedrooms to share between five of us, I wrote on my bed again. A friend gave me a desk that would fit in our little bedroom and I wrote *Re-entry* (1995) with a laptop on that desk. But when I bought a desktop computer and had to share it with my young teenagers wanting to type up essays and play games, I nearly went spare!

I've written lots of drafts on my bed. As a child I enjoyed writing in our paddocks, and I still enjoy writing drafts outside. Since I write much of my draft by hand, I can do it anywhere, even in the Outback. Children are shocked when I tell them this, but I find the tactile 'hands on' approach helps with my creativity. But it may not for others. Other practices that help me with creativity, getting ideas and keeping a narrative flowing are to use images, music, colour, and artefacts to stimulate the right side of my brain.

Tip

Have your own computer and uncluttered workspace. It does help, even if it is your bed or a cupboard.

Developing a Writing habit

This brings me to writers' block. It may come as a surprise, but I don't believe in writer's block. If I did it may give me an excuse not to write when it gets difficult. Especially at the beginning of a book. It is normal for a book to be hard to write. Why should we expect it to be easy? If a story isn't working for me or I can't get started, I go back to my journal knowing I haven't done enough research or thoughtful work on my characters.

When my mum died, I couldn't write my work-in-progress for six months. The book was *A Kiss in Every Wave* (2001) which reminded me of Mum, so whenever I tried to write it, I cried. That wasn't writer's block; that was grief. Often writers procrastinate – that gets called writer's block too. Some writers lack the confidence to keep going; that's not writer's block. Author Markus Zusak called this 'a lack of writers' faith' at the 2019 Adelaide Writers' Week. Some would-be writers don't have the passion for writing at all – that's not writer's block, but maybe 'I should be doing something else' block. There are genuine cases where writers are not well enough to write or a mental problem is blocking their progress, but if it were me, I'd hesitate to call it writer's block. Rather I'd name it for what it truly is. Then it can be overcome.

Anne Lamott (2008) discusses writer's block in her excellent book *Bird by Bird*: 'we all get it – but is it a block? The truth is you're empty.'[14] So replenish, fill up with reading, walking and all the things you know will help you rejuvenate.

Sometimes we just need a break, as PH Court suggested earlier.

A good tip to overcome obstacles in our writing is to write each day, not just when the wind blows. If not writing, do research or write rubbish. I'm surprised at how the story will progress into good words again after a few pages of drivel. The quick writing exercises in Chapter 3 will kick start sluggish writing. Limber up first.

I've also found prayer very helpful in getting a story started. First, I do the procrastination thing – clean out a drawer or actually pull the vacuum cleaner out of the cupboard. Then I say, 'I can't do this again', so I read the first page of my last book which was published and think, *okay that doesn't sound so bad, maybe I can do this again.*

Never underestimate the power of positive thinking. I try to be careful to 'tell my brain' optimistic and true statements which are backed up by a verse from the Bible. See Dr Caroline Leaf's book *Switch on your Brain* (2007) for more discussion on this. She undergirds what we've always known about renewing our minds, with the science of neuroplasticity. If we think we won't be able to start our novel, we probably won't. Simple. So, instead of saying I can't, tell yourself 'I can do all things in Christ's strength.' Then pray for help. It always comes. I'm learning to pray first.

Thinking like a writer is making our writing a habit, our work. And what work is that? We are communicating. We need to consider not only what we feel led to write but also our young readers. We need to keep them interested, which is quite a feat in our digital times. We need to know something of the forms, genres and media made available for children. What we do is transfer what we see and experience to the minds of our readers and we keep learning how to do it well. We don't wake up one morning wanting to play the violin and expect to immediately perform on stage. It takes ten years to be able to play music on a big stage. Writing a novel is similar; it can take ten years of reading and practice to write a novel that will be published. We need to be determined and steadfast.

Tips

- *Make* time to write. People who can't *find* time to write will never find it. Choose your writing time by deciding when you work best. For that period of time don't answer the phone or check social media. One writer I know has a voice message that says she's working and please ring back after 1 pm or leave a message. Once I tried a Do Not Disturb sign on the door when I had teenagers at home, but they knew I didn't truly mean it.
- Decide what keeps you on the chair. A cat on the lap? Music helps me stay put when I'm writing a draft. It also helps to tell myself that writing this chapter/s is the only thing I need to do today.

- Turn off social media and the phone if you can't ignore it. I find it best to pay bills or write that email at lunch time or when I'm finished writing for the day. This eliminates frustration.
- Declutter. Try to throw paperwork away and don't double handle. I'm still not good at this. Right now I need to de-clutter my desk even though I'm told I'll write better with the clutter gone. Discover what works for you; some are more creative in a stimulating environment.
- Try not to be concerned about the housework. Cornish brownies don't usually come to our house even though it is an antique Cornish cottage, so I keep a few hours on Saturday to clean up. Then I'm not using valuable writing time.
- Be encouraged that your writing is worth the time spent. I find it helps to know that my writing or my work is part of my worship. I believe God has placed us where we are to serve with our writing.

Beginning with a story

My writing career began when my husband and I were aid workers with a Christian mission/aid agency in Pakistan. My eldest child was a young teen and listening to stories was her favourite thing. One night she asked me to tell her about a kidnapping, since an aid-worker we knew had been abducted by freedom fighters. After this she asked me to write it for her. Without her encouragement I may never have had the 'nerve' to become a writer, but I knew she wanted that book: 'Mum, I want to walk into a bookshop and buy a book that my mother wrote just for me.'

For me, writing began with storytelling, and I still believe telling stories is a good way to begin writing a book. In lectures and workshops, I often ask students in groups to tell a story from words on a card they are given: a character's name, a setting and a problem. This grew from a story game my children and I played in the car crossing the Himalayan foothills or on a bazaar walk. They gave me a character's name, a setting and a problem. Then I had to fix the problem, though they helped in the process. 'No, Mum, he wouldn't have said that' or 'What's she wearing?' and 'Why doesn't she tell him the secret?' In this way I learned about strong motivations, having to think up a plot line quickly as three expectant faces waited. I still tell the stories of my novels, usually to one of my grownup children over tea or coffee, as I'm writing them, or beforehand. I find the writing process becomes smoother as a result.

Workout
Try telling a story to a child. Think of a child character, where that character lives and what's happening in their life right now. How will they resolve it?

Try asking the child to give you the character, setting and problem. It's more challenging, but it's amazing to see how you can make up a story with elements you hadn't thought of.

Reading

Reading is not just a fun activity for a writer's spare time; reading is an important tool for writers. I consider it part of my working day, even though I mostly read at night. I may have started writing through storytelling, but I began learning *how* to write by reading (as well as forging ahead to finish that book for my daughter). Oh, I took writing workshops later and learned how to hone what I knew, how to edit, how to decide what to rewrite, and more. But in those early days of writing the draft of my first novel, I kept reading.

AJ Cronin's *The Lady with Carnations* (1978) taught me that I hadn't developed my characters well enough; Michener's *The Source* (1965) disclosed how to take my readers on a journey and to think more about my plot; Geraldine McCaughrean's *The Maypole* (1989) showed me that words can sing. As I wrote her first line in my journal, I sighed at the beauty: *Day came in like Joshua, with ramshorn blasts of sun.*

I took novels apart to see how the structure worked: how many chapters, what was in them and how they ended, where the climax came. As Francine Prose (2006) suggests by the title of her book *Reading Like a Writer*, we have to learn to read like writers, what she describes as 'close reading'. It's a good idea to keep a log or journal of what we read (I also use Goodreads) and do remember to cite who wrote that beautiful quote you wrote in your journal. Ten years later you may forget it wasn't you!

Not only do we learn how to write when we are reading, but our brains are also computing how story works. We think of creative ideas because, as we are reading, our brains relax. I often think of the very way to fix the hole in my current plot when I'm reading a novel with no connection to the story or genre I am writing. Other brain relaxants, like going for a walk, having a shower, listening to music or looking at images, will also give me ideas for fixing plot problems.

In the beginning I learned to write by reading, passion, persistence and hard work, and I agree with Prose's additions: 'repeated trial and error, success and failure, and from the books we admire.'[15]

Tip

As well as reading like a writer, learn to see like a writer, hear like a writer, feel like a writer. For children's stories it's good to remember like a writer. Do you remember some of the key turning points in your childhood?

> We need to align ourselves with the river of our story, the river of the unconscious, of memory and sensibility of our lives which can then pour through us, the straw – Anne Lamott.[16]

A writer's journal

Not everyone believes in writing journals as I do, though only a few students groan when I mention them. Journals can take many forms: a hardcopy visual diary, a notebook, a computer file, a blog. I also use Pinterest as a visual journal. Some writers like to research and plan extensively, so a journal is ideal for that. Some writers are 'pantsers' – they write by the 'seat of their pants' with no planning and often little research beforehand. May I suggest that the pantsers' journals are in their heads? Even writers who say they don't plan ('it just happens') are thinking constantly about their story.

A journal, in whatever format, for ideas, scraps of information and images can be beneficial. I call this my daybook, which is with me most of the time. I use an A5 format so it's easy to slip into a shoulder bag. Ideas for future works or research not pertaining to the present project will go in here; also drafts of talks; quotes, images pasted from newspapers or magazines; photos or sketches.

The last few years I've also kept a journal for each novel I'm writing. In it go images, research, quotes, mind maps of characters and plot, ideas for structuring the work, exercises on voice and dialogue; editing. I often invite my main character, (especially if she/he is the narrator), to write in my journal so I can see how the voice sounds. I can't start in earnest until I hear that voice. I showed a friend my journal for *Kerenza: A New Australian* (2015). It is much like an old scrapbook album because that is what Kerenza creates in the story. My friend said, 'I wouldn't have time to do this.' I replied, 'I didn't have time not to.' I had a deadline and, while I was writing in the journal or pasting in old images from my research, the story was developing in my mind. I believe I wrote that story quicker because of the preparation in my writing journal. And when I rewrote the novel, all the information I needed to refer to was easy to find in the journal.

Early in the morning I draft in the journal, so getting on task later in my underground writing room is easier, since I just need to begin by typing what I've already written, and I can carry on with the story without stalling. Journals are also helpful in thinking about or evaluating our writing: where it needs to improve, what works and what doesn't and why. (More on this in Chapter 12.) Many writers think little about their craft and surge ahead on intuition and what they've subconsciously learned through reading. Others want to improve their craft and do their best. That involves evaluation, either by oneself or by trusted readers.

Besides creative journals, I also use a spiritual journal in which I may even mention the current project. I've been finding pieces for this writing book in my spiritual journals and daybooks from the last ten years!

Tips

- Use an index in your journal so you can easily find information. Leuchtturm1917 journals have page numbers and an index already marked.
- Write words every day. This is why a journal is useful. Don't wait for inspiration to strike. A Latin proverb states: 'When there is no wind, row'. So limber up with some 'quick writing'. See Chapter 3 'Keeping Fit' for practice writing exercises.

Writing in a group
If you are critiquing another's work:
- Read the work before commenting.
- If not stated, ask what in particular the author would like comments on (i.e. don't quibble about punctuation if it is an early draft and the author needs to know if her child character's dialogue is genuine).
- First, make positive comments about the elements you think work well in the creative piece (e.g. character development, setting, plot, voice, writing style).
- Then suggest areas which can be developed more. Be encouraging and honest.
- Always be mindful of the level of the writer. If a new writer, choose only a few things that can be worked on rather than everything you see, so as not to discourage.
- I suggest using pencil when making comments on someone's manuscript; it is less confronting than red pen.
- Be kind with humility. Never use critiquing as an opportunity to show how much you know. We are all learners who are writing better each day.

If your work is being critiqued:
- Try to take your draft as far as you can. Please don't ask the group to look at what I call a zero draft: your very first or messiest version.

- Be careful of defensiveness. It keeps us from the truth about ourselves and our writing, and perpetuates self-doubt. Constructive criticism can be liberating. There is no need to defend or justify your choices. If others didn't understand what you meant, it's possible an editor or professional reader mightn't either. Don't interrupt to explain unless asked.
- Keep an open mind, even if others do not understand your story. All writing can be improved.
- Bear in mind that people's comments are their opinions. There is no right or wrong way to write your story.
- Don't revise just to please others or you'll be revising forever; you decide whether a subjective suggestion is right for your story and character.

Choose carefully whose opinion of your work you listen to. And write. It sounds obvious but until you get the words out on the page, nothing will ever come of them.[17]

Riding the Wind

> i cannot speak the words
> screaming for release
> so i bleed
> onto the page
>
> one
>
> heartbeat
>
> at
>
> a
>
> time
>
> **Elizabeth Snow**[18]

2
Children's Literature

Why write for children?

A writing life enmeshes our whole life, our habits and values, our tools of trade, our thoughts and fears about ourselves, our abilities, craft and motivations. So let's ask ourselves: why put ourselves through this? What is our motivation?

I'll answer this with more questions: Do you want to tell a story? To entertain, or bring joy to a child's life? Do you think it would be easier than writing for adults? Do you write because you believe children need good books to grow on? Do you want to share the world the way you see it, to share your worldview? Do you want to get a message across? Do you want to reflect light and hope? Do you want to give glory to God?

Children's literature expert, Peter Hunt, makes the following observation:

> It is arguably impossible for a children's book (especially one being read by a child) not to be educational or influential in some way; it cannot help but reflect an ideology and, by extension, didacticism. Children's writers are therefore, in a position of singular responsibility in transmitting cultural values, rather than 'simply' telling a story.[1]

Do you agree with Hunt's statement? In what ways do you think a children's book affects the reader, if any? We're often encouraged to not push a message or moral as in Aesop's Fables, however, I see many modern books with obvious messages. As writers we do want children to be positively influenced by our stories, but I think the trick is to let the character and the story show what the character is learning and feeling. We don't need to thump a lesson home. Young readers are savvy; not only do they smell a moral, or a condescending attitude, but they can also work out the meaning according to their need and understanding.

From this discussion do you think we have a responsibility, as children's writers, which is different from that of writers writing for adults? Author and teacher, Elizabeth Fensham, writes here about her responsibility as a writer:

> My Christian worldview means I feel a clear responsibility to my readers ... and I would feel this for an adult reader as I do for the child reader. I do not believe in indulging any neurotic or self-indulgent tendencies. A novel can deal with the toughest of issues, but not to the point of destroying hope in my reader. But I am not didactic—or try to avoid this. For me, my views, like wine through water, are part of the warp and weft of my stories ... just there, because this is a part of me.[2]

Teachers, like me, often 'fall into' writing for children. They know children; they may also know where there are gaps in the market and have lots of ideas for books that would work with the curriculum. When I began writing I was teaching, but it was a teen voice that appeared first. Partly, this was because I was writing for my teen daughter at the time and helping ESL teens write English assignments.

Finally, here is some advice from Hemingway on why we write: 'Forget the "why", it's enough to know you want to write. Write'.[3]

Is writing for children easier than writing for adults?

I have heard authors who write for both children and adults say that children's writing is more exacting, as they have to capture the young reader's interest and keep it. Author, Nina Bawden, maintains the story line needs to be stronger 'but the only real difference between writing for adults or for children is whose eyes I am looking through'.[4] One could argue a strong story line would also apply to adults, but children often seem to have shorter attention spans and have lots of other interesting things to do like playing video games.

Listen to Roald Dahl in the 1982 BBC Archive video where he discusses this question. He states emphatically that it is harder to write a children's book of comparable quality to a fine adult novel. 'Children take books more seriously than adults,' he says. 'Adults read a book once and give it away. If a child likes your book that's not the end of it. They will read it and read it, maybe fifteen times! They even learn it by heart. And your book has to stand up to that.'[5]

It also has to stand up to parents having to reread it night after night.

So what is a good children's book?

> Beauty is defined by physicists as having simplicity, harmony, and brilliance. Those are also the properties that author Katherine Paterson feels are crucial to good writing; brilliance being 'the light that a book sheds not only on itself but beyond itself to other stories and other lives.'[6]

This is my favourite quote about children's writing. It is what I yearn for each time I start a draft. Please Lord, let me write something beautiful, something good, let it shed light and hope. The finished product is not always what I first had in mind, but it is the best I'm able to do at that time.

A good children's book should be able to be enjoyed by all ages as an art form. It will use themes that children can relate to, good characterisation, language, content that's suitable for certain ages, hope, enrichment, beauty. All these elements need to work together. There are some adult books that tell a story through a child protagonist, like *That Eye, the Sky* (1986) by Tim Winton, and *I'm not Scared* (2003) by Niccolò Ammaniti but the content, writing style or language is not suitable for children.

A good children's book will affect the reader in some way. This is how author and academic, Edward Veith (1990) puts it: 'A good book is one that has moved us emotionally. A book that is a work of art will explore the depths of human behaviour'.[7] Renowned reviewer, Katharine England, stated in a CBCA talk that a good children's book should change the reader.

What do you think of these statements?

- From CS Lewis: 'I put in what I would have liked to read when I was a child and what I still like reading now I am in my fifties ... A children's book which is enjoyed only by children is a bad children's story.'[8]
- Children's literature must be good literature that children can relate to. Author and teacher, Eleanor Nilsson, states that writing for children is primarily a question of subject matter and point of view.[9]
- Children read for pleasure and often to escape from difficult times. Paul Jennings states: 'Children need magical stories to help them deal with their lives.'[10] I'm sure he has cheered up many a child.
- A book with a child protagonist dealing with sexual abuse and/or violence in explicit terms would not be a children's book. Children learning to hope again after their Grandpa dies would be. See *Passing On*, an excellent picture book by Mike Dumbleton (2001) about a grandparent dying.

Knowing your market

Maybe the biggest challenge in writing for children is pitching your story to the right age level. Publishers and educationists have researched this and have developed certain age categories because they know a regular 6-

year-old mightn't be able to read a 30,000 word novel that an 11-year-old would enjoy. There are always exceptions (I know a boy who read Tolkien's *Lord of the Rings* when he was 5-years-old, whereas my son was 11) and for that reason an excellent story which falls between age categories may be accepted.

If a story about a cute bunny that needs to find his lost tail is 20,000 words long, it will probably miss the mark as younger children might not be able to read it and older ones who could won't be interested in the content. However, a long novel about rabbits like *Watership Down* by Richard Adamson (1972) can be successful as its content will suit the older reader. Content and length need to correspond. A 10,000 word story about learning to use the potty would work best if cut to a picture book text with maybe 100-300 words. A picture book with too many words won't work with wriggly pre-schoolers either.

Workout

So head into the library or bookstore and check out the types of book in the different sections, their length and content, for example picture books, early chapter books for children starting to read, junior novels for primary school (6-9 years), middle grade novels (9-12 years), novels for upper primary/middle school, lately also called lower YA (11-14 years) and for older YA (15-18+). Try to decide what makes them all different from each other. Read a few pages of each age level to see what makes the language in each level pertinent to the age of the targeted reader.

What do you think of the themes, content, language and the length in the different age groups you found? Your notes could start like this or you could draw a table:
- Picture books: baby, wordless, 100 words, or less.
- Picture Books: early childhood, classic, approximately 300-700 words.
- Picture books that are really illustrated stories for primary children, may have more than 800 words.
- Picture Books: YA, see the work of Shaun Tan and Colin Thompson.
- Short story anthologies.
- Short chapter books for early readers: 6-8 years, 1000-2000 words.
- Short chapter books: 7-10 years, 4000 words.
- Junior novels: 6-9 years old, 6,000 – 10,000 words.
- Novels for younger readers (middle grade): 9-12 years old, up to 40,000 words.
- Novels for middle school (usually called lower YA), 11-14 years old, 40,000 words plus (I've added this age level, though it is not a set category in the Australian market yet).
- YA novels: 12-18 years, or more recently (15-18 years) 40,000 – 60,000 words.
- Then there are series of books which may have less words. Particular genres, like fantasy, may be longer.

Children read up and down the age levels, so these categories or lengths aren't set in stone, but they are a guide. Your knowledge of them will show your market research.

Guest Author – Lorraine Marwood[11]
A Writing Hint and a Little About My Writing Journey

I believe my gift of writing comes from God who is endlessly creative. There are tingling surprises when I write. The challenge is to believe that when pen or type-pad are set into motion the writing will come; it will be just what is needed and will sing.

The excitement that comes from writing and reading is deep within me, a burning desire. When I first allowed myself to think as a writer, I relentlessly found out as much information as I could about practice, tips, other authors' personal journeys, competitions, steps to publication, small literary journals, writing exercises.

I believe that to be a writer one must be armed with as much information as possible, networking, joining groups is important too. In everything practice, persistence, reading, faith and prayer come into play.

I'm a great believer in notebooks, jotting down ideas, snatches of conversation, the very tiny unfurling of an idea.

So here's a quick idea to increase your stash of ideas.

Children's Literature

> Each day for a week at the end of the day jot down five surprising things: a sighting, a conversation, a thought.
>
> Here's an example:
>
> + Watching a big bird hop from small branch to small branch; would a bird ever snap a branch off?
>
> + The way thunder just rolls over the top of any other outside sound.
>
> + A teenage boy chatting to his mates down the street, holding a king-size packet of disposable nappies.
>
> I want to hold onto the idea of bringing God's delight and excellence to what I write. Uplifting, enjoyment, empathy and wonder at God's boundless creativity and love inspire my writing. I hope it will inspire your writing too.

3
Keeping Fit:
Writing and Storytelling

This chapter is not about keeping physically fit, although I will mention that since I have been walking regularly not only has my physical fitness and health improved, but also my mental capacity for keeping a plot in my head. Spotting what needs to be changed in my drafts has improved as well. Doing jigsaws also helps with this.

Our writing also benefits from developing a writing exercise habit which comes from keeping our writing fit. Some authors will set themselves a goal to write for five minutes each day; it often becomes much longer. I call this type of writing 'quick writing' – to limber up each day. It's good to write regularly even if we are not working on a project. These exercises improve our writing and often give ideas for story projects. I don't try to think too much, just let the right hand side of my brain have fun and write whatever comes out as quickly as I can. It's not only a good way of developing a writing habit, but also of learning to let our writing flow.

We want to write to achieve a finished product, but consider these exercises as just that: creative pieces that may not see the light of day, but through which you will be learning to write freely and nurturing a writing habit. You will even hone skills, but this needn't be a goal of practice writing either. At times you may gain an idea from an exercise that leads to a project, but this also isn't the primary goal. There's no right way to do this; just do it. Write. Play. Don't think too much, keep writing, don't edit. You don't even have to have a topic. Write whatever comes into your head. You will discover how your mind keeps providing ideas.

We are learning to be better writers by the hour. I recently had the joy of rewriting some of my early novels. I was shocked to see how poor my writing skill had been, and no doubt I'll think the same in ten years about what I'm writing now. I find free writing helps with confidence and working through technical problems. It also produces more efficient writing.

Often a student will write an assignment based on an idea from an exercise of quick writing that we did in class. I was honoured to launch the *Beast Speaker* series by Wendy Noble (2017), fantasy novels for lower YA which began as a writing exercise using hats in one of my classes. So let's start our keeping fit exercises with hats and who wears them. Remember to have a child or teen protagonist.

Keeping Fit

- Find some hats. Try one on. Who are you now? What is happening in your life right now? Is there any way to fix your situation?
- Choose an object in the room. Let it think and talk. How does it feel? Show this in a few sentences without mentioning its name. Others in your writing group can guess which object it was.

Riding the Wind

- One year my husband and I were house parents in an international boarding school in Pakistan, and a boy wanted to see how long he could wear his socks before people complained of the smell. He reached five weeks before we noticed. Does your character have smelly socks? Write about smelly socks for five minutes.
- Find an interesting object; for example, a piece of jewellery. Who wore it? Write a creative piece.
- Alliteration. Think of a letter of the alphabet and write a sentence with some of the words in it starting with that letter. It's good to remember that not all alliteration works well. As with all writing, a little of a technique is better than too much. Read it aloud to check.
- Write a paragraph without an 'e'. It must make sense. This kind of exercise forces us think of other words to use and so increases our ability to show emotion and images.
- Play with words. Write ten nouns down one side of a page e.g. daisy, aeroplane, gorilla, violin. On the other side write ten verbs e.g. slice, boil, sauté, stir, chop or saw, dig, plant, mow, fertilise. Then combine the words: The daisy sliced the sky into segments. The aeroplane mowed through the clouds.
- To practise showing rather than telling, try this game with writing friends. Put some pictures (postcards or calendar photos) on the table.

Keeping Fit: Writing and Storytelling

Write about one without indicating which one it is and don't describe obvious elements in the picture, but try to include the mood or tone of the picture in your writing. See if your friends can guess which picture inspired your creative piece.

- You are two and you want something. What is it? And how will you get Mum to notice? Try to capture 'twoness'.
- Imagine you are five. You are learning to read. How do you feel picking up a book you can actually read? Write about it in the voice of a child. Then try it in third person.
- Find pictures of animals. Choose one without telling your friend, and write a piece showing the thoughts and feelings of the animal without writing the name of the animal. Can your friend guess which one was chosen?
- A 10-year-old boy goes for a walk in the scrub and finds a box under a bush. It looks like it's been there awhile. What's in the box? Write a creative piece.
- You are 15 and a message is sent to your mobile phone and you know it is not meant for you: 'I am ready now to work on the relationship. If you are too then give me a call.' Write a creative piece.
- I remember walking home from school with my big sister. I was in Grade 1 and she was in Grade 8. We had to cross a paddock of cows. One

afternoon we saw the bull. We knew not to run but we dashed from tree to tree hoping he hadn't noticed us. Finally, we reached the gate leading to the house. Do you have a memory of a dangerous event? Write about it, keeping in mind a child readership. That is, try not to write the memory from an adult's point of view of remembering. Get into the scene, capturing a child's voice and emotions.

Workout

Make up your own keeping fit exercises. On a walk recently I found a lone shoe. I searched for the other, wondering if I'd find a body. Take photos of such things as they can be used as a quick writing prompt with friends or by yourself.

I also keep packs of pictures from calendars, junk mail, postcards or photos, such as pictures of people talking: What are they saying? Pictures of a lone person: What are they thinking? Pictures of action: What is happening?

Even opening a dictionary and choosing a word at random can get the right side of your brain excited. See what happens.

Storytelling and word games

> *Storytelling is essentially, crucially, primarily mostly about redemption.*[1]
>
> Brian Godawa, screen writer.

Stories heal. Scheherazade in *The Arabian Nights* proved that stories can truly mend hearts. For 1001 nights she told the deranged king stories to distract him from killing her as he had so many other brides, but when she finally asked him to stay her death sentence, he said the stories had healed him. He didn't want to kill brides any more. Telling our own story can be healing to ourselves and even to others in the same situation. I found that with *Dear Pakistan* which deals with culture shock. It's the truth in a story that heals. Stories can shake us up, make us think, make us smile, cry, imagine. Stories can make us see life or another person in a different way. Stories can show hope in the darkness, the light on the other side of the forest where victory awaits. On a practical level, I find the act of telling stories leads to writing and improving them.

Using storytelling to stimulate our writing

To help with planning I play a storytelling game with classes and workshops where I supply a character, a setting and a problem on a card and students singularly or in groups tell the story.

Another idea to help encourage plotting: I supply a picture of a character and give each student cards to prompt plot ideas. They then tell a story around the circle trying to remember to keep the story causal like a plot (each event must cause the next thing to happen) and keep the tension rising. The first person has the picture of the character and introduces the character. If she hasn't introduced some difficulty in the character's life or what they'd like to be able to do, then the second person does this. The second to last person knows they have to create a climax where the character finally gets what they want or tries for it, and the last person must resolve the action. This is more difficult than it sounds, as the story can easily (especially with very young people) start on a city street and end up on Mars with different characters and no causality between events.

Try these activities to improve your story skills

- Play the game *Dixit* with your writing group to improve your storytelling and get new ideas for stories. *Dixit* consists of illustrated cards which prompt storytelling.
- Storytelling games like *Never Ending Stories* by Living and Learning, Cambridge, UK can be helpful for plot planning.
- Packs of interesting photographs or postcards (which you can collect yourself) also prompt storytelling ideas.
- *Once Upon a Time*[2] is a storytelling game with cards which uses interrupt cards so that anyone in the circle can take the story further when they want to rather than wait for their turn. You have

to have an ending card to end the story. Can't wait to try this in a class.
- A good idea to improve word power is to play games like *Taboo* or *Balderdash* where players try to convey the meaning of a word to a group without mentioning that word or synonyms of it. This helps us to think of more effective words to use in our writing.

Workout

Stories are the axe for the frozen sea within.
Franz Kafka

Use this grid for a storytelling exercise and then write the story. Choose a character, setting and event and see what happens. Or make your own grid.

Try to show the character needing to do something which will either redeem or heal a character or a situation.

Character	Setting	Event/Problem
Wizard	Beach	Flood
Knight	King's garden	Shipwreck
Unloved princess	Walnut shell	Kidnapping
Poor sailor	A treehouse	A child is lost
Wolf	Forest	A rope is cut
Sheep dog	A ship	Storm
Trapeze artist	Lighthouse	A message found
Girl tree feller	Island	Bushfire
Elf	Cave	A jewel is stolen

Tips for telling stories

Stories do not need to be learned by heart as they change and develop with the telling, but I do learn the first line so I can start with confidence and I know the last line so I can finish crisply.

- Introduce the character and the problem. Build up audience sympathy.
- Be clear what your character wants, or what their problem is, and therefore, their motivation.
- Cause conflict.
- There must be something at stake. Suspense can be generated by a time limit, a secret, danger or raising the stakes.
- Include a dark moment.
- Rise to a climax.
- Resolve the story so that it does not rely on coincidence, but on the courage or cleverness of the character.
- Use facial expression, pauses, costumes, hats or a prop, and vary volume and tone of voice to help tell the story.
- Know the last line so you can end well.

Before I had a book for younger readers published, I told stories to children at school visits. These often later became published books, like *Yardil* (2004) and *Across the Creek* (2003).

Workout

Think up five story prompts of your own. I often get ideas from newspapers, articles on the web, objects I find, an image I've seen, places where I walk, fairy stories, folktales or any reading at all. There are more ideas for writing to keep fit on my website called 'Picture This' under 'About Writing'.

www.rosannehawke.com

God chose to communicate with us through stories. Stories are able to transcend the limits of ideological debate by allowing us to look at the world through another's eyes. Literature is an extraordinarily powerful medium; we learn through stories, we explore our world through stories and ultimately the act of reading them is an exercise in empathy. This is why I write. I am eternally fascinated by those whom God has made in his image and I want to explore the world through the eyes of others. My observations are filtered through the lens of my faith, therefore my faith is greatly integrated with my ambition to depict the world and all its people as Christ would see them: with compassion, empathy and love. I am driven to challenge the preconceptions I and my readers might have about certain types of people. Through my writing I try to ask questions about the world and its people, rather than answer them.

Claire Zorn[3]

4
Characters Can Write Your Story

Children ask me where my characters come from. If I say a character arrives on my page the child will ask, 'Where from?' If I say I made the character up, I get asked 'How?' And making up characters doesn't seem sufficient, not after the night I was asked by a 13-year-old visitor to town who said she'd just read *Zenna Dare* and wanted to meet Caleb. Caught on the hop I said, 'I made him up.' It didn't go down well. 'I'm sorry, he doesn't live here, he's just in the story.' Worse and worse. The girl was devastated. 'I want to meet a boy like him,' she finally said. How do you 'make up' someone like Caleb? Not possible. How do you explain how they turn up? Perhaps a few stories will help.

While living in Pakistan, my husband Gary was only arrested twice. I thought this was pretty good considering the way he'd dress up as an Afghan (he looked Afghan with his olive skin, green eyes and hooked nose) and go to the bazaar at night even when there was a war in the Gulf. He was adventurous, larger than life, maybe a bit like a grownup Joel Billings from *The Keeper*. The first arrest occurred when he was actually dressed in an Afghan cap escorting a Pakistani friend of ours to her husband. It involved our friend wearing a burqa and a bus journey at night. At one of the bus stations police picked him up because they thought he was abducting our friend. This was because she was wearing a Pakistani burqa and he looked like an Afghan. He couldn't possibly be related to her and so be a proper escort. It was all explained and they let him go in time to get back on the bus.

The second time took longer to get him released. It was election time; posters on electric poles warned against loud noises. We couldn't read those, but we knew to be careful. Gary wanted to have a fireworks display for a special celebration at the girls' school where I worked. For weeks he'd asked for permission from the proper offices but never got anywhere, so he presumed it wasn't important enough and decided to do it anyway. Rockets zoomed, fire burst into the sky. At every whoosh four hundred girls screamed with joy.

The army was swift. They descended at a marching trot and took Gary away. The teachers poured in to my house to pray. They wept as if they'd never see him again. So I rang our former landlord who was a retired army colonel. It took a bit of wrangling, but he managed to get Gary released before morning. Now, is Colonel Rafique in *The Truth about Peacock Blue* (2015) inspired by our friendly landlord? Is the adventurous father of Jaime in the *Beyond Borders* (2016) series inspired by my husband?

Inspiration from a person in our lives is not a bad thing. I've been asked to write a book actually based on a person's life – this will be nonfiction, so I won't mix the two. Readers who know my husband may think Jaime's dad is like him, but he has different talents, skills and family from Gary.

Some speak about creating characters, others of finding them. I think of meeting them. I know that when a character turns up, they have a backstory and they will live on when my story finishes. Joel in *Killer Ute* (2013) is thinking of new exciting things to do. Tamara from *The Messenger Bird* (2012) is pursuing her music in university. Ameera of *Marrying Ameera* (2010) is preparing to marry Tariq but will she get away with it?

But that first meeting: does it come from a memory, from deep inside my own personality? Or inspiration of a startling person I've met like Frank in *Marrying Ameera*? (2010). A passing acquaintance or encounter could even give me a simple idea and the character could emerge.

Having met them, I get to know and understand my characters and during that process they show me who they are.

Early on I discovered the classic book by Maren Elwood (1942, 1987), *Characters Make Your Story,* I learned more about the characteristics of characters. I wrote notes in an indexed book: how people walk, how they talk, how they look and think. I discovered that when you have characters responding characteristically to stimuli you have a story. I learned how to observe, listen, interact with children to discover those genuine details that make a character come to life, and therefore my story. I soon realised so much hinged on how well we know or develop our characters. The books I like the best have genuine characters peopling them, folks who have flaws, make mistakes, but learn to have hope and to love and forgive.

If I know my characters well enough, they will write my story, and my story will only be as effective as the characters in it. It's my belief that characters are the impetus for all other components in the story. The characters are more important than their problems; more important than plot.[1] Of course all elements work together in a story but what do you think lives longer in the reader's mind? Our lives are about relationships; people read a story to see what will happen to the people in it. Readers are interested in people.

One way I make sure I know my characters well is by drawing mind maps for the main characters, like the one on the next page.

Stylised mind maps were developed by Tony Buzan[2] and his research shows that the mind can think creatively and quickly generate new ideas when an image is drawn in the centre of a blank page. Connected ideas are added. Mind mapping works by association and engages the right side of the brain, where colour, music, images and creativity reign.

On the mind map I jot down anything about the character that comes to mind: name, personality, age, family background, reactions when angry, sad, how he/she speaks, favourite sayings, favourite things (clothes, food, music, books, sport, movies), dislikes, friends, pets, collections – anything at all.

Then I discover what the character wants the most, is frightened of, and what makes him/her unique. I even think about their strengths and weaknesses, for a flaw could lead to a character trait that the character needs to grow in, and that may be the place in his/her development the character needs to arrive by the end of the story. I enjoyed the characterisation in Anthony Doerr's *All the Light We Cannot See* (2014). Although an adult novel, I mention it because I'm intrigued how his characters are so strongly individual, quirky even, yet authentic. No stereotyping for Anthony Doerr.

When I was thinking of writing *Shahana,* a story about children living in a war zone, I couldn't start until I knew what she desired. When I finally realised she wanted to keep her little brother alive, then I had the story. Some characters need to find something, grow in some way or overcome a fear; knowing these things helps me with the story and heads me towards an ending.

When a young writer tells me they can't finish a story I usually find that they haven't thought enough about the character and what that character wants or needs to do or needs to learn. John Marsden says he takes his characters on a journey from ignorance to awareness.[3]

Workout

Here is some of the process I follow to know my characters: to get started, perhaps find a picture of a character or use an idea of your own, then draw a stick figure in the middle of the page. This stimulates the creative process in the right hand side of the brain. Draw a mind map for this character, let your brain travel as fast as it likes. That is, don't think too much, and write whatever comes to mind. Afterwards think about your character's desires, fears, motives, talents and flaws.

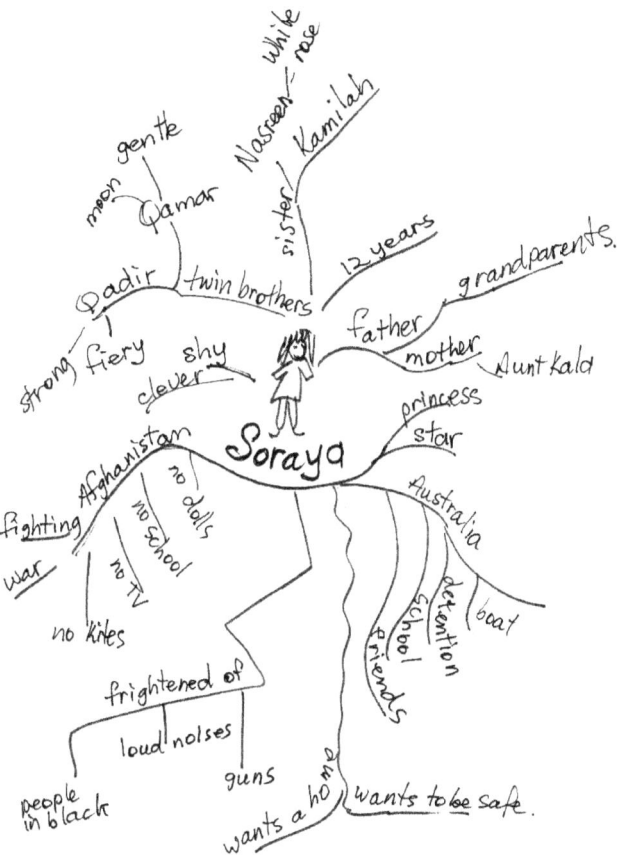

To think about

What is your main character's worldview? Ameera's father had a worldview that saw nothing abusive in arranging a marriage without telling her and forcing her to go through with it, believing it was the best thing for her and the family. What is the worldview of all your characters? What do they think about family, life, faith, society, friends, people who are different from them? Does the person who is causing trouble in your protagonist's life have a different worldview from him/her? What is your character's faith? What does she/he believe about life and spirituality? I often find characters are not rounded unless there is some indication of their beliefs and worldview. Is your character an outsider?

Here is a snippet from DM Cornish on faith and characters.

> I definitely would say my writing is faith informed: it is actually by faith that I do *not* say overt things about Jesus, hoping/trusting that He will come through gently in the manner of the characters, in the description and approach to what is good and what is evil, in writing characters with sympathy and empathy the human condition – the kind of mercy Jesus seems to show to people. This is my hope at least. DMC *Beluae Nunquam Superarum*[4]

We have to know our character well enough to understand their goal and motivation, and even the conflict in the story. Academic Debra Dixon writes of questions the reader wants answered: who (the character), what (the character's goal), why (the motivation), why not (the conflict). Her whole book *GMC: Goal, Motivation and Conflict* (1996) expands on these questions and is a worthwhile read to see how character leads plot and how they work together.[5]

Thus I try to create authentic, convincing characters and know what is of utmost importance to the character which will depend on the outcome of the story, and indeed will influence that outcome.

Tip
I try not to over-describe my characters. Razaq in *Mountain Wolf* (2012) is small for his age, but it is another character who mentions his green eyes and how fair and beautiful he is. Some editors will ask for more description of the character, especially for middle grade, but I have asked children and I'm often told they like to visualise by themselves what the character looks like.

Showing emotion
Everything in life is about relationship. Readers want to know what happens to people. They connect to characters they can relate to. Young readers like adventure but how will the character cope when such and such happens? There needs to be emotion in your story. The emotional core or heart of the story is the emotions the character and readers will feel. I try not to forget that these emotions need to be close to our collected human experience for the reader to connect with the character and therefore the story.

Always show rather than tell emotion with direct emotive words (He felt so sad) or with emotional adverbs in speech tags (she said angrily). Telling emotion can result in melodrama, that is, over-written emotion. Explore your characters' emotions in your journal. Emotions can be complex and characters often feel numerous emotions at one time. See if you can describe them without telling. An interesting book on showing emotion is *Creating Character Emotions* by Ann Hood (1998).

> i think you underestimate
> the strength of my emotion
> you see a raindrop
>
> – i am an ocean.
>
> **Elizabeth Snow**[6]

Workout

Practise these in your journal. Remember to have a child or teen protagonist.

- If you are a member of a writing group or class, introduce your character as if you were introducing a real person. See if you can answer any questions your friends ask you about the character, that is, their back story. Or you could interview your characters and see what they say. I am amazed how students who have just created a character using a mind map can answer any question put to them about this person. The character truly comes alive.
- To know your characters further, try writing them into paragraphs. What is your character thinking?
- Write for five minutes in first person as if you are your character. Write what he or she wants to do today and how they feel about it.

- What is your character's favourite object? Have another person come to ask for it but your character doesn't want to give it. Write a dialogue between them showing the conflict. (This dialogue idea from a Thomas Shapcott class.)
- What is your character's favourite food? Write a few sentences showing your character eating this food. Try to show how your character is feeling without telling.
- How do you react when you are angry? When you are sad? When you are excited? Show your character acting or speaking when feeling one of these emotions. Don't mention the name of the emotion.
- Imagine two people talking. What are they saying? Write a dialogue between them. Or maybe you are on a bus and you see two people talking. Imagine what they are talking about.
- What if your character found a key? Or another object that would suit your character. What does it open/do? Write a few paragraphs showing what your character does with the object.
- Draw a map of the first house you remember. Your character lives in this house. Put her in one of the rooms and show what she is doing.
- What is your character's favourite place? Show him or her there doing a favourite activity. Find authentic settings for your character.

How does your character talk?

Have a character write in your journal. Interview them. Does your character speak a certain way because of his background? Is English her first or second language? Is another language spoken at home? Does your character like talking or not? Is there a quirky saying your character uses?

Names

Since names are so important, I choose my characters' names for reasons that suit them, for example, Raw's name in *Wolfchild* (2017) is the Kernewek or old Cornish word for 'wolf'. Kamilah's name in *Soraya the Storyteller* (2004) means 'perfect' in Dari; she was the perfect gift her father gave the family before he was taken away. I use name books or websites to find the names I need. I like Oxford's *Everyman's Dictionary of First Names* as it includes name origins.

Care should be taken to ensure the name suits the character and family cultural background as well as the time in which they live. If it is a wildly different name for culture, time and place, it should be noted why. In fiction, heroes quite often need strong names, so think of hard consonants such as Kate, Brett. A weakling may have a name like Ollie Smith. Of course, as with all writing, you can do whatever you like, but it needs to be set up. Write with purpose.

If we spend the time getting to know our characters well, it will pay off: our character will keep the story on track. Knowing your characters' goals and motivations will enable you to finish it.

What stories was your character told?

I grew up on Bible stories and fairytales. I ate through the whole twelve blue volumes of *Uncle Arthur's Bible Stories* and the row of Oxford's *Myths and Legends of the World* which included many folktales and fairytales. Maybe this is one reason why I include such stories in my work. They are part of my worldview, even the Bible stories which I knew then were true and now know are part of a true fairytale, from which all the others possibly grew.

Another reason is to show what sort of cultural and family background my character has. Ameera's father told her folktales about elicit love versus obeying parents. All the stories about love were Romeo and Juliet tragedies. Did he do this to groom her for an arranged marriage? In the YA novel *Neverland* (2018) by Margot McGovern, Kit was told a particular story by her father that haunts her into her teen years. She has to recover her memory to discover why she was told that story. Perhaps some stories shouldn't be told. That was one of those.

Tip

Push your characters, make them suffer. Explore what they are capable of. We will suffer in this life. It is what grows us and develops us. In the same way our characters have to suffer to develop and for the reader to have hope in their own situation.

What do you think?
Write comments to share with your writers' workshop.
- Do characters need to change or grow by the end of the book for the story to be satisfying?
- How can we be sure not to stereotype our characters?
- Do you have any tips on how you get into your young character's mind?
- In what ways do child characters differ from adult ones?
- How do you think your characters can be authentic? How important is authenticity?
- Who is your character in conflict with?

Guest Author — Lisa Shanahan[7]
The Work of a Writer

Most of my books have started from some small, messy ordinary moment that would have been easy to overlook. Like many writers, I always carry a journal — so I can write anywhere. In the main, the things I write are just snatches; things I hear, things I see and things I feel. Snatches of conversation. Snatches of description. Snatches of ideas.

Sometimes I collect words that leap out, words like *squinch, spangle, gauzy, jaunty, limpid, velvet, mayonnaise*. Sometimes I note down tiny little snatches of overheard conversation from strangers, like the dark-haired business man who was reminiscing about the thrill of picking up his son from preschool when he was still little. 'Now,' he sighed, 'he's 15-years-old and he speaks three words a week.' Or the time recently, when a very old woman cycled tremulously past on a pink bicycle, with her front wheel wobbling, just as I stepped out onto the road. 'I'm practising,' she cried, smiling exultantly right into my astonished face.

I have a particular ear for tender, poignant moments. Like the time when my youngest son said to me, after the traumatic death of our second dog Lolly, 'I don't know why God created the tortoise and gave it one hundred and fifty years, just so it can take one step a day and why he allowed dogs to have such a short life.'

Some of these tiny snatches go on to become books or scenes in stories. But most of them don't. And that's okay. Because what I'm really doing with these snatches is tuning in. I'm tuning into the world. I'm tuning into other people, tuning into joy, sadness, hope, curiosity, fear and wonder. I'm tuning into small, messy ordinary moments, hoping to hallow them, to treasure them up, to see them for what they really are. Because if following Jesus has taught me anything, it's that small, messy ordinary moments count. That small, messy ordinary moments often turn out to be of astonishing, stupendous importance! And that one tiny story well-told can sometimes make all the difference, that it can flip the way a person views their whole entire world.

Just recently, I was writing in a favourite café, when a tall, thin, older woman came shuffling in for a cup of coffee, accompanied by a paid carer. The older woman had a long, limp, grey pony tail and she was wearing blue denim shorts, with embroidered white daisies down the seams, paired with black court shoes and white socks with shamrocks. She clearly had some kind of catastrophic brain injury. She couldn't speak. A string of 'bbbbbbbs' just kept coming out of her mouth. I couldn't imagine how frustrating that would be, to be so desperate to make a connection with people but to be so completely thwarted.

She sat nearby, clicking her immaculately, pink-painted fingernails against the tabletop, hoping to catch our attention. She was like a small child, bursting to be seen, desperate to be noticed. And when she was noticed, when someone shot her even the smallest smile, her whole face, which was so rubbery and expressive, became suffused with sudden, ecstatic joy.

I was struck by the mystery of it all – how luminously alive this woman was, how incredibly and exuberantly free! And in some ways, how much more so than every other person in that cafe, including myself and including her carer, who sat slumped across the table, yawning, rolling her eyes at the café manager, clearly embarrassed by her noisy, effusive client, impatient for the work day to be done.

In that moment, I felt the invitation, the gentle nudge, to keep looking past the first shock, to keep looking past that first glance, to keep looking past the second when I might want to turn my head away, when I might want to avert my eyes, because I'm crushed by the sight of another person's suffering. To keep looking past the pain and the pity. To keep looking at this incandescent, grey-haired woman, who is shuffling out of the café with a walking stick, taking baby steps in her shamrock socks and black court shoes, wearing a bubble-gum pink t-shirt, who can't say a single sensible word, who will take literally hours to walk home, but who will greet every person she meets as if they were royalty, as if they were the best friend she has always been longing for.

Keep looking.

It's the vocation of every writer. The calling for every follower of Jesus. To keep pushing past the first cursory glance, to not divert our gaze, to stay open to deeper realities.

Keep looking. It's the invitation at the heart of every work of art. It's what we hope people might carry away, from a novel, a poem, a play, a picture book — the quiet summons to look once more at the world and all the people in it, with freshly illumined eyes.

5

Character and Plot

Plot is what the character does to get what she wants.

John Dufresne[1]

When I was 10 years old, looking out my window, I could see the trees lining the creek past the wheat paddocks on the flat. Further to the east there was a rise and tight scrub. I wanted to go to these places, to see what was beyond, to explore. A few years later, I took my dog, a stick to scare off dingoes, a cordial bottle of water and we explored. Writing is like that for me: the urge to explore new places, to discover what will happen. So let's explore together.

Try writing a short story with no plot. The reader would probably get to know the characters well. Will the characters be at the same spot at the end of the story as in the beginning? Think of what a plot does for a story. Some contemporary writers for adults don't think plot is imperative but EM Forster believed there is a need for plot and that the novel tells a story.[2] Queen Scheherazade in the *Arabian Nights* avoided dying because she knew about plot and how to create suspense in a story: that pleasurable anticipation awaiting an outcome. She could tell a story well enough to stay alive. Thus plot is how a story is told.

Think about how we tell a joke: the initial set up, building up, the punch line. In a story we think of orientation (and exposition, that is, backstory), development, resolution. Aristotle named it beginning, middle and end, like three acts of a drama.[3] You'll soon find that every writer has their own way of thinking about plot and letting it work for them. In the beginning I found it difficult to organise events; I basically just wrote to see where the character and the story would take me. I've learned since that I need some idea of where the character needs to be by the end. It usually changes, but it helps me to keep writing with purpose.

New writers have to begin somewhere. I often get asked, 'How do you let it take shape?' I used to ask that too. Now I wonder if it has more to do with intuition and experience. I suggest to students to introduce the character, and the conflict; then play out the story, making sure one event leads to another (I didn't understand this at first), keeping the tension rising with conflict and disaster until there is a climax with the character achieving the goal and a satisfying resolution.

What children expect from plot

A plotless story may work for adults as a literary experiment but would children like a plotless story? I suspect they wouldn't. They'd keep asking, 'When is something going to happen? Why doesn't the character do something about what the villain said?' Maybe there wouldn't even be a villain. I suppose many of our days seem plotless but we mustn't impose that on children who want an exciting story.

Child readers may not understand all about writing technique but they do know when they don't like a book. Children like something to happen. They like to know early on who the main character is and what their problem is. They want to like and be interested in the character. They like to think ahead and decide how the characters may achieve their aims. They want to be involved in the characters' lives. They want to see an adversary of some sort; the villain can do dastardly things as most children like tension and suspense. They can even be scared when reading and relish it. Younger primary school readers like a happy ending where the character is successful in achieving the goal. They like to imagine themselves as the hero winning against evil or a problem, whether it be a fantasy with dragons or a seaside holiday where a boy learns to face his fears.

What is plot?

> *We can think of a plot as a series of causally related events, involving some sort of conflict or tension, leading to a climax and resolution.*
>
> John Hodgins[4]

Plot is not just the events that follow each other as is often the case with storytelling. It's the 'what' that leads to the 'why' and the 'how'. EM Forster (1962) talks about killing the king. A plot is a narrative of events, the emphasis falling on causality, 'the king died and then the queen died,' is a story. 'The king died so the queen died of grief', is a plot.[5] But why did he die? I suggest that if there is poisoned wine on the king's bedside table the plot thickens. There is always a reason. In a plot we ask 'why'; readers always want to know why.

Plot is about the word 'why' and not the words 'and then' as in oral storytelling. Events in a plot must be causal, making the next event happen. If you find a scene you have written which does not move the plot forward like this, then delete it. Academic and author John Gardner (1991) suggests that although character is the emotional core of great fiction, plot must become the focus of every good writer's plan.[6]

The basic plot of all good stories is this: you have a central character who wants something and goes after it despite opposition, and as a result of struggle comes to win or lose. Plot is thus the journey that your character embarks upon, and therefore, the reader also. Aristotle wrote that plot was more important than character (he devoted nine chapters to 'the primacy of' plot in his book *Poetics*), though he did say the tragic dramas were meant to touch our hearts, to move us emotionally. Although he believed characters alone don't make fiction, action by itself doesn't either. The plot still relies on character in my opinion. The plot would be different with another character on centre stage. The character decides the plot and the plot can also shape the character and help hold the story together.

The plot starts to form for me as I ask questions (often in my journal): what does my character want? What is motivating her? What or who is preventing that? What does she do about the obstacles? Why? This forms the basis for the conflict. Even pantsers will know much of this before they start writing. What are the results? What climax does it lead to? Does she get it in the end? My plot develops more as I write.

Most simply of all there is still a beginning, an end and a lot happening in the middle. It may sound simple, but author Jane Yolen (2006) shows in *Take Joy* that the beginning must set the stage for something not as yet understood and begin the suspense. The middle develops gradually and the end must be both surprising and inevitable.[7] It was that middle bit which caught me out as a new writer. How to make everything happen after the beginning? It's what children ask me the most: how to make things happen. I even asked my university supervisor how to plot and structure and he said to look to my character. The character will tell me. Of course he was right, but I wanted to know how to organise it.

Hodgins (1993) suggests that to avoid lifeless plots we must put more effort into understanding and exploring the characters.[8] If the main character has a life of her own, she is likely to suggest a situation that will challenge her to use all her resources. By responding, the character is already suggesting a direction of action. It can be risky letting characters take care of the plot, but if we have a strong sense from the beginning of where the story needs to go, it will travel better.

An accessible book to read about how to plan a plot while keeping the characters in mind is Debra Dixon's *GMC* (1996).[9]

Some say conflict drives the story forward. I still believe the character does, but it is her goal choices and especially inner motivation plus the presence of an antagonist, that is, *characters* that make the conflict happen.

Process

There are many different ways to write a story. Some make a plan (e.g. mind maps, storyboard). Not all writers plan – for example, when writing *Re-entry* (1995, now *Dear Pakistan* 2016) I had no idea what the resolution would be and the publisher was asking for a synopsis which needed the ending to be included. I just had to keep writing to see what would happen, and hoped that the publisher hadn't noticed it took me a month to reply. Gillian Rubinstein said in a talk at the South Australian Writers' Centre that one of the joys of writing is to take 'an idea and a few snatches of character, and see where it leads.' A plot can start anywhere, as Professor Thomas Shapcott often said in my writing class. Now, however, I find that if I know enough about my character it is much easier to see where the plot will go. The character makes all the decisions in the story, including what will happen in the plot.

Carol Wilkinson, who wrote *Dragonkeeper* (2003), showed at a launch how she meticulously plans her plot on a wall-sized whiteboard, by drawing a story board in the form of a grid. She enters in the major scenes that will be in each chapter. Some authors design it first (some call this outlining), some let it pan out. Gillian Rubinstein said that she starts where she feels some connection, maybe with the climax, and puts the fragments together later. This happened for me in *The Messenger Bird* (2012) where I had fragments or sketches, even sections of the story, and then I had to see where they fitted, if at all. But I do some outlining too so I know a general direction where I'm headed even though it may change and I could get a surprise. Overall, I think a certain amount of magic happens. At the end I have no idea how it all comes together.

Madeleine L'Engle states, 'When the words mean even more than the writer knew they meant, then the writer has been listening. And sometimes when we listen, we are led into places we do not expect, into adventures we do not always understand.'[10]

Workout

Review the mind map path to planning a character in Chapter 4. Now draw a mind map of possible events with your character in mind. Start with what they want to do or need to do or learn, and see how your brain will think up ideas of how this goal can be achieved. A plot will emerge.

What do you think?

Q Not all authors plot their books in the beginning; what could be the advantages and disadvantages of not planning?

Q Make a mission statement about your story. Can you say what your story is about in a sentence or two? This can keep you on track while you are writing and become the basis for your pitch later on.

Q A plot could look like a formula if spoken about as a list of events to tick off. Should we distort events or alter characters to make a story fit a pattern?

Plot patterns

There are many books promising various numbers of models for plot lines. In the reading of fairy tales we find readymade models of plots. Like the screen writer, Brian Godawa, Joseph Campbell who wrote *The Hero with a Thousand Faces* (1968) believed there was only one major story; that all stories boil up from the basic, magic ring of myth.[11] Vogler (1999) explains in *The Writer's Journey* (based on Campbell's book) that all stories consist of a few common structural elements found universally in myths, fairy tales, dreams and movies, that is, 'The Hero's Journey'.[12] This format of plot is seen in the book as a form and not a formula.

The Hero's Journey

This is a version of 'The Hero's Journey' in relation to my novel *Across the Creek* (2004). I read Vogler's *The Writer's Journey* before I wrote *Across the Creek* and I can see the influence of The Hero's Journey format in the story. If you look at CS Lewis' *The Lion, the Witch and the Wardrobe* and also the story of Joseph from Genesis, you'll be able to see the same pattern. I don't suggest this to be a formula to rigidly stick to, but it can be a pattern to look at if we find a plotline is not working. The skill to cultivate is to not let our plot become predictable.

In the beginning Aidan lives in the normal world.
1. **Call to adventure**
    Aidan hears a voice calling, and crosses the creek using stepping stones.

Riding the Wind

(Narnia: Lucy finds a way through in the wardrobe.)

2. **Refusing the call**

    Aidan is fearful and refuses to complete a task in the land across the creek.

    (Lucy continues to play.)

3. **Crossing the threshold**

    Aidan returns after a few days and walks across the creek again.

    (Narnia: Lucy goes through the wardrobe.)

4. **Testing of allies and enemies**

    A dragaroo attacks Aidan. He escapes it and the Cornish knockers in the mine.

    Is Raff, the piskey, his friend?

    He may not be facing only physical enemies.

    (In Narnia: the witch is the enemy; beaver & fox are friends.)

5. **Approaching innermost core**

    Aidan enters enemy territory, to face the Cornish spriggans and, later, ancient Australian spirits.

    Aidan is changing, becoming less fearful.

6. **The supreme ordeal**

    The hero has to overcome a supreme test.

    Aidan faces the mer-giant. He must stay awake or he can't save Jenice.

    (Narnia: Lucy in the river. With the other children she faces the battles and the wolf, thus developing capacity as a ruler.)

7. **Reward**

(For surviving and taking up destiny.)
Aidan can take Jenice out of the land.

8. The road back

Aidan discovers his courage when facing the knockers in the mine again.

9. Resurrection

Aidan finds the dragaroo's weak spot and overcomes it.

(Aslan comes back to life in Narnia.)

10. Return with elixir of healing

In the end, Aidan returns home with Jenice and they are welcomed as heroes. Both were thought to be kidnapped or dead and now are alive. Aidan learns he can be brave.

(Lucy et al crowned kings and queens and understand who they are.)

Thus the hero who doesn't understand all about his life sees destiny, goes through his journey, is victorious, discovers his identity and learns about his life after a battle or struggle.

Here is a similar pattern of plot based on an idea by Jane Yolen.[13]

- A beginning
- Immediate consequences
- The plot thickens – make things happen
- Re-establishment
- Plot thickens some more
- More plot thickening, deepest emotional level
- Resolution, inevitable and surprising.

All the different types of plots are to show you that there is a variety of possibilities.

This is Hodgins' view of formatted plots:

> Rather than think of plot as a prescribed formula … to which you must make your material 'fit', I suggest that you think of it as a general pattern floating somewhere in the back of your consciousness as you write, ready to come to the rescue when you are looking for the reasons a story doesn't satisfy, refuses to move forward … or simply bores you.[14]

Tips

- Let the plot take on its own shape: one that suits the character and the story.
- Don't think of too easy a resolution. Think of an unresolvable situation and have your character solve it. My professor used to say to push characters to their limits, see what happens. Karen Foxley's *A Most Magical Girl* (2016) does this very well. Just before the end when Annabel has to save London, the shadowlings catch her and she is without her magical means of protecting herself. There is no way she can survive. She is pushed to the wall and there is no escape. Or is there? I couldn't see it at first; I was devastated. Yet Foxley turned it around. I like to be surprised like that. When I find my character is between a rock and a hard place I return to my journal, reflect and do mind maps

on my character's personality and abilities because the character does have the solution. At times I have told the story to someone to untangle the plot. If this fails, I ask readers to brainstorm it with me. At one of these times I discovered I had already written the climax and so the character couldn't go any further. I wrote another chapter leading to the climax and the problem was solved. See a diagram in Chapter 9 where I resolve such a problem.

- Be careful of episodic plots. In *Poetics*, Aristotle[15] said they are the worst type of plot, where the sequence of episodes are neither necessary nor probable. I first wrote *Taj and the Great Camel Trek* (2011) as a diary, then realised it didn't work since Taj would not have been able to write English. So I rewrote it as a novel. It took many drafts to rid it from being episodic, that is, it had read like a diary with no causality between some of the scenes. This had been helpfully pointed out to me in an early rejection letter.

Workout
Check your plot
- Does your protagonist have a goal and motives that the reader will care about and so get involved?

- At the opening of your story does your plot invite the reader in at a point of change or when the character is in trouble?
- Does your plot have events that are causally connected?
- Are there conflicts, obstacles; from minor hassles to disasters? The real interest is in the way the character handles (or copes with) the conflict. Is the tension only occurring from misunderstandings of what people say? Once can be fine, but a plot built only on misunderstandings will make the story melodramatic. Have strong reasons for tension and conflict.
- Do you have a climax point? Everything has been leading to this.
- Is the plot too complicated for younger age groups? Subplots? Long flashbacks? Or is a flashback used too soon before the reader can gain rapport with the main character and the main story?
- Is there some insight into what all the struggle has been about for the character?
- Is a complication or climax overcome by coincidence? Even if it seems to happen like that in real life, it doesn't work in a story. If a character needs to get down from a mountain, he needs to work it out for himself, not have a character who's never been mentioned turn up in

a helicopter. This would reduce interest and credibility.
- Endings can be surprising, but seem obvious once the reader has read it. It can't be disappointing, and I believe there needs to be hope, especially if the characters don't achieve all they set out to. It doesn't have to end up too sweet, but the possibility of future resolution can be shown. In my novel *Sailmaker* (2002), the old sailmaker's dog dies, but there is the hope of a puppy. The dog was not a main protagonist. That would have made a different story with the dog dying earlier in the book perhaps so the characters could work through their grief.

write

write about the winter
the creeping cold
the darkening trees
the breath that curls and whispers
of warmth
write about desire
its soft touch
its weight
write about the fire
that burns like hunger
write about sickle-shaped leaves,
pale strains of music
write about the grey stain of shame
the bent knee of repentance
write of hope
in birth, in water,
in each bright star
remind us why it matters
remind us to be still
write us down
beneath our slumber
where we wait to be awoken
write
that we remember.

Elizabeth Snow[16]

6
Writing Short Stories

The first page test

Many times I am asked how I 'do' it, how I write a children's book. Children are more particular. A Year 2 boy once asked me, 'How do you get all those words on the page?' There is little difference in the process of writing novels for children's and writing for adults, other than the age of the main protagonist, voice, content, style and length. The most important things about writing are the same: creating great characters, an engaging story, using interesting words, showing love, hope, beauty, and truth about life. The big question to ask ourselves is not if we're a good enough writer to write an adult or 'real' book, but whether our writing is good enough for children. UK Academic and author, Andrew Melrose, says that we shouldn't just write for children. Write well for them. Give them the literary experience they deserve.[1]

Would your writing pass a child inspection test? Try out the first page of your story on some children – expect honest answers and you may receive them. Here are a few:

'Nothing happens, they're still eating breakfast at the end of the page.'

'There's no problem yet. (Kids know these things).

'Who is the story about? I can't tell.'

'It's boring because there's no dialogue.'

'Nice descriptive sea words, Nanna, but it's a bit slow. You need a shark in there.' Eeek! I did manage to include a shark in the land-locked book *Kerenza* for Amelia: it appears as a metaphor.

Your young readers should never be in doubt about who your main character is, how the character speaks, what's bothering him/her, and what he/she is doing about it. Your readers should never, ever be bored on the first page.

Let's start with short stories as it is a form we've probably all had a chance to write. I didn't write hundreds of short stories like speculative author Sean Williams. My children wanted novels, but I did write a few short stories. One called 'Dingo Fence' was accepted in a magazine for teens called *Pursuit*. It's a good idea to write stories and try to get them published or enter them into competitions – it all helps when it's time to publish a novel. As usual I always read the format I am attempting to write. So as you read a short story decide what it is that works for you. Is it the character? The setting? The plot? Why? Decide how the author achieves reader rapport with the character. What happens in the beginning, then how is the development handled? What form did the story take? How much time is given to the ending? Read with a writer's eye. Try drawing a graph of the story's tension. Does it rise and fall, while insistently travelling up towards the climax?

I think of short stories as having a 'rule of one' (though, as usual, any writing rule can be broken if you do it well and with purpose). Stories for children are written to be read in one sitting and usually have one main character with one point of view. They tend to have one theme, one plot, one main event or problem, one main setting, one time frame like a snapshot of a character's life, one tone or feeling, one climax and ending. This is because they are short. Here I'll refer more to stories that are 1000 words. There is fast fiction of 500 words and even competitions on the web for 50 word stories or 6 word stories. Here is a 6 word story: Much loved dog kennel for sale.

Even wordless books like Aaron Becker's *Quest* (2014), Jeannie Baker's *Hidden Forest* (2005) and Shaun Tan's *Arrival* (2006) tell a great story.

Choices will need to be made, such as, when will the story start, in which particular time frame of the character's life will the story occur? Which character will take the stage? Some of the best short stories for children are simple in structure, so don't try to include a subplot, flashback or too much background. Choose words carefully. A well-chosen word can show more than a phrase or sentence.

As with all stories, there is a basic structure of introducing the character and problem, the development of how that problem or issue is handled, and a satisfying resolution. The ending doesn't necessarily need to have a twist. I think of the structure of a story, whether it's a short one or a novel, as a letter 'S' – the beginning of the lower curve is where the character and problem is introduced; the tension/conflict rises up the stem of the 'S'; the climax is at the top, and then you have the resolution. A difference between a short story for children and a novel is that short stories have one main rising tension and climax with no chapters.

Characters pre-exist for me. In a short story in particular, we write about a certain time slot in the character's life – but the characters were living before the first paragraph, and will be after the end. I think this is true for novels too, unless the story starts at birth, but it is more obvious in a short story.

To be convincing, characters have to fulfil readers' expectations.

- They need to be consistent in their behaviour. If they act inconsistently it should make sense and show character insight.
- Characters need to be motivated in what they do, that is, have a reason for their actions. What are their goals? What is it your character wants to do or find or learn about in these 1000 words? It won't be a big decision that a novel would normally handle.
- They need to be authentic or lifelike. The character must be capable of change. Maybe we will see only the desire for change appearing in a short story. It's possible in a short story that characters will understand something new about life or themselves by the end.

Tips

Explore the character's emotions and thoughts. I often do this by having them write a diary page in my journal. Imagine your character's friend forgot to enter her into a competition and she could have won. How does she react? How do your characters act when frightened, sad, happy?

Make sure you write action. 'Resist the urge to explain' every detail about your character on the first page. Young readers like characters who want to do things. How they do it will show a lot about the character, so you won't have to *tell* the reader about them.

We need to help the character come alive for the reader and so suspend the reader's disbelief, to coax them to believe the character is real.

What do you think?

If you have written short stories for adults, what do you think is different about writing short stories for children? I came up with this list.

- Age and point of view of protagonist. The protagonist needs to be a child.
- Content/themes that children will relate to.
- Children's stories may be shorter.
- Sentences may be shorter depending on the target age of readers.
- Children enjoy new and interesting words and concepts so don't be afraid of using them. But convoluted phrases and sentences with too many conjunctions (using 'and', 'but') can be confusing for very young readers. Though author Jackie French argues that most children's books are not suitable for them because they are too simply written. 'We have confused the books

that a child would be interested in, with the ones that they are able to read. We have set the bar too low with the material we give our kids.'[2] She goes on to say that a truly great kids' book is also an adult book.

Workout

Draw a map of where the action will take place in a scene. Think of your character there. What is he/she doing?

Bring in another character. Something is wrong. Show the conflict between them. Have these two speak together and try to have them speak differently from each other by using their styles of speech or particular words. If one is menacing, show it without using an emotive adverb such as 'he said menacingly'. Please don't tell emotion, show it in a creative way.

Beginnings

Since you may only have 1000 words to play with in a short story don't start with the back story or exposition, that is, the set up for the story. Exposition needs to be spare but relevant. And most exposition can be shown in scenes through dialogue, the character's thoughts and actions. Use your journal for writing the backstory, theme, and what's just happened before the story started. Then let the story start.

Some beginnings focus on: introducing a character, showing a problem, dialogue, a time. Beginnings are difficult for me, so I don't wait until I have that first fabulous sentence to start. I leave a space and start writing where I feel comfortable. After I've finished the first draft I go back and write or rewrite the beginning. I use this technique with novels too. My first chapters usually have to be cut or rewritten or switched with the second one.

Endings
Endings need to be satisfying and logical with the child character making choices, that is, having agency, to bring about the resolution. Check out these endings.

- Happy ever after. This is beneficial for young children, especially at bedtime.
- Hopeful ending, even if the character doesn't achieve everything she wanted to. Often used in upper primary or YA readership.
- Dead end – unhappy ending. Not suitable for children's writing. Most topics can be written about for children, even death, but it has to be handled sensitively. Ending with a death would be distressing, but starting the story with a death can work well as the character and reader have time in the story to process the emotions of the event. Though if the death has recently happened it may be a larger idea more suitable for a novel.
- Twist – ironic. Twist endings don't always satisfy and can make the story sound contrived, created only for the ending. So I suggest not to force a twist ending but if it happens naturally, it can work, as I found when writing *Kelsey and the Quest of the Porcelain Doll* (2014).

- Surprise. Some element of surprise is helpful but again, don't push it, let it also happen naturally.
- Returning to the theme.
- Returning to the title. This is the last line of my novel *Sailmaker* (2013):
  > 'Yep. As the sailmaker says, you just have to ride the storm through – things tend to float right side up sooner or later.'

Workout
Try writing to an ending for fun.
- That's how the school burnt down.
- I'll never let Flippy out by herself again.
- I had to laugh. Kris did look funny.
- Or make up one of your own. You can always change the ending afterwards.

Did this work to get a story idea or was it constricting? Did the story have a life of its own or did you find you were trying to make the story fit the ending?

Reflecting on our writing
Author Michael Morpurgo reflected on writing his short stories in the book *Singing for Mrs Pettigrew: A Storymaker's Journey* (2006). The book includes eleven short stories for children and after each one Morpurgo reflects on the story, his process, his art. Quite fascinating. I believe this is a helpful exercise for our own writing.

Workout
After you have written a short story, reflect on some of these questions.
- Why did you write it?
- Where did the first idea originate?
- How did you develop the character?
- Why did your character make certain choices?
- What do you think works well in the story?
- What could be improved?
- Have you read it to someone? What did they say?
- What have you learned from writing this story?

There is more discussion on reflecting about our writing in Chapter 12.

Reviews
Writing reviews can be a good way to ease into the publishing scene. There are many review sites online. See the Reading List for children's & YA literature journals online like *Reading Time* and *Viewpoint*.

Here are some tips on writing reviews from Wendy Noble, author of *Beast Speaker* (2017) and reviewer for *Good Reading Magazine*:
- Never, ever, reveal the ending.
- Give enough detail to whet the reader's appetite.
- Make sure you mention the genre of the work.
- If you like the book explain why, and vice versa.
- Always be respectful. Your job is to critique the work to enlighten future readers. It's not your job to attack the author.

- Don't copy anyone else's style. Find your own voice.

Guest Author — Sally Dixon[3]
An excerpt from 'Where is Midnight?'

The story so far: Molly and her family have to leave their house because of the threat of the bushfire – but Molly's cat, Midnight, is nowhere to be found.

Mum doesn't say anything at first. Her face is grey like the smoke-filled sky.

'I couldn't find Midnight,' she whispers. 'He must've been sleeping in a secret corner. I searched and searched, but there wasn't time…' Mum's voice trails into nothingness.

I kick the car seat in frustration. Tears trickle down my cheeks.

I want Midnight. I need Midnight. I love Midnight.

I cry all the way to Nanna's house. Elise blows butterfly kisses my way, but it doesn't help.

Dad is already there. He comes out to meet us. I sit and sob and don't look up. Dad reaches in and unbuckles my seatbelt. Strong arms wrap around me as he lifts me out of the car. He holds me tight and murmurs, 'I'm sorry, Molly-Moo.' I bury my face against his shoulder. My tears make a wet patch on his white shirt.

> 'Midnight is a clever cat,' he whispers. 'If any cat can find a safe hidey-hole, he will!'
>
> His words help a little, but I can't stop crying. I cry until I fall asleep in Nanna's spare bed.
>
> I miss Midnight.

Just to reassure you, this is not the end of Midnight's story.

Opportunities

Visit the websites of magazines for kids. You should find information on themes, lengths of stories and age levels, for example, *The School Magazine* http://theschoolmagazine.com.au

Jackie Hosking's *Pass it On (PIO)*, an e-zine on writing for children, has a list of opportunities for stories at https://jackiehoskingpio.wordpress.com

Read some anthologies and keep checking publishers' websites or e-zines like *Pass it On* for opportunities to contribute. At times you'll find a novel existing of short stories. This is not an easy thing to do and if not carefully planned the novel could become episodic. In Phil Cummings' novel, *Danny Allen was Here* (2007) each chapter is a short story but collected together they become Danny Allen's story.

7
Writing Picture Books

There are many picture book manuscripts in an old folder in my underground writing room. I went to picture book workshops and discovered the way to format them, but that isn't the whole story. A picture book needs to have an innovative, interesting idea which will enthuse the illustrator before it manages to become a book to inspire children and their parents. There was one story that I kept revisiting. It changed from a fairy story to a cultural story about a girl living in a mountain kingdom in Northern Pakistan. I still had trouble because I didn't know what this girl, Shazia, could want to do in the story. I needed a plot line. Then one morning in the newspaper I saw a snow leopard cub asleep in a bed with a very tired zookeeper. And I knew what Shazia wanted. It became a story of conservation on three levels: snow leopards, the Kalasha people and their forests. I called it *Yardil* and it received about twenty rejections, mostly because 'who would want to read about a group of people who number only 3000?' This was before the Australian National Curriculum had an Asian component.

Yet even when I told this story without illustrations, children liked it, so I kept trying until finally a small publisher said yes. 'This is the sort of thing we like to do: stories about cultural groups that no one knows about.' So never give up; as long as you're committed to making it the best you can, there will be someone who will appreciate it.

Think of a recent picture book that you are fond of. Why do you like it? What do you like about the style of writing? The illustrations? The ideas/theme? How is it different from picture books you enjoyed as a child?

What makes a good picture book?

- Do you think characters can be developed enough in a picture book? How?
- Is the central idea conveyed in a way that is arresting and innovative even though it may be a topic already written about?
- Are the words interesting and memorable with rhythm, repetition and metre? How do they sound when read aloud? Do they conjure images? Is there simplicity and harmony?
- Do the illustrations take an equal share of the storytelling? Do they suit the text?
- Is the story and content applicable to children?
- Structure and simplicity. Simplicity doesn't mean 'dumbing down'. Sometimes texts that seem the simplest have taken the longest to write. Mem Fox's *Green Sheep* (2004) for instance. See her reflection on writing *The Green Sheep* on her website.[1]
- Emotional core – does the reader care about the characters and the story?
- Is the story, as Katherine Paterson said, a thing of beauty with simplicity, harmony and brilliance?[2]

One of my favourite picture books which fulfils all the above is *Banjo and Ruby Red* by Libby Gleeson and Freya Blackwood (2016). Banjo is an old farm dog and Ruby Red is a proud hen who never obeys Banjo when he rounds up the hens. It doesn't look like they'll ever be friends. With onomatopoeia and charm this story grabs your heart, as one day Ruby Red doesn't show. Banjo finds her and keeps her warm. A special relationship ensues.

What do you think?

Q Author and academic, Eleanor Nilsson, suggests it is subject matter and POV that make a book suitable for children.[3] Do you agree? Is there a certain style, and structure? For example, flashbacks for children under the age of 9 or 10 can be confusing.

Q Nilsson says to be true to your own story.[4] What do you think this means? Madeleine L'Engle makes a similar statement about being obedient to the story.[5] Does L'Engle's statement go a step further?

Q Skills are learnable. You also have to desire to write and have talent. What do you think is the proportion of inspiration to hard work that is involved in writing a picture book?

Some categories of picture books

- Wordless books: e.g. *Window* by Jeannie Baker (1991) (for younger readers), and *The Arrival* by Shaun Tan (2014) (for older readers). *Journey, Quest* and *Return,* the wordless trilogy by Aaron Becker (2014). Prior to creating the books he illustrated scenes in animated movies, including *The Polar Express* (2004).

- Baby books: e.g. *Baby, Baby* by Phil Cummings and Greg Holfeld (2006) and *Baby Dance* by Katrina Germein and Doris Chang (2015). These may only have 50 or less words.
- Preschool: counting, first times, books by Pamela Allen, e.g. *Mr McGee* (1989); *Hairy Maclary from Donaldson's Dairy* by Lynley Dodd (1983); *I'm a Dirty Dinosaur* by Janeen Brian and Ann James (2013) and *Be Brave, Pink Piglet* by Phil Cummings and Sarah Davis (2015). These last two are stand-up favourites of my grandsons.
- Early childhood (4-8 years): including fairy tales, realism, and fantasy e.g. Allan Baillie and Jane Tanner's *Drac and the Gremlin* (1988); *Rose Meets Mr Wintergarten* by Bob Graham (1992); *Boy* by Phil Cummings and Shane Devries (2017); and *Potato Music* by Christina Booth and Pete Groves (2010). These form the category of classic picture books which are usually between 300 and 750 words. Though some publishers opt for less than 500 words.
- Older readers: e.g. Shaun Tan's work, for example, *The Red Tree* (2001) has a classic picture book's number of words but is suitable for upper primary. See also Colin Thompson's and Amy Lissiat's humorous and thought provoking *The Short and Incredibly Happy Life*

of Riley (2005). *My Dog* by John Heffernan and Andrew McClean (2001) deals with ethnic cleansing during war. My picture book *Mustara* (2006), illustrated by Robert Ingpen, has a thousand words and is for mid-primary, also not a classic picture book. Yet when I rewrote the story of Mustara as a chapter in the novel *Taj and the Great Camel Trek* (2011), I found that the text in *Mustara* was more picture book-friendly than I had thought. The prose in the novel brings out all the nuances that Robert Ingpen's illustrations portrayed.

Today my cat can't decide what to do: inside, outside; outside inside. *Dog In, Cat Out* by Gillian Rubinstein and Ann James (1991) for early readers deals with this very occurrence. It has approximately 50 words using only 4 different ones: dog, cat, in, out. However, the illustrations show the full hilarious story. Think of a book like this when you write a picture book to remind you to leave room for the illustrator to create a story too.

Read widely as there is much variety in picture books, for example, *Where Does Thursday Go?* by Janeen Brian and Stephen Michael (2001) is a philosophical story for younger readers.

Illustrations

Usually the publisher chooses the illustrator, however after *Mustara* was accepted the publisher asked me which illustrator's style I thought would suit the story. Rather flippantly I suggested Robert Ingpen but was told not to hold my breath as he was in demand and overseas at the time. However, he enjoyed the story and said he would do it. He worked quickly, and quite soon after he had accepted, an A3 story board arrived with small sketches of all the spreads. With Lenore Penner's and my latest picture book (which is actually an illustrated fable), *Chandani and the Ghost of the Forest* (2019), we suggested to the publisher an illustrator we knew, Lara Cooper, and the publisher accepted Lara on the basis of her portfolio.

One of my favourite classic picture books, *John Brown, Rose and the Midnight Cat* (Jenny Wagner and Ron Brooks, 1977) doesn't give detail on what has happened before the story starts. It's a good reminder not to add too much detail in the text. Some illustrators say there's nothing for them to create if there is too much detail. They don't want to just illustrate but interpret, develop and enlarge on the story. Do visualise the illustrations as you write, but one of my publishers told me that if authors give detailed instructions for illustrations, she tells the illustrator to feel free to ignore them.

A picture book can have a subtext, that is, the text can tell a different story from the illustrations, as in *Drac and the Gremlin*, by Allan Baillie (1991). Here the text sounds like a sci-fi story and yet the illustrations show children playing in their backyard. In Amanda Graham's *Educating Arthur* (1994), many of the pages start with the words 'Arthur helped', but the illustrations show he is creating chaos everywhere. So in a case like this you'd need to mention the rationale for the illustrations but not in great detail.

Tip

Only include any suggestions relating to the illustrations that are vital to the meaning of the story. Authors who cannot release their work to an illustrator and trust they will do their best may need to reconsider whether they should write picture books. I have found that the illustrators of my picture books have done a good job in not only interpreting the story but also adding the other part of the story in their own style. This is an occasion of not being possessive about our work. Our stories are given to us, and we need to be able to relinquish control, however hard that may be. I don't mean we have to agree with suggestions we feel are wrong for the character or story, but a picture book is a collaboration of the visual and prose, and so illustrators may want to introduce another element of the story and use their own family and pets as models.

Also, authors who can't release their picture book text to an illustrator will be seen as difficult to work with. So a publisher could be alerted to such behaviour in a cover letter that outlines exactly how the author wants the text to be illustrated, even including photographs of children and dogs they want the characters to look like.

In some databases the illustrator's name is entered first. It is after all, a *picture* book, even though the author may have had the first idea.

Collaboration

My daughter and I have collaborated on writing two picture books, *The Wish Giver* (2008) and *Chandani and the Ghost of the Forest* (2019). Our process involved Lenore first of all writing the draft, then myself writing the second draft. Then we workshopped it many times to improve it further. It has happened that Lara Cooper has used one of my granddaughters as a model for Chandani because she has dark skin, hair and eyes like Chandani. We didn't expect this though.

Now illustrator Mandy Foot and I are collaborating on *The Book Horse* (working title). On Facebook I shared a story about women librarians taking books on horseback to outlying farms during the depression in the US. I noted that there's a story there. Mandy answered and said, 'Yes, let's do it'. We both did research. Then we workshopped the story, the characters, who they are and the setting. We've had a lot of fun. Mandy did a draft illustration to show the characters of the horse and the main human character, Will. I loved it. After that I was able to write a draft of the text, which we workshopped and I rewrote many times. As this writing book goes to print *The Book Horse* is still a work in progress but we can't wait to see it come together.

Some authors and illustrators have collaborated and then found a publisher, for example, Libby Gleeson and Armin Greder with *Big Dog* (1991) and many others; Jane Jolly and Sally Heinrich (2015) with *One Step at a Time* (2015) and *Big Papa Sky* (2017); also Ruth Starke and Greg Holfeld with *An Anzac Tale* (2013) and their graphic novels. During the process, Ruth and Greg kept in close communication with the publisher, Working Title Press.

Collaboration may not be a good idea if you are new at the game, but publishers are often willing to take a risk with authors and illustrators whose work they know. As you'll see from Christina Booth (below), at times a publisher may ask for a different kind of illustrator than you had in mind.

Writing a picture book
Layout

Look at examples of picture books. What can you notice about the layout, number of pages, how much text is actually needed, that is, how many pages in each book? Odd pages are always on the right.

Did you find they are all printed as multiples of four? If there are 28 pages (book pages usually start on an odd number, for example, page 3), and if you call double pages 'a spread', there are usually only 12-14 spreads and so you may only need 12-14 paragraphs of text and 12-14 illustrations.

Pages 1-2 are often imprint (details of publication) or title pages. Sometimes the imprint page is at the end. Ann James' and Janeen Brian's board book, *I'm a Dirty Dinosaur* (2013), doesn't have a title page, and the imprint page is at the end.

Try dividing a picture book text into pages like this diagram. In this chapter I've included part of *The Wish Giver* (2008) text to show text formatting.

Sally Heinrich

Themes and ideas

A picture book text needs a strong, innovative idea to carry it through. Take *Boy* by Phil Cummings and Shane Devries (2017). The main character is the hearing-impaired son of a king. When his father and army go to war against a dragon, the boy writes in the dirt, 'Why are you fighting?' A conversation ensues and the boy brings peace to the kingdom. This book won the 2017 Australian Psychological Society's (APS) Children's Peace Literature Award. What an interesting idea, using fantasy and a boy with hearing loss to show how peace can be wrought. Other ideas close to young children's hearts can work too. Another picture book about hearing is *Olivia's Voice* by Mike Lucas and Jennifer Harrison (2016) which shows one day at school in Olivia's life.

Choose topics children are interested in. Think what young children like: animals, people, toys, trains, diggers and so on. What could be happening in a child's life? Mum having a baby? Lisa Shanahan wrote a picture book called *Daddy's Having a Horse* (2005) which is an original way of introducing young readers to a new baby.

Children won't sit for a story if they're bored. It's best to keep away from inanimate objects such as toothbrushes. I used to make up stories to get my kids to brush their teeth, but I don't recommend it for an enriching picture book.

Remember what you liked, and talk to children to find out some ideas. Children often read to be entertained. Some disagree with this, saying that reading is serious for a lot of children. That means writing for them is a responsibility; our writing can make an impact, enrich lives and bring joy.

Do you think we should feel responsibility as writers for children? Recording artist, Keith Urban, says his music is a responsibility; he talks about the blessing, the love.[6]

Workout

Write three fears you have now. Then write three fears you had as a child. Is there a story idea in your list? A successful story about fear and its resolution is Libby Gleeson's and Armin Greder's *Big Dog* (1991). A problem to be solved produces narrative tension.

What other problem could there be in your story? The first time to do a task or go somewhere? Something lost is found?

In my journal/notebook I keep ideas and research to do with the subject I want to write about. Hanging around children, listening to what they talk about is enlightening.

Character

We must know our character. There may only be one or two main ones in a picture book, yet they can still be developed well by text and illustration.

Read the information and tips on character in Chapter 4, then write notes or do a mind map on the type of person your main character is. For example: age, name, family, personality, likes and dislikes, favourite animal, favourite colour? Fears, wishes, background. What is their favourite food, games, what they dream, a particular characteristic or hobby? All this will not go in your picture book, but you will know, and it will give you confidence to create an authentic character. I do this exercise now as a mind map for every book I write.

Tips

- Make sure the character is involved in action, either in the text or illustrations.
- Show emotion by actions or words. Quite often the illustrations will show the emotion. Don't tell information in your story that the illustrator could be showing. There is no need to refer to how happy the character is or what colour their clothes are unless it's a book on feelings or colour. Picture book creation is a 50-50 partnership.
- Impart information about the character through dialogue, action and illustration.
- Personality can be conveyed through a like or dislike, actions, or habit. What does their nickname say about them?
- The character could improve or learn something new or overcome a problem or fear.
- Be careful of having too many characters for young readers to follow. An exception to this is Ronojoy Ghosh and Mem Fox's picture book *I'm Australian Too* (2017). It has a different character on each spread. This works as the theme holds the characters together, as does the text. The beautiful illustrations by Ronojoy Ghosh develop the characters on the page.
- If there is a villain like the wicked queen in *Snow White*, she/he/it should arrive early so the reader knows of the threat and will be aware of his/her/its power/tension. If the hero doesn't

know of the threat, all the better. This happens in *Fox* by Margaret Wild and Ron Brooks (2000). The animals, a crow, a dog and a fox, have the same feelings and angst as people do. Children often enjoy seeing a 'bad' character become good. (Fox doesn't though.)

- A thought on animal characters: animal characters can work if written well, for example, Mem Fox's *Wombat Divine*, illustrated by Kerry Argent (1995), shows Wombat wanting to be in a nativity play. His personality is portrayed just as a human person's would be, although he is illustrated as an animal, and I think that is the secret to having animal characters work well. *Koala Lou*, also written by Mem Fox, and illustrated by Pamela Lofts (1988), is another successful classic of love and belonging.

Plot

For a picture book, keep the plot simple: a quest pursued, a task achieved, or a problem overcome. Keeping a plot simple can be harder than it sounds. We tend to have linear thinking in Western culture (Indigenous and Eastern cultures have more circular logic). In the West, even our sentences have a subject, verb and object: a beginning, middle and end. I, too, tend to follow Aristotle's beginning, middle and end plan. When the middle part gives me trouble, I remember what the character wants to do and why, and how that will influence the character's choices. Then it is easier to find that resolution.

A simple plan to follow could include the following:
- Orientation/beginning: set scene, introduce character
- Middle: events – the problem or quest, and what leads to the next thing.
- Climax and ending: ends happily, back to normal.

This is not meant to be a formula for picture books, but it can be beneficial to start the story right into the action. It's not a good idea to start with waking up, unless your story is about a day in the life of your character. Gain interest and sympathy for the character early. If the character has to go through a problem the readers will want to keep reading to see what happens.

Keep the narrative smooth as children are eager to read the story, not to see how cleverly you have arranged it. No need for flashbacks, time changes, or inner thinking by the character. I was told recently that my picture book text had too much dialogue: a reminder that a picture book is not a novel.

Have the ending in mind – there can be a surprise ending but this is not necessary. A picture book for young children must have a strong and happy ending.

This is why I wonder if Ron Brooks & Margaret Wild's *Fox* is actually for very young children as the reader does not see Magpie return to Dog. The hope that she will get home is there, but for younger children a picture of Dog and Magpie together on the end papers would assail any fears. A teacher told me it works well with her Year 2 class as they discuss jealousy in friendships.

The resolution can often be the most difficult part of a picture book, maybe after getting that brilliant idea in first place. You've set it all up, now how does the character get it all to work out? Again I do mind maps and think a lot. It finally comes. A picture book doesn't take a weekend to write although that has happened to some authors or song writers. Picture books can take as long as a novel in thinking time and polishing the words. Mem Fox said *The Green Sheep* (2013) manuscript took a year.

Workout
Plot
Try some mind mapping or brainstorming on your story. What are the different ways it could end? How will your character end it? Since the resolution is often the hardest part to write, how will it resolve in an interesting way?

Try story mapping. Story mapping is like mind mapping, but you draw the events along the way.

Setting
Write 'I remember ...' five times down your page and write some places or events you remember as a child. Do any of these give you an idea for a setting in a story?

It's always a good idea to use a setting children can relate to, for example, the beach, the back garden or places where they go.

Tips on language

Be visually aware. Understand the relationship between verbal and visual narratives. The story will be read aloud so it must sound right. Nilsson calls writing for picture books a concentrated style where the story is written in a condensed way with the detail lying under the surface for the illustrator to develop.[7]

We need to encourage the child reader to want to turn the page. Each spread is like a chapter, so finish each odd page with the promise of an interesting event on the next page. Each spread needs its own story arc, rise and fall.

- Be precise in your choice of words; keep it tight, as each word counts. Leave room for the illustrator to supply details and to interpret the text. Young children 'read' the pictures as well as the text.
- Think about the placement of the words; read it aloud to check. It can sound rhythmic without having to rhyme.
- Sentences shouldn't be too long, so eliminate complex clauses.
- You can write simply without 'writing down'. Your readers are clever.

- Be careful with description. Leave room for the illustrator to be creative and to interpret the story.

Some writing techniques
- Repetition – young children like repetition of words and ideas e.g. Lynley Dodd's *Hairy Maclary from Donaldson's Dairy* (1983). It's fun for them to join in on telling the story. Repetition must be used with intent and not sound as if we couldn't think of a better word.
- Alliteration is repetition of the same letter, for example, the slithery snake slid towards Sara. Be careful though – too much of a good thing can sound cheesy. Make sure the words are necessary and are not just included to see how many words starting with a letter you can write.
- Assonance: repetition of sound. Check out Janeen Brian's excellent use of assonance in *I'm a Dirty Dinosaur* (2013).
- Rhyme. For me, rhythm is more important than making words rhyme. Rhyming can work if done well. For good rhyme look at the work of authors such as Max Fatchen, Pamela Allen, Lynley Dodd. Have a look at Max Fatchen's *Meet the Monsters*, illustrated by Cheryl Johns (2004), and Ann James' and Janeen Brian's *I'm a Hungry Dinosaur* (2015). Whenever I have read this one to preschool children they want to dance. And they want cake!

- Rhyming text is the least published form of picture books, only 24 per cent. Not only is rhyming text often little more than doggerel, or using meaningless words because they fit the rhyme, but it is also difficult to translate into languages other than English.
- If you are a whiz at rhyming verse and have written your first picture book in verse, then consider sending it to Jackie Hosking's Rhyming Manuscript Service[8]. She also has an e-publication called *Rhyme Like the Experts*[9] which some of my students have found very helpful.

Drafting

Do rewrite a lot. Professional writers can re-write picture books more than 20 times to have the language just right. I rewrote *Yardil* (2004) 20 times, if not more. And if given the chance I'd rewrite it again. Remember to keep all drafts in numerous formats with back up. Don't be afraid to cut text. In a picture book less is definitely more. Depending on your target age try to keep the word count between 300-700 words. And less for early childhood. Though, as with all stories, they are as long or as short as they are meant to be, as my agent once said.

Read the story aloud. Read it to children to see if it works; when I'm reading *Yardil* to children they relax too soon before the end. I learned from that to allow my next picture book *Mustara* (2006) to resolve more quickly.

Author Eleanor Nilsson (1992) suggests rewriting without referring to the first draft.[10] Would you like to do that? Can you think of the benefits?

Other matters in picture book writing

- Humour works well, especially slapstick, but most jokes based on meanings of words can go over the heads of younger readers.
- It's best not to overdo the moral or a message you have on your heart. Some new writers really want children to learn something. Maybe they feel they have done a good job if the children can take away a message from the story. Let the story speak for itself. A picture book is not the place for getting a point across. The story is the reason for writing a picture book. And if it is an enriching one the reader will understand and be blessed without explanation.
- Best not to have violence in a modern day setting as it can be too scary. See Shane Devries and Phil Cummings' picture book *Boy* (2017); it's about war and peace but in a way a child can understand. Also, Phil Cummings and Owen Swan (2015) show WW1 in a way children can understand in *Anzac Biscuits* (2013).
- Total tragedy is unacceptable. The story should end happily for young children. *My Dog* (2001) by John Heffernan and Andrew McClean doesn't end totally happily but it is for primary school age children. Younger children would

like to see the mother come home. I keep mentioning *Fox* by Margaret Wild and Ron Brooks (2000) as it is an arresting picture book about the worth of constant friendship. Year 2 readers cope with the fact that the story finishes with Magpie hopping back to Dog from the desert after Fox has tricked her into leaving Dog. But younger children ask, 'Will she find him again?'

- Family issues like death of a loved one or Alzheimer's disease have been dealt with successfully in picture books. See *Newspaper Hats*, another collaboration by Phil Cummings and Owen Swan (2015). Georgie is visiting her grandfather in an aged-care centre:

    > Georgie walked through the doors that opened like curtains.
    > 'Will Grandpa remember me today?' she asked.[11]

    It's a beautiful book, illustrated sensitively to suit the content. And although Grandpa doesn't always remember Georgie, he can remember how to make newspaper hats. Again this has been written in an accessible way for children to process what may be happening in their family as has *When I see Grandma* by Debra Tidball and Leigh Hedstrom (2014). Any subject can be written about; it is the way it is treated that makes the difference for a child's picture book.

- Good still needs to win over evil. Though if you labour the point that virtue is rewarded and vice

punished, your story may sound moralistic. Let the story work its magic on the readers. It will call for thoughtful writing that shows and doesn't just tell.
- Don't write anything that will bore *you*.

Formatting a picture book manuscript

The manuscript is typed on A4 paper, double-spaced, with page numbers. Check publishers' individual websites for submission guidelines when submitting to them. Most publishers accept submissions via email. If publishers suspect you haven't read their submission guidelines, they may not read your manuscript. Not every author sets their picture books manuscript out with page breaks as *The Wish Giver* (2008) example is here. I didn't do so for *Mustara* (2006), but I do it now as I think it can give the publisher that added confidence that the writer understands a picture book layout. Of course if they love it, they won't care even if it has wombat paw prints all over it, which is what happened to Jackie French's first novel submission.

Here is the first part of *The Wish Giver* draft.

The Wish Giver
Rosanne Hawke and Lenore Penner

Pages 1-2 title pages

Page 3
In the heavens, a boy lives on the biggest, brightest star. When children wish upon his star he makes their dreams come true.

Pages 4-5
One night the boy was looking at Earth and he noticed Layla. She lay curled in her bed. The moonlight glistened in her eyes. She held Morgan, her bear, so close her tears were like rain drops on his fur.

Pages 6-7
Layla squeezed Morgan. 'The children in my new class don't talk to me,' she whispered. Another tear rolled down her cheek and splashed onto Morgan's nose. 'No one sits with me at lunch.'

Pages 8-9
The boy on the star leant closer to listen, and suddenly his foot slipped.
　　Down,
　　　　down
　　　　　　down he fell.
Like an autumn leaf he landed in Layla's garden.

Author Phil Cummings kindly read it and suggested we keep the story totally in Layla's point of view. Of course it was a better idea (why didn't we think of that?) and here is the rewrite. See how much tighter it is. After submitting, the editor restructured the content on the pages to fit a 28-page picture book instead of a 32-page one which we had written.

The Wish Giver
Rosanne Hawke and Lenore Penner

Pages 1-3 title and imprint pages

Pages 4-5
Layla lay curled in her bed.
The moonlight glistened in her eyes.
She held Morgan, her bear, so close
Her tears were like raindrops on his fur.

Pages 6-7
'The children in my new class don't talk to me,'
Layla whispered to Morgan.
Another tear rolled down her cheek and
splashed onto Morgan's nose.
'No one sits with me at lunch.'

Pages 8-9
Layla stared through the window.
She could see the biggest, brightest star.
She brushed the tears from her eyes.
Was she dreaming?
She thought she saw something falling
   down,
       down,
           down.
Like an autumn leaf it landed in Layla's garden.

Synopses are not always necessary for a picture book since the text is short enough to read in one sitting. However, I think it is a courtesy to include a short cover email to say this is your manuscript for perusal, with your details included. A well-written cover letter/email (or a badly written one) can determine whether the editor wants to see your story.

Find Mem Fox's tips for writing picture books on her website[12]. You'll also see some excellent and entertaining information regarding reading aloud to children.

Poetry

When I was working on *Wolfchild*, I knew that Morwenna sang so I tried writing her lines. My professor, Thomas Shapcott, a renowned poet, said that songs must sing, and mine didn't. Poetry must be music in words. There must be song, surprise and beauty. So I wrote the music of Morwenna's song, then I found the words to fit the tune.

To have a picture book that will be read aloud time after time, we need to take notice of rhythm and our choice of words. Rhyming isn't always the way to go. Children's poet and picture book author, Janeen Brian, in a guest lecture at Tabor Adelaide (2011), stated that children's poetry needed simplicity, word pictures, senses and feelings, tight compact lines, strong nouns and verbs, and details. She also mentioned a hook in the first line and to leave a memory in the last line. This is a fabulous summary of not only writing poetry for children but also of writing in general.

She has generously given permission for me to include some of her poems here. See how each one says something about the reader's world.

Huff-notes[13]

Huff-notes
need a window clear,
a deep warm huff
that fogs, and fingers
to clear the mist with shapes and words.
Be quick!
See-through, drizzly
huff-notes
don't last.

Colours remembered[14]

With a flick
    a flip
    a twist
    a flutter
autumn leaves pattern
sky and gutter
with colours remembered and
colours combined
from sunsets
of long ago
summers.

Snowflakes[15]

From their cloud cocoons
snowflakes unfurl,
stretch lacy wings
and butterfly
down winter sky.

I remember a dad time[16]

It was a gentle time
with a long jetty,
a sharp knife
and slivers of squishy cockles.
His sure fingers
slicing
bait
which I would thread
on a hook
as if making
a garment.
Sun crowned our heads,
I in his shadow
freckling away,
swinging legs,
aching to reel in – and in – and in.
Sure each wavelet
was a fish, dad!

> Mostly it wasn't.
>
> Mostly it was
> just a dad time.

Guest Author— Christina Booth[17]

As a Christian who writes children's literature, mostly picture books, I often consider how I glorify God in what I do. It isn't always the words we write that can carry God's message to the world but how we deal with people, how we respond to the negativity that sometimes comes our way in this industry and how we act as professionals within the business of creating children's books.

As my work has never had an upfront obvious Christian message I know that people do not reject my work or want to change it because of that but even if it did it is very important how that work is written and presented. No writing can be preachy or orientated primarily towards a particular lesson, Christian or not. No publisher will take that on. Christ taught us with stories; the Bible is full of stories in the Old and New Testaments and it is the way humans interact, pass on important information and learn from one another. We desire stories.

Often Jesus told stories that were not understood by even his closest followers on the day.

Stories need to be carried, they need to grow and evolve and become a part of us so that they can enhance, change and adapt our lives. It is the same for children's writers. In my work I always like to focus on hope, a strong message from the Christian heart and one, Christian or not, that is sought by most. We must focus on telling the story and allowing its revelation to come naturally, not to spoon feed or thump people on the head.

How do we respond to a rejection? I've had a few. The biggest rejection: not illustrating my own story. I had to take a healing journey with that as well as work out how to respond to the publisher who made that decision. It wasn't because I was a Christian, she didn't even know me, and it rarely is anyway. God took me on a journey. He always works with whatever life dishes up to us. I learnt so much about being an author who had to hand my work over to different eyes and creativity. This was such a huge blessing as I now have a much better empathy for authors when I illustrate their work. I am able to work as a team and with care for their feelings, feelings I wasn't aware of before. What a gift! It made me a better illustrator, even if I did start out angry about the decision.

We must consider our work. What am I trying to say? Who am I saying it to? Is this the best way to do it? What other angles and perspectives, points of view should I take? When I am rejected or my work is criticised, what journey is God taking me on to make me better at my craft and our gift? Will I let him? Can I, in the midst of anxieties, changes, editing, rejections and negotiations, be a pleasant person to work with, not taking it personally, and continually developing an attitude that will eventually be recognised as easy to work with, responsive to direction and a happy part of the team? We don't have to sell ourselves short, no one should, but we should do all in the love that God has graced us with. Let's shine in our work and our work habits and then God will be glorified in all that we do.

8
Writing Chapter Books

How I came to write a chapter book

Originally, I didn't choose to write a chapter book. I correctly suspected it was too difficult by far, but I heard a publisher was looking for short books for early readers, first chapter books. I understood they were to be 5000 words and thought I could manage that: maybe ten chapters of 500 words each or so. I just needed an idea that would last the distance but not be weighty enough for a novel. My gaze fell on my cat.

My cat named Q could collect hairpins. True or false? True. I continually found my youngest daughter's clips and hairpins in his food bowl along with paper clips and twisty ties and didn't at first realise he was the one putting them there. He could also open doors with simple handles. Some years before, another cat of mine had strolled in with a feather stuck to his whiskers so I used both these ideas to write a story about Luke and Breanna who had a clever cat who, they would discover, could collect things. This was the subplot and the plot involved Uncle Max's pigeons from next door going missing and everyone, except the children, blaming Q the cat. There was a time restraint. The children had to find the culprit by Friday when their dad would be finished the ploughing and would have time to take Q to the animal sanctuary to live. It was already Tuesday.

I sent the manuscript off and I received a kind rejection letter saying yes, they were looking for chapter book manuscripts but only 2000 words, not 5000 words.

However, they would be willing to look at it again if I cut it accordingly. When you receive a letter like that, always act upon it. It's not truly a rejection letter but a letter of invitation to have another shot at it.

Cutting can be exciting after the first spate of terror. I deleted the whole subplot of the children discovering that the cat can collect things. Two thousand words shrank to a paragraph of summary:

> Everyone looked at Q. He was just a young black cat with half a white moustache and a white 'Q' on his forehead. But Q was not ordinary. He collected bobby pins. Whenever Breanna or Mrs Tamlin couldn't find one, they checked Q's food dish and there would be their lost hairpin.[1]

Q's collecting crops up naturally again in the story and I discovered I didn't need the subplot. The other 1000 words were cut by eliminating unnecessary words, repetition and shortening sentences to suit a 6-year-old readership.

Next time I sent the manuscript it was accepted. I didn't dilly dally as I wanted the publisher to remember me and also not to fill their list before my new version had a chance to be read again. It became *The Collector* (2004), beautifully illustrated by Anna Pignataro.

Chapter books are not short stories or novels

Besides picture books, I think chapter books are difficult to write mainly because writing 1000 to 2000 word books might appear to be simple, but it isn't at all.

Not only does the chapter book need to have a story arc or shape like the overall structure of a short story, but each little chapter also has to have its own story arc, its own rise and fall. Also in a chapter book we are writing for children who are learning to read and we mustn't bore them. Children who are learning to read need good literature.

Author Joy Cowley argues that children learning to read need a real story that is interesting, entertaining, educationally and emotionally supportive, a story that is child-centred.[2] Cowley is not talking about class reader sets here but lively fiction to inspire children to love reading forever. We can inspire a lifetime of joy in reading. How amazing is that! It's what I hope to do.

One of my favourite early chapter books for technique is *I Want Earrings* (1997) by Adelaide author, publisher and agent Dyan Blacklock and illustrator, Craig Smith. In this story Carla wants to wear earrings but her parents don't give permission. How will she manage to resolve her problem and get those earrings? Blacklock introduces Carla to us and what she wants most in the world. Carla meets other people with earrings or piercings of different sorts which give her opportunities to ask her parents for those. They always say no with a reason. Their final reason is that no one in their family has earrings or piercings. When Uncle Harry turns up Carla's dream comes true. Or does it? This is one early book for children which is slightly open-ended, but will cause lots of discussion. I also enjoy the way Carla's character is lifelike and her emotions are shown rather than always told. Plus it's funny. The characterisation, structure, plot and language of *I Want Earrings* is worth studying.

Some types of chapter books

Some of the books listed below are still in schools and libraries and useful for learning how to write chapter books even if they are not being published now. Easy to read books and many educational readers are considered boring and disheartening by children. So keep that in mind if you write for the educational sector.

Examples of early chapter books:
- Omnibus: Solo 1000 words – light hearted, uplifting, family, humour, short sentences, shorter words. These are discontinued now, but still kept in libraries and schools. Approximate age 6-8 years.
- Omnibus/ Scholoastic Mates – light, funny yarns, showing the matey side of Australia with colour illustrations e.g. Phil Cummings and Greg Holfeld's *Chook Shed Snake* (2009) and *Barnsey* (2010) by Allayne Webster and Tom Jellet. Approximately 2000 words. Age 6-9 years.
- Lothian/Hachette: Start Ups, 2000 words, e.g. *The Collector* (2004). Discontinued but still in libraries.
- Penguin: *Read it Yourself* 1200 – 1500 words. Age 6-8 years.

- https://www.penguin.com.au/young-readers/ages-6-8
- *Zac Power* series, edited by Susannah McFarlane and written by a team of writers under the pseudonym HI Larry, including Hilary Badger (the first), Meredith Badger and Chris Morphew. Susannah McFarlane has many successful series. (For more capable readers).

There are many others too, so do look on the web and in your library. These are usually the books kept in boxes as children like to read in a 'series', such as the *Alice-Miranda* series by Jacqueline Harvey (though these are longer books written for middle primary). Never underestimate what a child may like to read.

Tip on length: keep a balance. Write until you've finished the story, but note which series have a certain word count. There is no point writing a long story for very young children if they are not going to be able read it, and it won't be accepted for publication.

Characters

Characters can and must be developed in a chapter book. I suggest not too many characters – maybe only two or three, and a few supporting ones. Try to choose a distinctive detail about a character. There can be strong emotions and intense relationships. There may not be as much room for character development as in novels, but the story and characters must be believable. Readers expect dialogue and action. Adults still play a part in these stories.

Read how one writer introduces her characters. Here is Tammy from Janeen Brian's *Rock and Roll Ducks* (2005): 'It was a piano and Tammy loved it… The piano didn't belong to Tammy. It belonged to Grace. Next-door Grace.'[3]

I like to discover what my characters want. Tammy wanted to play music. When you discover that, you have a story. Knowing their fears can help with the plot also. Minor characters may just have a phrase describing them. Here's Tammy's uncle in *Rock and Roll Ducks:*

> The next day Tammy's uncle came with a surprise. He had five ducks in a box.
>
> 'Can you look after them for a week?' he asked.
>
> Tammy's uncle kept pets. But he was always going on holidays, so he needed people to look after them.[4]

Language

Notice the sentence structure in the examples above: sentences are shorter than in books for older readers. The structure of the sentence is simple with no extra phrases to confuse new readers. However, children are never too young for delightful images like the piano in *Rock and Roll Ducks*: 'It was like a big, friendly animal. When its lid was up, it smiled with all of its teeth.[5] This is probably how young readers see the piano themselves. I did.

Emotion is shown well in Blacklock's *I Want Earrings*. When Carla is told she can't have earrings, she feels like stamping her feet. When she is told the fifth time that she can't have earrings, she won't speak to her parents for the rest of the day. The author has resisted the temptation to tell the reader what emotion Carla feels. Instead, she shows it through Carla's actions.

Eleanor Nilsson suggests being guided by the requirements of the story rather than watering down words to suit the needs of the audience.[6] So use the words best suited to the story. The structure of the sentences may need to be less complex. As an early reader I found the Beatrix Potter books difficult to read due to the extra phrases in the sentences with 'and' and 'but'. I still vary the length of my sentences as the snippet from *The Collector* shows earlier. Otherwise the rhythm will be stilted or non-existent. So be careful of using sentences with complex clauses or starting a sentence with a present participle like this: 'Lying on the ground with her face in the dirt, Jess could see the fluffy white clouds scudding by above.' Apart from being impossible to do, young readers may lose track of where Jess is by the time they get to the bit about clouds.

Illustrations

You don't need to worry about leaving enough of the story for the illustrator to show as with picture books, since in story books the illustrations are just that:

pictures which illustrate the story rather than interpret it as in picture books.

Structure

Chapter books are different from short stories in that they have chapters with a story arc as well as in the overall story and they are tricky to write. To work out the structure of a chapter book, I 'pulled' one apart to see how the author created it. Let's deconstruct or pull apart the structure of *I Want Earrings* since we know the story. I often used this method as an exercise when I was an emerging writer.

In *I Want Earrings* there are 1000 words and six chapters; that's approximately 170 words for each chapter. In the first chapter, Carla asks for earrings and her parents say little girls don't have earrings in their ears. In Chapter 2, she finds her friend Rosa has earrings and tells her mum, but her mum says that no one in their family has earrings. In Chapter 3, she sees a girl with a nose pin; she asks for that, but her mum says no one in their family has a nose pin. In Chapter 4, she sees a boy with a ring in his eyebrow. When she asks about it, her dad says no one in their family has a ring in their eyebrow. In Chapter 5, she sees a girl with a ring in her belly button. The same thing happens.

Think of a resolution to this story. There is one chapter left, only 170 words. How do you think Carla could get her earrings?

The resolution: in Chapter 6, Carla's long lost Uncle Harry visits. He has a ring in his ear. Carla is very pleased to see him.

Plot and the character's journey

A plot will be more successful if it arises from character, for then the action clarifies character. For a chapter book you may need to outline a plot beforehand. Types of planning include mind maps, story maps, story boards or lists. Joy Cowley (2010) encourages plots built from a simple idea.[7]

Timing: the story usually takes place in a day or two or in a week, so have a single dramatic idea and timeslot.

Theme is the underlying idea, or what lies behind the story. When you can't think of a theme this often is what prevents you from finishing a story (besides not knowing what your character wants), as there isn't that driving force in the story. Everyday experiences can work well as themes for this age group, making friends, pets and family; a new activity.

Nilsson acknowledges that chapter books can be difficult to write as we have to come to grips with the problem of developing our material. The way to do this, she suggests, is to expand on one theme or small idea, not throw in more ideas to achieve length[8] which I did in my first attempt of *The Collector* (2004).

Ending

Be careful the ending is not flat. Have an ending resolved by the main character. This age of reader needs certainty about what is going to happen. Work it out at the beginning, then you can drop hints along the way, so that when they get to the end it will seem to be the only possible way it could have happened. A sense of joy and wonder for this age group works well, so why not write a happy ending.

Humour

Humour is always important in stories. Cowley states that for a young child, laughter is the natural reaction to a feeling of wellbeing, and she suggests to write situational humour rather than putting people down[9], or using humour at the child's expense. Situational humour arises from relationships, family connections, emotional reactions and misunderstandings. Most TV comedy is based on situation humour, but always consider the child's perspective. Phil Cummings (2009) uses this type of humour in *Chook Shed Snake*. Dad is hunting the snake when a hen pecks his leg. He thinks it's the snake and chaos erupts. Young children also enjoy slapstick humour. They are also interested in their bodies and therefore enjoy humour to do with bottoms, poo and fluffs. As they get older, they will enjoy puns and double meanings and jokes based on misunderstandings. Joy Cowley gives some tips on writing humour.

> Humour requires crisp, vibrant language. Play with words. Be aware that they are the tools of your comedy. So are the gaps between them. Often what you don't say is as funny as what you do say. Learn to be ruthless when pruning. Funny stories demand a cracking pace.[10]

Workout
More practice on writing for different ages. Find a picture of a child character that you find interesting. This won't necessarily be your character, but it can be the inspiration to get you thinking about a character. Think of an idea for a story, like moving house, starting school, or facing a change in the family or in life.
- Write a page of it for 5-6 year olds. Use dialogue, emotions, action.
- Read aloud.
- Now write it for 7-9 year olds.
- What's different in the language and content?

Workout
Think of an emotion
Many exercises are worth repeating regularly; this is one of those. Write a paragraph showing your character having an emotion. Maybe they are playing their favourite sport. If your character is angry, how will his/her emotions affect their game? Don't mention the emotion or any synonyms of the emotion. Show the emotion by expression, actions, thoughts, or dialogue. Read it to a friend and see if they can guess which emotion your character is feeling. If they can't tell, rewrite it.

Workout
Don't be afraid to cut text
When I was first asked to cut 5000 words down to 2000, it seemed impossible. But after careful thought I could

see how it could be done. Cutting and pruning always results in brighter blooms and tighter prose.

This is a cutting exercise. Return to the first picture you saw or choose a new one – this character finds a button, or whatever you know your character would find, maybe a key or a stone.

- What does your character do?
- Whose button/key/stone is it? How did they lose it? What can it be used for?
- How does the personality of your character show in what they decide?

Write a creative piece about your character finding the button – perhaps a page or more.

Now cut your text by a third or even in half while still keeping the integrity of what you've written. Cut out subplots and flashbacks, extra adjectives and adverbs and long descriptive sentences. What do you think of it now? Have you cut too much – is there a word or two that needs to go back in? Play with it. I often do this on a subsequent draft after the first or second edit.

Guest Author — Kat Apel[11]
Why I write what I write

Two unplanned themes that seem to have worked their way into my writing are kindness and self-acceptance. How much better our world would be if we practised kindness … to everyone! If we didn't use our words as weapons, but thought more before we spoke or tweeted; remembered that real people have real hearts – real hurts.

Closely intertwined with that is self-acceptance; being comfortable in your own skin. Less comparisons and discontent. Being the best YOU! Enabling others to be *their* best. I hope my faith makes me kinder, more considerate and compassionate. Similarly, I'm hoping that my books help to make the world a kinder, better place. If my words help others to see those around them (and themselves) as individuals, and of value – if they promote kindness in actions – then that is a beautiful thing.

9

Writing Novels for Middle Grade, 9-12 years

When I returned from Pakistan in the 1990s, I did relief teaching as well as working in the Tyndale Christian High School helping ESL students with their English-rich essays. One day a 15-year-old boy came in for guidance. As he put his bag on the floor it fell over and his books spilled out. One was Roald Dahl's novel *James and the Giant Peach* (1961) that children usually read in primary school. He stuffed that book back in his bag like a flash, his face colour heightened. I felt sorry for him; he needed easy-to-read books that had teenage content and covers.

Around the same time I relieved in a Year 1 class in an 'at risk' school. One little guy was jumping on the desks and when I asked him to stop he swore at me. His face bore a mixture of anger and fear as if he knew he would spend lunch in detention. He ran before I could say a word. I reported the incident and gave my five cents' worth about the boy's needs. On the way home I wondered how he would fare if he didn't receive the help he required.

These two incidents meshed in my imagination and a 14-year-old boy who had trouble learning and controlling himself appeared. I worked hard to capture the 'in-your-face' personality of the 6-year-old boy I met while developing a story with content for older boys that was accessible and interesting enough for ESL students to read. The boy's name became Joel Billings. The first publisher rejected the manuscript because she didn't like Joel as a person. I knew I was onto something. Kids with ADHD often come off second best; they generally don't endear themselves to teachers or other students. The publisher who did accept the book had been a teacher; she recognised Joel Billings and, like me, wanted to give boys like him a chance to be a good mate.

This, *The Keeper* (2000, 2013), was my first novel for younger readers but it didn't start that way. I thought it would be lower end YA, but the publisher suggested that Joel be 12 instead of 14; that it be a book for younger readers rather than older, since the text was easy enough for them to read. In payoff I asked if the cover could portray the man, Dev Eagle, as well as Joel. I wanted older boys who couldn't read well to be able pick it up without embarrassment.

Categories of junior fiction

As with all age categories of books and especially broad ones like 9-12 years (middle grade), there will many different age levels represented. Some novels may be more suited to older readers like Wendy Orr's *Dragonfly Song* (2016) or my *Taj and the Great Camel Trek* (2011) at 50,000 plus words. Some may be shorter (10,000 words) and more suited to younger readers like *Audrey of the Outback* (2008) by Christine Harris or *Rain May and Captain Daniel* by Catherine Bateson at 20,000 words. *The Naming of Tishkin Silk* (2003) by Glenda Millard can fit somewhere in between. Children read up and down; some 9-year-olds can confidently read *The Hobbit*, some 12-year-olds would rather read a series like Andy Griffith's humorous *Treehouse* series.

Check out the series books in the library; many are kept in boxes within easy reach of the children, such as the pre-mentioned *Zac Power* series edited by Susannah McFarlane; Jacqueline Harvey's *Clementine* series; Emily Rodda's *Deltora* or *Star of Deltora* series; Kate Forsyth's *The Impossible Quest* series and Rick Riordan's *Heroes of Olympus* (2010). There seems to be a series for everything: fantasy, super powers, sport, fairies, horses, midnight library, horror, ancient Egypt, robots …

Series are often generated by marketing concerns: they can be quicker reads that produce quicker sales. Many times, though not always, they rely more on plot than character development, which is often a different emphasis from literary or stand-alone titles.

What are your thoughts on novels for 9-12 year-olds?

- Do you think settings should be familiar? Can they be set in other cultures?
- How much research would be necessary for a novel for this age group?
- How much of a story is taken from life? Should we stay true to the real events?
- How do you plan?
- Should you write for yourself or for your audience?

- What do you think will interest children aged 9-12?
- What structural and writing devices are 'acceptable' for this age group, e.g. flashbacks or metaphors?
- To what extent, if at all, do you think the author needs to be in control of the characters? Is an author ever in control of characters?
- What have you noticed about the language of some middle grade novels you have read?

These are some of the concerns I have to consider when planning to write a middle grade novel and which we'll address in this discussion.

Choices

Full length novels give us more scope to write without restraint, to have a plot with a subplot, and develop characters so well that readers feel they actually know them. I certainly find this easier to do in a novel than a picture book or a short story. Some writers find getting the plot to work and discovering the resolution is more difficult in a novel. Again, I find the resolution more difficult in a shorter work, but resolving the conflict well in a novel can be difficult for all of us, so don't be deterred.

Any genre can be used for a middle grade novel. Any time frame, past, present, or future. Any setting that children may find themselves in. I've just read *How to Bee* (2017) by Bren MacDibble set in a future where bees are extinct. Children train to be 'bees' to pollinate trees in orchards. Fascinating.

Characters

- Creating your character, or letting them come to life is the most important thing in novel writing. Know everything about your character (see Chapter 4). What do they want, and so why do they make their choices? Show their inner motivation rather than tell it. Please don't dump all this information on the first page but develop the character through dialogue and action.
- Some writers don't wish to know everything about their character so that they can get a surprise while they are writing, but I find it helpful to know enough so I can write with conviction. See what works for you.
- Characters must have weaknesses to be genuine people. Have a point of change, and appreciate weaknesses or flaws and how they can work for the character.
- Creating relationships between people who are different from each other can be interesting.
- Parents can still be present as characters in novels for middle grade readers. In *The Beginner's Guide to Revenge* by Marianne Musgrove (2012) Romola lives with her mum and writes letters to her dad who is a soldier. In Catherine Bateson's *Rain May and Captain Daniel* (2002) Rain May lives with her mum.

Riding the Wind

Gwenda Millard's Silk family in *The Naming of Tishkin Silk* (2003) is a loving, extended and colourful family.

- Villains are usually well-drawn in this age group and it's still easy to tell which people are the good guys and the bad guys. Older readers in this age level can cope with a 'villain' who's not meant to be a bad guy, like a father. See Tristian Bancks' *Two Wolves* (2014) and my *Killer Ute* (2013). On a different note, Elizabeth Fensham's *Helicopter Man* (2005) sensitively portrays a dad with a mental illness.
- I don't suggest basing characters on people we know as we won't be able to push them past boundaries in case it hurts our friend's feelings. Some readers think we are writing about them even when we're not (that is, they see themselves in the main character), so it isn't necessary to do it on purpose.
- The character is not just me even though elements of myself will appear in the character, but I've found I have more freedom if I keep a distance. The characters have to be independent enough to have a life of their own. Nor do I think I know them better than they do themselves – best to give them space to be themselves and be ready to be surprised.
- We already know how important names are. I choose names that not only suit the character in sound and background but also in meaning. Be

creative with nicknames. But maybe only certain characters use those nicknames. Details like this can help readers know who is speaking in dialogue.

Point of view (POV) – whose story and whose perspective?

The first novel I wrote for my daughter had to have twins, she said. Portraying twins realistically is difficult for anyone let alone a new writer, but my daughter was adamant. I didn't know it at the time, but those twins were indistinguishable from each other and I jumped from head to head as if they were the same person. A few other characters managed to show their thoughts as well. It was repeatedly rejected, of course, so that was when journalist friend, Ken Packer, introduced me to point of view and how it can work best in a novel. 'Choose one point of view,' he said, and 'stick to it.'

Which POV will you use and who will tell the story? Since writing *A Kiss in Every Wave* (2001), was difficult in first person I changed to third person, keeping Jessie, the main character, in sight. Then I found I was floundering as the narrator. I didn't want my voice to be overpowering and make the narrator sound older than fourteen. I decided that another teen character in the story should write it in third person. Once I knew that person was Elijah, the narrative flowed better in his voice. When writing my early novels I found it easier to write in third person when I knew who that third person was.

Who is telling your story? Is it the main character using first person (I, me), or another character in the book using first person telling the main character's story? Is it in third person (he, she) told by a narrator where we see only through the eyes of the POV character? Some call this limited third person POV as it acts in the same way as first person. I found this worked best in *Wolfchild* (2017) and in *The Tales of Jahani* (2016) since they were historical. Yet I used first person in *Taj and the Great Camel Trek* (2011) even though it is set in 1875. I wanted readers to identify with Taj and so make the history of an exploring trek more immediate for them. When I originally tried first person for Taj it made him leap off the page.

Tips

It's best not to mix points of view in the same paragraph and certainly not in the same sentence. I leave a blank line or a line space between paragraphs, that is, a new section, to show a different point of view if I want to change it to tell the story. Many writers say the story is more important than devices and if you need to change point of view do so, but be careful that you do it seamlessly. It's my opinion that if you have set out to write a story in one point of view there is always a way to get information to the reader without changing that point of view, such as through an email, a note, or dialogue. I also believe we can show another's perspective in different ways, without giving them the point of view, that is, by how they act, what they say in dialogue, what's overheard (though be careful of too much listening behind closed doors if it doesn't fit the story).

To maximise the emotional impact for younger readers it can be best to keep to one viewpoint. This is unless you have decided on a structure of telling the story from two different points of view giving these characters' alternate chapters as in *Jehan and the Quest of the Lost Dog* (2017) where Jehan has his chapters and Lali, the dog he rescues, has her own. In this way Lali can tell the story of her pups before Jehan knows about them. Different sections for each character within a chapter can be used as Catherine Bates does so well in *Rain May and Captain Daniel* (2002). Whatever you decide, be consistent.

A story is shaped largely by the character's perceptions of life, so when the viewpoint is changed, it alters the language, attitude, everything about how the story is being told. Changing viewpoints unexpectedly is disconcerting to the reader and can also show poor narrative technique. Of course, you will read stories where there are multiple points of view but, if it has been done well, you may not even notice. Check out Ursula Dubosarsky's *The Golden Day* (2011). This one is almost in omniscient POV where multiple points of view can be appreciated. It's good to remember that it is best not to break out of guidelines for writing fiction until you can write with skill and innovation.

If readers are confused by reading your story and there is an indirect feel to it, there may be a problem with its point of view.

Dialogue

It is important to nail dialogue, for it to sound genuine and show the characters' voices. To have dialogue sound genuine we need to cut out a lot of extra sounds that people actually say, like 'um, erm, well'. In dialogue the two people talking should also be distinguishable. How do you think we could do that? Dialogue should show new information about the characters, show conflict, express the theme, show tension. It depicts change, reveals character and advances the plot without telling. It can even expose a secret.

Some Dialogue Tips

- Dialogue actually means speech between two people, so I try not to have too many people talking at once. Though there will always be exceptions. Anne Hamilton's *Daystar: The Days are Numbered* (2016) has seven main characters. After a while it can be seen why seven are needed but I don't suggest trying this as a beginning writer.
- Speech tags: Don't be afraid to use 'said' as it is neutral to readers. We probably don't need 'asked' either if there is a question mark. 'She replied' or 'he told me' work as speech tags too.
- One of my pet dislikes is qualifying the verb 'said' with an emotive adverb, for example, 'he said angrily'. Telling the character's emotions is not skilful writing. The character's thoughts,

speech and actions should show the emotion, not be told by the speech tag.
- Be careful of talking heads, that is, people talking without the cues of body language or setting. Show where the character is and what he/she is doing. 'He fiddled with his helmet strap'. This is called a 'beat' in Browne and King, *Self-editing for Writers* (2001)[1]. But only use actions which show characterisation. Those beats are actions interspersed through a scene of dialogue. Beats remind the reader of who the people in the scene are and what they are doing. But don't interrupt the dialogue too much. Only give the reader enough detail to picture the action. Beats also need to reveal character, advance the plot, not interfere with rhythm of the prose, nor be distracting.
- Use the setting: The rain drenched her shirt. 'I'll never get there in time.'
- Ellipses for trailing off or for hesitation … dashes for interruptions—
- When writing a speech tag I generally write the character's name first, then the verb 'said'. 'Said John' is old fashioned and I think it sounds weaker. When I'm writing contemporary fiction I write 'Sally said' instead of 'said Sally' as it sounds stronger to me. At times in historical fiction I'll write 'said Sally' if it suits the character.

- Long stretches of dialogue can be broken up by summarising some of it in the middle, for example: Then she went on to say how it had all happened. This is useful when the reader already knows what has happened, but another character doesn't.
- Avoid whole sentences of dialect or misspellings to show speech. Show it rather by rhythm of prose, by not using contractions and by a few words or figures of speech from the character's language. Look at the word 'instead' in this sentence: 'It is a good idea but we'll use Mustara's reins instead. He will find the way home.' An English speaker wouldn't say 'instead' at the end of a sentence, but Urdu speakers put the most important part of the sentence at the end. Some more examples can be found in *Taj and the Great Camel Trek*. See Marianne Musgrove's *Frieda: A New Australian* (2016) which shows how a character with German background speaks in dialogue.
- Use contractions and sentence fragments in dialogue in contemporary stories otherwise it can sound too formal. This is unless you have a character who likes to speak that way or English is their second language.
- Be careful of using dialogue to tell all the story – that's what the narrator is for. Also don't have a character tell another what they both know just to tell the reader.

- Avoid repetition of a character's words. If a character has just said he won't go, there's no need to have his mate repeat it, 'You're telling me you won't go?' In my own edits I delete a lot of extra words in situations like this.
- Characters don't talk alike – is there a phrase one says differently from the other? Does one use questions a lot? In *The Messenger Bird* (2012) I used POV and tense as well as a different style of speaking for Tamar and Gavin. Their sections are both in first person but Tamar's speech is more thoughtful and flowing in past tense because that is where her head is; Gavin's speech is short and upbeat in present tense. He rarely uses 'I' and that's the sort of bloke he is.
- Don't let one character dominate the dialogue. You'll get a feel for this, just as you do when a friend goes on too long about his day. Have another character interrupt if one is a natural talker like this.
- Listen to people speaking. Do they interact? How? Have you noticed that people don't necessarily listen to each other? A character may finish speaking and the other one may finish what he was speaking about before. What's not said can be as important as what is. This happens in my novel *Finding Kerra* (2018). Blake often speaks as though Jaime hasn't asked him a question. Why? He doesn't want to answer it.

One character may finish the other's sentence. Speech moves forward as both concealment and revelation. Grieving people, for example, are often not articulate. What they want to say and don't say (like Blake in *Finding Kerra*) might be more important than what they do say.

Workout

Writing for different ages. This is an exercise that's worth repeating often. Think of a child character, say, 9 years old. Find a picture, in a magazine perhaps. Now think of a scenario that a 9-year-old child may be involved in. Where is your character? What is happening in his or her life right now? Write a few paragraphs. Try to include some dialogue. Then write the same creative piece but the same character is now 12 years old.

What changed? The scenario? The language? The tone? What else?

Some good books to help with dialogue are Dufresne's *The Lie That Tells a Truth* (2003) and Browne and King's *Self-editing for Fiction Writers* (2001).

Scenes

> *Scene is at the heart of the story and dialogue is at the heart of the scene.*
>
> Dufresne[2]

A scene takes place in real time; the reader can see events as they unfold. In scenes, events including action are seen as they happen rather than described after the fact. Scenes have a setting. Often scenes involve dialogue but it's good to have physical action to remind readers where the characters are and what they are doing.

Some writers simply summarise what's happened, but it is best to write a scene to show it happening. Take your readers there. Scenes give immediacy to the story.

Even if you have to write some exposition about a character's past or about a house, it can be done in a scene. Instead of describing the history of a house you could have a character showing the family portraits to a guest, for example.

Keep summary for those moments when you need to link scenes or to give a small piece of information that doesn't warrant a whole scene.

Tip

Make sure that all the important plot points in the story happen in scenes. Don't let important events happen offstage, or be summarised by a character later. The reader will be disappointed. Be brave, write in scenes.

Workout

Once, when we were living in the UAE, some bigger boys asked our 5-year-old son if they could ride his bike. Our son didn't know them and wasn't sure if they'd return it, so he laid it on the ground and sat on it. Finally they moved on. I just gave you a summary of an event. Turn the following summary into a scene and finish with one of the boys riding off.

> Jason received a scooter for winning an award. He was excited and took it down the street to try it out. When he reached the deli he saw that Greg, the class bully, was there. Greg stepped in front of him and asked for a turn. Jason knew that Greg wouldn't look after his new scooter and didn't want to give it to Greg …

Taking language to a new level

Description and images will be subject to the character's viewpoint. It depends on who is doing the seeing and how they are feeling. I enjoy reading sparkly sentences or 'golden lines' (as US author Ralph Fletcher called them) in children's literature. Glenda Millard is a master of them: Here are a few lines from *The Naming of Tishkin Silk* (2003). Griffin is not an ordinary boy and on his first day at school he is interrogated by the rough crowd.

> He looked up at Scotty and his band of supporters. They stood on a forest of battered legs with scabby knees and filthy, unlaced sneakers, arms folded, waiting edgily for a sign, a word from their leader.[3]

Keep description short, sprinkle it like salt; and remember, a little salt adds to the taste but too much can cause a heart attack.

At times I am asked to read a manuscript where the writing is good, but it lacks sparkle. It needs a new way of seeing. Comparing feelings or items by making images is what lifts a story beyond the ordinary. Again, too many images will spoil the effect. The trick is to know when enough is enough. Some writers who are very good at imagery pile in four or five images in one paragraph, until the text becomes too slow to read. An extended image can work where one idea is built on throughout the page perhaps, but too many images that don't relate to each other remind me of a traffic jam at peak hour.

Also be careful that images and metaphors grow from your character's interests and the setting she/he lives in. If she lives in the country and has never seen the sea, then don't use beach images. Below are some images from my beach novel *Sailmaker* (2002).

Simile
(when an object or feeling is *similar to* another thing). 'Guess we must look like a huge flock of alien birds invading his territory.'[4]

'Like' is used well in this example from *Danny Allen Was Here* (2007) by Phil Cummings: 'Danny wandered the kitchen like an archaeologist searching for treasure …'[5]

There are also many ways to show a simile without using the word 'like'. Again from *Danny Allen Was Here*: 'Everywhere Danny looked, he saw dirty dishes and mixing bowls stacked in leaning towers. They reminded him of the ruins of an ancient city'.[6] See how these two images, leaning towers and ruins, relate to each other?

Metaphor
(when a thing is regarded as a symbol of something else; when an object *is* another thing). Jesus Christ constantly spoke in metaphor, images and stories. He didn't distrust the images of the imagination.[7]

- 'Seagull at a picnic, that's you – eyes wide open.'[8]
- I've managed to patch up my sandcastle life after Nancy's visit. Built the sand up round the edges. Then Zoe turns up. I see the tide coming in high and fast.[9]
- I think of the sandcastle in me and how easy it is to crash it down – any thought, anything I hear. Even Shawn Houser can do it. Vern makes me feel like I've got to have rock, not sand.[10]
- She could have asked me sooner – saved a lot of sandbagging in my head.[11]

Using the setting for images
In *The Slightly True Story of Cedar B Hartley* (2002) by Martine Murray, Cedar beautifully describes an old couch and how it has weathered over the years and then compares this description to her grandmother, saying that is what time has done to her. You must read the page for yourself (page 81). The description of the couch does more to describe Cedar's grandmother than if the author had described the elderly lady directly.

Workout
Show not tell
It is always good to practise showing the reader what you are seeing rather than thoughtlessly telling the reader everything in your head. Imagine your character is cleaning his or her teeth – can you show information about your character by the way he/she is doing it, and by the words you choose to use? What emotion is your character feeling? How would you show that?

Dialogue is effective in establishing characters. Find a picture of two people or use characters you are developing from your current story. What are they saying? Without telling everything, show the interaction between them in their dialogue. Show their emotion without telling or explaining it to the reader.

Children in the 9-12 age level can understand showing and not telling and enjoy practising it themselves. Some very young children might not pick up on the clues to a character's feelings, so at times, especially in a chapter book or picture book, a writer may need to say that the character is sad. Again, I wouldn't overdo it as illustrations are excellent at showing a character's emotions.

Senses
Smell, touch, sound, sight, taste. Most writers will show what a setting looks like. They'll even show what a character looks like. Sight is probably the sense that is mostly used for showing or comparisons. So practise writing with different senses.

Elaine Forrestal wrote a novel called *Someone Like Me* (1996) where the sense of sight was totally eliminated. The point of view character is legally blind, yet this is never mentioned during the story. Once I realised this and read it again, I saw how skilfully Forrestal had used all the other senses. Only near the end is the reader told that Tas has a sight impairment.

Workout

- You have a sight impairment and are 10 years old. Write a creative piece showing how you will run a race.
- Write a creative piece showing your child character doing her/his favourite thing but leave out one of the main senses we rely on.
- Your character has a hearing impairment. Show how your character has a conversation with a hearing person she doesn't know on the bus.
- Try describing an object without mentioning it by name.

Structure

There are several things children will not put up with in a book. You have to have a proper beginning and an end; you cannot have flashbacks. Then you can't have a lot of description: keep it to a minimum. And you must be very careful with words. I find I use fewer, and they have to fit the case exactly and be chosen with extreme care.
Rumer Godden[12]

Workout
Reading to write

As a beginning writer I learned to read a novel to see how the structure worked. Read a novel for younger readers. What form is it written in: diary, prose, emails? Decide how the characters are introduced. How soon did you realise what the character is grappling with at the moment? Is the story chronological or does it use flashbacks? Does the tension rise throughout the story? Try making a graph of the main events. Is there a rise and fall in each chapter? Do chapter endings lead or link to the next chapter in some way? Are there too many cliff hangers?

Structure and plot work together but have different roles: plot, as we've seen, is the causal journey of events in a story; structure is the organisation of the plot and controls the order in which the reader receives information, that is, how we order that material. It affects how the reader reacts to the people and events in your story. The structure can even control the amount of reader involvement. It also shows how the writer sees the world. Pakistani novelists often don't write a chronological story. Indigenous novelists often don't use a linear structure either as they have a more circular style of thinking. The structure contributes to the theme or meaning. Genres like Choose Your Own Adventure, for example, give lots of scope for involvement.

Structure is not a technique that can be picked up immediately; it's another one of those mysterious things you learn as you do it and get a feel for it. Unless, of course, you resort to formulae. Flannery O'Connor states in *Mystery and Manners* (1984): 'the more you write, the more you will realise that the form is organic, that it is something that grows out of the material, that the form of each story is unique.'[13]

Ever been to an IKEA shop? Now that's a journey. They organise those shops so you experience merchandise in a certain order. Structuring a plot is the same. Your POV character is the floor designer who decides what sort of emotional journey the reader will have. Your character has choices. Decide what structure would suit your character and his/her story. The beginning, middle and end don't necessarily need to be in that order if you are writing for 11 plus.

Some structural choices

- Will you tell the story chronologically? Or will you start in the middle and flash back? A flashback must serve the present story. It must never overwhelm it, nor be too long. If your flashback goes on too long, start the story earlier so the flashback isn't so long, or maybe you'll find you don't need a flashback at all. Also, flashbacks can be confusing for many readers under 10 years.
- Will you use diary form, for example, the series *Diary of a Wimpy Kid*, or *My Australian Story* series?
- Alternating points of view: Catherine Bateson's *Rain May and Captain Daniel* (2002).

- Emails/letters: John Marsden, *So Much to Tell You* (1987).
- Interviews: *Brontide* (2018) by Sue McPherson tells the story of four boys (12-17 years) through interviews where the boys tell their stories. It reads as though based on fact and maybe it is. Innovative but will tug at your heart. For mature readers.
- Emails/official documents and diagrams: *Illuminae* (2015) the first title of The *Illuminae Files* is a space opera novel set in 2575 written by Amie Kaufman and Jay Kristoff. Even though it is YA, I mention it here as, no doubt, Year 7s who like sci-fi will read it. I found this fascinating as the story is told/structured through censored emails, classified documents, interviews and diagrams. The two main characters Kady and Ezra are in different space ships and can't meet, yet a relationship develops.
- Short stories which together form a larger story: Phil Cummings, *Danny Allen Was Here* (2007).
- Mixed media, journal entries, news clippings, diagrams: Andy Griffiths, *Treehouse* series (2011); Gary Crew, *Strange Objects* (1990). *Miss Peregrine's Home for Peculiar Children* by Ransom Riggs (2011).

When I've finished a draft I first of all read it through while wearing a 'structural hat'. These are some of the things I look for first. Structural edits are discussed in more detail in Chapter 11.

How is your beginning?

The beginning defines the major character and goals, the initial action or situation, the problem that needs to be solved. Plot is all about motive. And in plot everything happens for a reason. The first paragraph shows us what has been, who is there, and something happens. There is a sense that the entire story grows out of the beginning, as in my novel *Across the Creek* (2004):

> Aidan knew he shouldn't wander alone near the abandoned mine, especially not to the creek where Jenice Trengove disappeared last year. It was as if the water was calling him, 'Ai-dan. Ai-dan'.[14]

Of course Aidan goes across the creek, and finds Jenice as well. The whole adventure is foreshadowed in the first few sentences.

Interesting beginnings make us read on. Some raise a question. Some foreshadow a problem. Some establish the narrator's voice. Good ones make us curious. You may only have the beginning to induce a child to buy your book. Or a publisher to send it to their official reader.

Start with an exciting event, though not the most exciting – a story is a bit like a relay race. You have to start with a good runner (maybe the second best) and leave the fastest till last to catch up. Try to begin at a high point in the character's life, the point of change;

perhaps starting a new school, moving home, a relative dies.

Development

Then I look to see if I have developed the material strongly enough. The character pursues her goal and the conflict is explored. Action, rising tension and opposition keeps the character from attaining the goal. Who or what is trying to stop the character from achieving her goal and why? Is it because he wants what the main character wants? In the Moghul historical fantasy *Tales of Jahani* (2016) Jahani needs to discover who she really is. The main antagonist already knows who she is and doesn't want her to find out as he wants what she will receive when she discovers her identity.

Some points I try to be careful of in the middle:
- Are episodes of excitement/fear/amusement evenly distributed?
- Have I left any character out for too long?
- Can I end some chapters on a note of suspense? This leads to curiosity and turning the page. However, I try not to don't overdo it; I read one novel where this device got so tiresome, I felt manipulated by the author.
- Is length of the chapters balanced? Is the tension gradually rising towards the climax? I often draw a letter 'S' in my journal, as in the diagram here, and list the events in the story along the back of the 'S'. Then I can see if one event has

more tension than another and I shift it further up so it will occur later in the story.
- Is there a moment of despair before the climax to heighten suspense where the character is thinking she'll never achieve the goal?

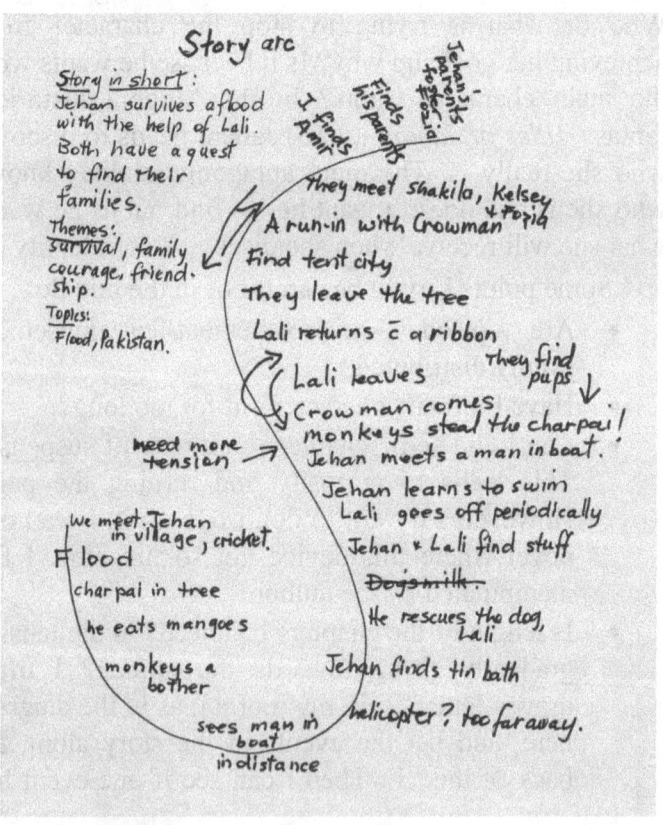

Tip
Moving from chapter to chapter
Does each chapter lead to the next in some way, not necessarily a cliff hanger, but a more subtle link? If a character is thinking of her friend at the end of a chapter, maybe the next chapter will show that friend in a scene. Or if a character falls out of a tree at the end of a chapter, the next chapter should show what happens next. It's not the best idea to always break a scene in half at the end of a chapter and finish it in the next. I try to only split scenes near the climax where I need the suspense a split scene causes. To do it all the time might make the reader breathless. Usually it's best to finish the scene in one chapter and start a new one in the next.

Endings
The resolution is the logical conclusion of all that has happened in the beginning and the middle. At times I have the ending in mind and will be writing towards it. At other times I won't see it until two-thirds through the first draft. Endings as well as titles are difficult for me. Afterwards I see the ending or title has been in the manuscript all the time. It could be hiding in the opening paragraph as in *Don't Call Me Ishmael* (2006) by Michael Gerard Bauer or in a phrase a character says.

I try not to spend too much time on what happens to the character after the resolution. I made this mistake in the draft of *Sailmaker* that went to the agent. She rang and said, 'Get rid of that last chapter, you have two endings.' I knew I needed some of the information in the last chapter, so I thought of including it earlier as a summary rather than a scene. Then there was no confusion about the true ending.

Structuring a novel can even be like conducting an orchestra. When I had finished a draft of *The Messenger Bird* (2012) I made a 'score sheet' of the characters in columns: In which chapters did they enter? Were they left out for any period of time? I could see if there was an imbalance of sound and make adjustments.

The key in structure is balance and simplicity. Simplicity is a harder goal than it sounds but structure does improve with practice – it's like an artist using her eye for colour and form.

Workout

- Take a plot line from another source such as a fairy story, folktale, Bible story or Shakespeare and play games with it. Jackie French has an excellent Shakespeare series: *I am Juliet* (2014) *Ophelia, Queen of Denmark* (2015) and *Third Witch* (Macbeth) (2017).
- Try changing the form and structure: decide at which point of the story you will start, for example, if there's been an accident and a boy has fallen off his horse. Start with the event and carry on? Or start earlier and relate how the accident happens chronologically? For older readers, you could start much later and flashback to the event. Will emails or embedded stories work well?

- Decide which structure would work better for younger readers? For upper primary?

Other forms of novels

This chapter has focused on the prose novel for children but there are other formats of novels, for example, novels written in the form of diaries, verse novels and graphic novels, none of which I write. So I'll suggest some examples to check out.

Verse novels

There are many review blogs online directing readers to interesting children's books. You can check out Megan Daley's reviews and many others on her blog: 'Children's Books Daily'.[15]

One of my favourite verse novels for younger readers is Kathryn Apel's *Bully on the Bus* (2014). This is an inspiring and wise book. Leroy is being bullied on the bus by an older girl. How will he make the bully stop? Apel's *Too Many Friends* (2017) is also a great verse novel for lower primary, helping readers to navigate friendship at school.

Also see Sally Murphy's *Roses Are Blue* (2014) and *Pearl Verses the World* (2009). Murphy writes light and darkness gently. The writing appears effortless but is carefully crafted by a talented wordsmith. Her book *Toppling* (2010) won many awards and deals with dominos, friendship, child cancer and hope.

Lorraine Marwood's *Star Jumps* (2009) won the Prime Minister's award for Children's Literature in

2010. It's set on a farm during a drought. Ruby wants to save the farm. Lorraine Marwood's *Ratwhiskers and Me* (2008) is a historical verse novel set in the goldfields of Victoria.

Sheryl Clark's *Farm Kid* (2007) won the Patricia Wrightson Prize for Children's Literature in 2008. It was good to see a verse novel treated equally with prose ones.

Wendy Orr's *Dragonfly Song* (2016) has a clever mix of prose and verse. The verse appears to show the main character's feelings. The switch from prose to verse is so seamless I didn't realise I was reading verse. Beautifully constructed. Have a look at *Swallow's Dance* (2018) set in the same world.

Poet Kate Deller-Evans (2011) wrote an interesting paper discussing junior verse novels, called 'Out of the drought: Australia's junior verse novels.' This can be found in the online journal *Write4children*.[16]

Graphic novels

Graphic novels are gaining increasing popularity. Have a look at *Captain Congo and the Maharaja's Monkey* (2009) by Ruth Starke and Greg Holfeld. This book has the size of a picture book with all the characters portrayed as animals. Captain Congo and his offsider, Pug, investigate the raja's death and find the court rife with intrigue, especially against Prince Beki. There's a race against time to uncover a dangerous plot. *Anzac Tale* (2013) is another graphic novel by this talented team.

Dan McGuiness has created many graphic novels and comics that are popular, for example, the *Pilot and Huxley* series (2010).

Rock Hopping (2016) by Trace Balla was Children's Book Council of Australia (CBCA) book of the year for younger readers in 2017. Clancy and his Uncle Egg go hiking in the Grampians to find the source of the Glenelg River. They have many adventures and learn a lot about flora and fauna. Exquisite illustrations show details of what Clancy and Uncle Egg see.

The Arrival (2014) by Shaun Tan is wordless and shows the story of his ancestors coming to Australia.

Genres

Any genre can be used with middle grade. I'll share here what I've learned from writing some different genres and give examples of books in each section. Genre can be a loosely used term as many books blur the edges of genre and my students may disagree with where I have slotted books. Ultimately a book is its own story and shouldn't be forced into a box, so these are just a guide. You decide.

Discussion usually comes up in class about what constitutes a literary novel as this, too, can be seen as a genre. Perhaps all good children's novels which develop character well and shine brilliance into the lives of the reader are literary novels. I have heard it said that character-driven novels are likely to be literary, while genre-driven or plot driven ones may not be. Possibly quick-sales books and quick reads are not either. You can decide this too. The important thing is that children read. Not all kids appreciate at first what adults call a 'good book for children'. The hope is that one day they will.

The CBCA judges' report of 2018 has this to say about literary novels for children: For a work to be literary it does not have to be a difficult read. It must be engaging and provide keys that peel back the seen but not understood layers of a young child's existence and success in their world.'[17]

Realism
There are many subgenres of realism, including contemporary drama, which was what I began writing. Much of my work has remained realistic in this way, for example, *The Keeper* series (2013) is a realistic portrayal of a boy who wants a dad. My cultural work set in Pakistan like *Jehan and the Quest of the Lost Dog* (2017) can be called a subgenre of realism.

One of my recent favourite realistic novels for middle grade is the junior novel *The Elephant* (2017) by Peter Carnavas which tells the story of Olive and her dad, who suffers from depression. His depression is like a huge elephant that enters the room with him. Olive must get rid of it. Another book dealing with a father's illness is Elizabeth Fensham's *Helicopter Dad* (2006).

Lisa Shanahan's *The Grand Genius Summer of Henry Hoobler* (2017) is a glorious novel about a family on holiday and a boy overcoming his fear of riding his bike. Catherine Bateman's *Rain May and Captain Daniel* (2004) is another favourite showing Rain May and her mother making a new life for themselves in the country.

Ursula Dubosarsky is a writer to read for writing style and innovation. Her novels include *Abyssinia* (2003) and *The Golden Day* (2011).

Don't forget the classics like *The Secret Garden* and *Tom's Midnight Garden.*

Cultural diversity

Beginning to write in Pakistan inspired me to write about cultures outside my own. *The War Within* (2016) and *Liana's Dance* (2017) are set in Afghanistan and Pakistan respectively and even though *Dear Pakistan* (2015) is set in Australia it deals with the culture shock that a teen feels on returning to Australia after being brought up in Pakistan. In *Soraya the Storyteller* (2004) I was trying to make sense of why a country like Australia would treat asylum seekers unjustly.

Journalist and novelist Deborah Ellis' work is widely acclaimed with the *Parvana* series (2002) and many more since.

Meme McDonald and Boori Monty Pryor have written books with Indigenous Australian main characters including *Njunjul the Sun* (2002) and *My Girragundji* (1998).

Set in Australia, Ruth Starke's book *Nips XI* (2000) is about a boy, Lan, who is tired of being called a 'nip' and that he isn't allowed to play cricket. He forms a team with his Asian friends and calls it Nips XI. It is funny and empowering. *Noodle Pie* (2008), also by Ruth Starke, is another favourite of mine as it cleverly shows the journey of a second-generation Vietnamese-Australian boy as he returns to Hanoi with his refugee father for the first time.

Allayne Webster's *A Cardboard Palace* (2017) deals with homelessness, forced begging and trafficking in Europe in a way suitable for middle grade readers. Webster's characters are strong and flawed and tend to steal your heart, or, in her YA fiction, to break it.

Figgy in the World (2015) by Tamsin Janu is an award-winning book set in Ghana. Janeen Brian's historical novel *Yong* (2016) is one of the few books about the Chinese experience in South Australia and *That Boy Jack* (2013), also by Janeen Brian, deals with Cornish history in South Australia. Marianne Musgrove's *Frieda: A New Australian* (2016) is about a German immigrant girl settling into Adelaide in 1914.

The *Through My Eyes* series depicting child characters living in war zones is thought-provoking for upper primary. Titles include *Naveed* (2014) by John Heffernan, set in Afghanistan and *Malini* (2014) by Robert Hillman, set in Sri Lanka.

Tips on writing a cultural story
If you are not from the culture you want to write about or you haven't lived in the culture, be very careful that your story and setting is genuine; do your research. Be sure you are meant to write this project, and plan early to have your manuscript read by a person from that culture. Check that characters are not stereotypical but ring true for the culture depicted and if they don't, show why. For example, Ameera in *Marrying Ameera* (2010)

is brought up as a Muslim but she has a Christian mother. Any lack of fervor for her faith is blamed on her mum by Ameera's relatives.

Even though I write novels set in Pakistan, possibly because I miss it, I do not feel I should write an Indigenous person's story as it is not my experience and Indigenous writers are writing their own stories. I do have supporting characters who are Indigenous as some of my novels would have an important part of the story missing if there weren't an Indigenous person present, like Caleb in *Zenna Dare* (2014). *Zenna Dare* was passed by Ngadjuri elder, Fred Warrior, as suitable to publish. If you don't have contacts within a cultural group, your state writer's centre would be able to help you find a test reader for your work.

It is becoming the norm for publishers to want a cultural story written by a member of that cultural group, if possible, though I believe I can still bring empathy for underappreciated cultures so that young readers will have a better understanding of the diversity of lives and cultures here and in the world.

More issues on representing others and writing Indigenous stories are dealt with in Chapter 13.

Historical

In writing *Taj and the Great Camel Trek* (2011) I found it difficult achieving the balance between the true historical account of Ernest Giles' expedition to Perth in 1875 and the fiction of Taj's perceptions. On the one hand I wanted young readers to be able to experience the trip as it really was, but on the other it needed to be a story that engaged the reader's imagination and interest. Always the biggest question for me was how close to what actually happened should I write it? And did I have any right not to? Was I writing historical fiction or creative non-fiction?

In historical fiction, history propels the story but mustn't swamp it. It was difficult to come to terms with the fact that the story mattered more than the history. Author Kevin Rabalais (2009) said at a conference that he didn't look at his research when he wrote *The Landscape of Desire* (2008), and when he couldn't remember if what he was writing was something he had learned through research or something he had made up, he knew he was writing a novel. I realised then that the story had to become Taj's and the history was the backdrop. Also, I came to accept that the historical events may need to be rearranged slightly to make a good story arc to sustain children's interest. The camels didn't race across that desert – it was an agonising trek continually searching for water. Tension increased when I rearranged a few events, which I note at the back of the novel.

Kate Forsyth's historical novels include *The Puzzle Ring* (2009), a time-slip adventure set during the days of Mary, Queen of Scots; and the award-winning *The Gypsy Crown* (2007), set during the English Civil War.

My novel *Kerenza: A New Australian* (2015), set in 1911, is based on family history, stories my father told after Sunday lunch.

Sonya Hartnett's historical novel *The Silver Donkey* (2004) tells the story of two girls who find a deserting English soldier in France. Her novel, *The Midnight Zoo* (2010), is the story of two Romany boys who find an abandoned zoo after leaving their deserted village during WW2. See what you think of Hartnett's *Children of the King* (2012). This counts as a historical novel as it is set during WW2, but it also links to the story of the lost princes in the tower without quite being a time-slip. I read her books to see what new ways she'll make me see the world. In this one a character's heart bounced like a trout.

Alan Tucker writes and illustrates many titles of history, including *The Bombing of Darwin – The Diary of Tom Taylor* (2002) as part of the *My Australian Story* series.

Morris Gleitzman's WW2 novels starting with *Once* (2013) are also noteworthy. *The Boy in the Striped Pyjamas* by John Boyne (2006) is a controversial children's book set in Nazi Germany.

Also see Alison Lloyd's work including *Meet Letty* in *An Australian Girl* series (2011) and *Do you Dare: The Bushranger's Boys 1841* (2014).

Biblical historical fiction
I Used To Be Dead (2017) by Colin Pearce is the story of the 12-year-old girl who Jesus raises from the dead. It explores quite a few themes: divine power, Tahlia coming to life and faith, friendship, culture and child marriage. Also included is multi-culturalism and the prejudice that many had in first century Capernaum – it's not a new thing. But one of the crowning

achievements of this novel is its humour. Not only do children enjoy it but also adults.

The classic tale, *The Bronze Bow* (1961) by Elizabeth George Speare which won the Newberry medal in 1962, explores the life of Daniel who lives in the same time as Jesus Christ. The Romans crucified Daniel's father and he hates them to such an extent that he joins a band of Zealots in the mountains, men who want to rise against the Romans.

Morris Gleitzman's *Grace* (2009) is not Biblical history but a modern telling of Grace who is being brought up in a religious cult. She knows something is wrong and sets about to help her parents see it too. I especially liked the way Gleitzman sensitively portrayed Grace's faith. Although Grace knew that complete control over others was wrong, she did not lose her faith in God.

Fantasy
Fantasy didn't come easily to me. *Across the Creek* (2017) began as a short story and I thought of it as a fairy tale. To turn it into a novel meant I had to think about fantasy as a genre. Although it is labelled fantasy, I still see it as based on Cornish folklore, which, as a colleague pointed out, is the foundation of fairy tale and fantasy. Fantasy can tell us a lot about ourselves as we write it and can give readers a distance when the character is dealing with difficult problems in their lives. Aidan is learning to be brave, brave enough to go on a quest to save lost children, a recurring theme in the

Australian psyche and literature. He also misses his friend, Jenice, who disappeared.

NZ author Sheryl Jordan's work comes to mind. Her middle grade novel *The Mark of the Lion* (1995) is fantasy and seems allegorical as it made me think of Christ's story of redemption. CS Lewis' *Narnia* series is fantasy, but he was adamant that the books were not allegorical. He believed that in an allegory each element would need to have a counterpart as in *The Pilgrim's Progress*, but he said he couldn't work that way:

> 'It all began with images; a faun carrying an umbrella, a queen on a sledge, a magnificent lion. At first there wasn't anything Christian about them; that element pushed itself in of its own accord.'[18]

Some high fantasy titles include *Rowan of Rin* (2005) and *Deltora* (2008) by Emily Rodda. Rick Riordan's *Percy Jackson* series (2006) draws on Greek mythology. Then there is *Harry Potter* and much animal fantasy, such as the *Warrior* series by the pseudonym Erin Hunter (2003), written collectively by three authors. *Have Sword will Travel* (2017) by Sean Williams and Garth Nix is also popular. There are so many great fantasy titles but here are just a few under the following headings.

Time-slip

Kate Constable's *Crow Country* (2011) is an excellent read, dealing with a white girl putting to right an event that happened years ago between her ancestor and an

Indigenous person. Crow wants reconciliation and Sadie is called to do it.

Playing Beatie Bow (1982) by Ruth Park is a classic time-slip set in Sydney as is Jackie French's *Somewhere around the Corner* (1994) taking the protagonist back to the depression era.

Check out *The Fire Watcher Chronicles* (2017), a time-slip trilogy by Kelly Gardner. I've enjoyed her YA historical fiction. *The Timeslip* series by Belinda Murrell (sister to Kate Forsyth) inspired by pieces of jewellery, including *The Lost Sapphire* (2017) is also popular.

Ransom Riggs' *Miss Peregrine's Home for Peculiar Children* (2013) is called a time-slip, an intriguing mixed-media book, using old photos that Riggs found in antique shops. And don't forget the classic *Tom's Midnight Garden* (1958). Not as fast-paced as children's literature today but still an informative read.

An interesting type of time-slip is NZ Sherryl Jordan's *Rocco* (1990), which uses time-slips to the future. This is YA but older primary readers may still enjoy it.

Historical fantasy

Time-slips can also be considered historical fantasy, like Kate Forsyth's *The Puzzle Ring,* but here are a few fantasy titles that are set in a historical period without a slip in time. *Wolfchild: A Year and a Day* (2017) is based on the Cornish legend of the land of Lyonesse that sank during the 1099 flood. Lord Trevelyan was the last person alive who fled the land. To keep the research at my fingertips I used a notebook and an index so I could easily find animals, flora, food and what everyone did in each month of the year in 1099. I think of this as based on a legend but it is labelled as fantasy.

The Tales of Jahani (2016) are set in Moghul India in 1662. When I told fantasy author and illustrator, DM Cornish that I cheated with the world-building because I used a setting I knew, he took me to task. 'It is still world-building,' he said. 'You created a new world for me.' Indeed, I've realised much world building is based on a historical period, very often medieval European and 18th century European industrial, as in steampunk.

Magical realism

A few reviewers said there is magical realism in *The Messenger Bird* (2012) due to Tamara being able to see a young violinist from the past who also lives in her house, from 120 years before. I'm not sure about this, as a defining characteristic of magical realism is that characters are not surprised by the magical element intruding into their world and in *The Messenger Bird* both Tamara and Nathaniel know something strange has happened.

Gabrielle Wang calls the genre of her books magical realism. Her definition of magical realism is a story set in the real world where a magical element is introduced. See her novel *The Beast of Hushing Wood* (2017), which is a lovely blend of adventure, fable and magical realism, and is beautifully illustrated by the author.

With this definition, Kirsty Murray's *The Four Seasons of Lucy McKenzie* (2013) also has magical realism, with Lucy being able to enter a painting at will and go back in time to help save the farm from a bushfire. This could also be called a time-slip. It is always interesting when genres intercross. And how would you classify *When a Monster Calls* by Patrick Ness (2011)? Realism with a metaphor the size of a tree? Magical realism? A fable?

See Ann Greer's MA thesis for a detailed discussion on magical realism.[19]

Fairy tales

The retelling of fairy tales as novels is mostly a YA genre but upper primary like them too. Kate Forsyth's historical novel *The Wild Girl* (2013) tells the true story of Dortchen Wild, the girl who loved Wilhelm Grimm, with the fairy tales she told him as they grew up together in war-stricken Germany.

Shannon Hale's *The Goose Girl* (2003) is based on the Grimm fairytale of the same name. Hale has many other titles.

Fable

What the Raven Saw by Samantha-Ellen Bound (2013) is a delightful fable about the bird, Raven, and the mystery he must solve.

Cassandra Golds' award-winning *The Three Loves of Persimmon* (2010) crosses genres: historical, fable, magical realism, romance. Golds' lyrical writing is perfect for fables. She has other beautiful titles to sink into.

There are many other genres including humour, mystery, adventure, romance. I've even seen crime titles for upper primary with 12-year-old sleuths as in Adam Cece's *Wesley Boon Super Sleuth* (2015). So have fun checking them all out and see what you would like to write. A tip in choosing is to think about what you like to read.

Non-fiction
Although this book deals with fiction I mention non-fiction here as many children's authors also write non-fiction. See Janeen Brian's *Hoosh* (2005) about camels in Australia and Alan Tucker's huge body of work including the award-winning *Iron in the Blood* (2002). Chris Faille and Danny Snell's picture book *Jeremy* (2013) is about a rescued baby kookaburra. Danielle Clode's work includes *Dinosaurs to Diprotodons* (2018) about Australia's amazing fossils. Kristin Weidenbach and Timothy Ide created *King of the Outback* (2017), the story of Sir Sidney Kidman. Kathy Hoopmann's *All Cats have Asperger Syndrome* (2006) is an excellent way to foster understanding of others. Alison Lloyd has written both fiction and non-fiction. A non-fiction title is *Wicked Warriors and Evil Emperors* (2010), the story of China's First Emperor, shortlisted by the CBCA. Her most recent book is *The Upside-Down History of Downunder,* (2018), illustrated by Terry Denton.

Some books crossover from fiction to non-fiction as in Ruth Starke and Robert Hannaford's *My Gallipoli* (2015). Check out the Notable list of the CBCA's Eve Powell Award to find many more fine examples.

> **Guest Author: Alison Lloyd**[20]
> **Stranger than Fiction:**
> **the process of writing children's non-fiction**
>
> History is wonderful stuff for children's books. It is full of stories you couldn't make up if you tried. In contrast to fiction, this genre requires the author NOT to make things up. Ever. (Speculate a bit, yes, as long as you spell it out.) So for me, writing non-fiction requires a more accountable and documented process.
>
> I start with an idea and I browse children's books around the subject. This is partly to avoid duplication, but also because children's books give a quick overview. I'll also read a couple of adult books. I draft a pitch to the publisher, with a blurb and tentative table of contents. That helps me define the project's scope, structure and approach. Fortunately, Penguin have said yes to three of my non-fiction proposals.
>
> Then I hit the libraries – local, State, and university. Some university libraries will let you borrow. Others have an online catalogue and nothing stopping you from reading off their shelves. The National Library's Trove is also great for colonial newspapers and online resources. I used to take notes on paper, but I've decided digital notes are easier to search. I use

Microsoft's One-Note, which has the handy function of taking clippings off web-pages too. At the same time, I build up a bibliography in the free version of Endnote, with a note on which library I got the book from. I break both the notes and the bibliography into sections that match the book's parts. If I rush and skip this laborious stuff, I will rue it later. I am embarrassed to admit the hours spent trying to verify source-less quotes and facts I don't want to leave out.

Note-taking can be creative. I might note how funny sailing vocabulary is (poop deck?) and think of a catchy title or a pithy comment. I try to put these bits in CAPS or colour-coding so they stand out later from the facts. I begin drafting as I'm researching. I use Scrivener to write because it's much niftier than Word for structuring the manuscript and keeping side-notes.

As the book builds, I need to read through the chapters sequentially, to make sure there's a narrative flow through the whole book – yes, in non-fiction too. Publishing timeframes have required me to send the manuscript off in chunks before the whole is drafted. Writing then becomes a collaboration with the illustrator, editor and designer, with each of us responding to the others' work. We fix, add, cut, tweak, and re-arrange. In the end the text should fit the pages and the pictures, read well, have the right permissions and still not stray off the straight and narrow path of accuracy.

For me, non-fiction is not always stranger than fiction, but it is more stringent.

10
Crossing Borders:
Writing for Middle School and YA

My writing career began with YA literature as that was the age my eldest daughter was. She was the one who encouraged/pushed me into writing so she could have a book her mother wrote for her. It grew out of our storytelling sessions, as many of my titles have done since. I have included this introductory chapter to YA writing as some writers start writing for younger age groups and then realise they are more suited to the older age group.

What I was writing twenty years ago as YA is now more suitable for 11- to 14-year-olds today, Years 7-9 or middle school. I believe another age level is emerging. My novel, *Shahana, Through My Eyes* (2013) is more suitable for Years 7 and 8 than Year 5. Yet it was published as middle grade (9- to 12-year-olds). *The Bone Sparrow* (2016) by Zana Fraillon was also published as middle grade, but is often included in YA lists. When this happens it's called a crossover, but I also believe it can mean a new age level is needed. When I speak to school librarians about this they agree. There are probably not enough books yet that fall over the line to warrant publishers starting a new age category for middle school (Years 7-9 and, in some schools, Years 6-9). Some YA titles fall over the line at the top end. So New Adult fiction (18-25 years) has started featuring characters over18, studying in university or holding a job, and having adult relationships. Some of the upper end of YA are exploring this content as well, for example, Vikki Wakefield's *In-between Days* (2016) and Allayne Webster's *You're My Centre of Everything* (2018).

So what is YA literature? Firstly, I don't refer to YA as a genre as there are many genres included within YA; rather I call YA a field of writing. Some of the series and genre books found on YA shelves are labelled teen fiction and are not true YA literature. YA fiction is usually stand-alone literary and innovative fiction that explores the human condition for young people between the ages of 12-18. The protagonist is a teenager and the content is interesting to an adolescent audience, often including high school life, identity issues and coming of age. Some say YA began as a marketing ploy or as a gap for those readers who had outgrown children's books but weren't ready to jump into adult-themed works. However, it has become a strong field of writing which is widely read, and by more adults than many realise.

I've called this chapter 'Crossing Borders' because young adults are crossing the border between childhood and adulthood and one hopes that YA literature fulfils the needs of these young people at this important time in their lives. Also I feel I'm crossing a border in writing it; I am not a young adult or adolescent. Sonya Hartnett, Simon French and Melinda Marchetta were when they wrote/published their first novels. Also, crossing borders gives me the idea of characters that we meet who cross borders in our novels – they need to realise their potential or find the secret to their growth. When we are writing we can cross borders to stretch ourselves, and our characters, to discover what we can explore.

Australia is a leader in YA fiction. I wonder if this is because Australia as a country is like a young adult, still finding her direction and identity. Ivan Southall writing in the 1960s and 1970s filled that gap between children's fiction and adult fiction and in 1985 the children's editor at University of Queensland Press, Barbara Ker Wilson, began the first YA fiction list.

The age of the protagonist often places a novel in a category, but not always, as I've mentioned before. Tim Winton's *That Eye, the Sky* (1986) has a child protagonist and yet isn't a children's novel because the content is adult. Adult readers understand what the boy sees and hears whereas a reader his age possibly wouldn't. Markus Zusak's *The Messenger* (2002) has 20-year-old protagonists and yet I wouldn't call it a YA novel, though young adults will read it. It has adult themes as does *That Eye, the Sky*. Other than her two children's/YA novels, Sonya Hartnett's books were never meant for YA, nor were many of John Marsden's meant for children under 18 and parents are understandably concerned when their 11-year-olds read books with older concepts and content.

The differences between a YA novel and an adult one seem to be growing less, but usually in a YA novel there will be an adolescent protagonist and intensity of feeling. The novels may not be as long and the plot may be more single-minded. The content of YA literature needs to be what concerns teenagers, with suitable language/dialogue that they can relate to. The novels often involve young people finding their identity and place in the world, thus the characters can be self-absorbed until they sort through the problems in their lives.

Often YA novels deal with an issue that young people are troubled about or have experienced. For example *Promising Azra* (2017) by Helen Thurloe deals with forced marriage in Australia. *Risk* (2016) by Fleur Ferris, a police officer, deals with online grooming of girls by criminals and luring them into believing they are corresponding with teenage guys the same age as themselves.

The Pause by John Larkin (2015) deals with suicide. The structure of the novel is innovative and shows what happens if a person should pause before they jump, and if they don't pause. He has had feedback about young people whose lives were saved from reading *The Pause*. This seems to support the belief that young people can gain help and encouragement from reading about a character in a similar situation and how they survived. However, Tolkien[1] claimed that escape was one of the main functions of fairy stories. This has led many to argue for literature as an 'escape', distracting readers to better equip them to confront their problems. When my son was unwell, he wanted to read fantasy, not 'sick lit' about an ill person. There is the point that literature is not only an escape but also a window to learn about others, to grow in empathy with people different from ourselves.

Tip
To be authentic and creative it would be best not to narrow on only one problem/issue in a YA novel as that wouldn't portray real life.

Information to keep in mind when writing for young adults
Adolescents are developing their self-identity, their worldview, looking for the ideal society, asserting their independence and trying to make sense of who they are and where they fit in the world. Friends tend to be more important than family in this age group and adolescents will often conform to peer groups in order to belong. They are also growing in sexual interest. They will have personal problems.

Characters in a YA novel are learning to cope but may not necessarily resolve their problems. There is not necessarily a happy ending. Mood and tone of the writing and story will differ from middle grade titles and there may be some disillusionment.

By readers' own choice awards it seems that many YA readers enjoy a more personal viewpoint, even stream of consciousness, exploration of emotion and issues that involve adolescents.

Thinking about YA fiction
Q YA literature can often be contentious. Do you think it is important to deal with issues that teenagers are obviously thinking about like dying, sex/dating, relationships, gender, drinking? With young children's fiction almost anything can be written about as long as it

is done with sensitivity and respect. Could that work for YA literature as well – is it the way topics are written about that makes a difference?

Q When does honesty and being 'true to your character' move into areas which induce librarians to claim a book is too graphic or dark for their shelves?

Q Do you think young people are more interested in intimacy and emotion than plot? What ramifications would this have on you writing a YA novel?

Q What kind of YA novel would you write?

There is much discussion regarding YA literature on the web. There is a good early overview of YA in Mark Mordue's article called 'The Secret Life of Us' (2003).[2] In 2011 there was an interesting discussion about the opinion essay, 'Darkness Too Visible' by Meghan Cox Gurdon which YA authors debated.[3] I understand what Gurdon meant about a mum standing in front of a bookshop shelf filled with black-covered books laced with blood, trying to find something good for her teen to read. There are a lot of sensationalised teen novels and series, however, there are enriching YA novels too, though you often have to order them.

Author Regina Brooks (2009) outlines five ways to engage YA readers.[4]

- Be genuine
- Avoid preaching
- Read YA literature
- Just write, don't worry about publication at first
- Be innovative

Publisher Anna McFarlane, when working with Pan Macmillan, said YA fiction is often very emotional – because emotions are very close to the surface when you're 16 or 17. She also wants to see wisdom in YA fiction, charm and truthfulness. There has to be a reason for the content.[5]

Emotion

All readers like to be moved. A good book changes one's thinking or emotions in some way. Readers also like to laugh. It's very difficult to write humour but Michael Gerard Bauer and Barry Jonsberg have done it well in their YA novels. *The Life of a Teenage Body Snatcher* by Doug MacLeod (2010) is set in Victorian England and is hilarious.

Workout

What emotion do you remember feeling as a teen? What caused it? Think of an incident when you were forced to do something, by a parent, teacher or peer. How did you feel? Write a paragraph in your journal.

In a paragraph, show an emotion your teen character is feeling while doing his or her favourite thing. Don't mention the word itself or any synonyms either. See if a friend can guess which emotion you were thinking of as you wrote.

Tip

I wrote about this earlier but it's worth mentioning again. Be careful of emotional adverbs, such as, 'You're wrong,' he said frustratedly. Here the emotion is tacked onto the sentence as an adverb and should be shown in another way, either through the dialogue itself or in body language or actions. Too many adverbs used like this can show that a writer hasn't thought enough about the emotion in the piece, or the author is imposing his/her own emotion onto the characters rather than letting the characters feel the emotion themselves.

Workout

Create a character using a wanted advertisement, a mind map or image. (See Chapter 4 for more on mind maps.) Or interview your character to discover their secret life. Imagine you are introducing your character to a friend and answer questions about them. Make sure you know the desires, needs, fears, flaws, distinctive attributes of your character.

Details count and can make your character live on the page.
- What smells does your character like, dislike, or notice?
- What does your character want for Christmas?
- What charity would your character like to get involved with?
- Is your character culturally insensitive? An unreliable narrator?
- Listen to a song your character would like.
- Which recording star does your character wish they could meet?
- Why does your character have his/her name?

- What does your character believe? What sort of prayer would your character pray? Or why doesn't she believe?
- Write a list of likes and dislikes for your character.
- What is your character's bedroom like?
- What is making your character miserable/joyful/angry/rebellious?

Here are some questions about your character to consider.
- Who will your character **interact** with?
- Write a **back story** for your character. This is for you to know, so your character is a real person to you, and you will be able to refer to events from their past during a dialogue that is just a snippet from the back story. When we first talk to people, we don't dump our whole back story on them.
- **Motivation.** What is your character's motivation, that is, the explanation for why your character will endure certain difficult circumstances?
- What **blocks** will an antagonist put in your character's way? This will become your conflict.

Most aspects of the novel or story will grow from character, that is, plot will grow from the character's wants and fears. The ending will come from what your character needs to learn. The structure will grow from what you know of the character also. The dialogue has to be your character's voice if he/she is the narrator.

POV and tense are also chosen on the basis of who the character is. When I was writing *The Keeper,* believing I was creating a YA novel, I began writing about a boy called Winston in third person and in the past tense: 'Winston couldn't wait to get on with things. This was something he had to do on his own too, not with Gran breathing down his neck.'

I knew Winston was a hyperactive boy, but the draft wasn't working. I changed his name to Joel and began again using first person POV. That was better, but Joel still wasn't jumping off the page like a landed fish. Then I changed to present tense: 'Wait? Nah, not me. I can't wait to get on with it. This is something I have to do on my own too, not with Gran breathing down my neck'[6] All of a sudden Joel was in my face and I could hear his voice.

Point of View (POV)

Since point of view is what many new writers, including myself, have trouble with, I include some more detail about it pertinent to YA novels here. How do we decide who will tell the story? Ask the question: Whose story is it? Then we need to decide how that viewpoint will be shown. Will we use a first-, second- or third-person narrator? Third person uses 'he' or 'she': Tom took his fishing gear to the jetty. Second person uses 'you'. Some young adult literature is written in the second person which is the way a lot of young people speak: You take your fishing gear to the jetty. Perhaps the 'you' is meant to be the reader or that the narrator is speaking to someone out of view or even a habit of the character if used in dialogue.

First person
First person uses the pronoun 'I': I took my fishing gear to the jetty. First person narrative defines the story's style, content and structure. You need to have the narrator's speech pattern, the cadence of his/her language and idioms down pat. The tone of voice sets the tone for the story, so develop an engaging one. The story can be told by the protagonist or by a witness. The first person narrator may be thinking the story, or telling it to someone, writing it as a journal or a letter, or speaking it aloud, or as in some young adult literature, recording the story mentally as it is happening in present tense.

Is your narrator to be trusted? Should the reader believe everything that's said? In *The Keeper* Joel doesn't know the recent family history that his gran does, which means the reader doesn't know for sure either. By comments his gran, and even his friend Mei, make the reader wonders if Joel is a reliable narrator. In Barry Jonsberg's *It's Not All About You, Calma* (2005), the reader sees the plot develop through Calma's eyes but, since she thinks everything is about her, the perception is faulty. This comes to light near the end of the book where Calma realises she has not seen the full picture and has accused an innocent man of a crime.

How much time has elapsed between the event and the telling? Has your narrator changed in between? Is your narrator withholding information to create tension?

A problem with first person is that it can feel self-centred. Look at successful titles like *Looking for Alibrandi* (Marchetta, 1992) and *Don't Call Me Ishmael* (Bauer, 2006). Successful first person narrators talk more about others than themselves and we learn about the main character indirectly. Authors find grammatical structures that avoid the over use of 'I'. Look for some of these in your reading.

Third person

In a story written from third person point of view the narrator could be omniscient (where the author knows everything about everyone, including their thoughts). This was a popular choice in the nineteenth century. Or the narrator could be objective, (where the author knows only what is seen and heard), or the narrator can use third person in a limited sense where the author knows all about one character and can show the thoughts of this one character, but knows no more about the other characters than this main one. This is called third person limited (or subjective in some how-to books).

The first person viewpoint is popular in YA fiction, but third person limited, where the narrator knows about only one main character, is almost as intimate as first person viewpoint. It has the advantages of first person point of view where the reader gets into the head of one character, and some of the advantages of third person, where there is some distancing. I used this in *Mountain*

Wolf (2012) for this distancing effect as I felt the content could have been too confronting in first person.

Third person can also be a good choice when writing about events inspired by fact or memory. I certainly found this with writing *A Kiss in Every Wave* (2001) when the material was too painful to write about in first person.

Second person viewpoint addresses 'you' the reader. This viewpoint is not just for how-to books; it works well in some picture books where a narrator speaks to you, the reader or a character in the book speaks to you, the reader. The narrator may also speak to 'you' but 'you' is a character in the book. Rebecca Burton's novel, *Beyond Evie* (2010) uses a 'you' viewpoint yet is not addressing the reader but a deceased girlfriend.

Tips

Make sure your characters don't know information that they shouldn't. It is impossible for one character to know exactly what another is thinking unless they are told. They can sense or surmise from actions, appearance and words, but they cannot be certain. This uncertainty can sustain suspense in your story.

Watch too that your third person narrator doesn't describe things that he can't possibly see, for example, 'Dick was determined to beat Ben to a pulp. His muscles rippled across his back as his face turned red.' Dick can't see his own back muscles, nor his face becoming red either. He must feel within himself the emotion which causes the heat.

Check that you haven't changed the POV when you didn't mean to. The story is shaped largely by your character's perceptions of life. When you change the viewpoint, you alter everything about how the story is being told. Readers can become confused if you change viewpoint accidentally in a paragraph. Use a line break or chapter break if it is necessary for the story. To maximise emotional impact it's best to keep to one viewpoint if you have one narrator.

Workout

Find a picture of two teens and write a paragraph from one character's perspective. Then try the other. Which one telling the story did you like best? If you wrote in first person, now try it in third. Which works best for the character?

> 'All my young adult novels have been gifts,' Sherryl Jordan noted in the *St. James Guide to Children's Writers.* 'I don't think them up. They hit me over the head when I least expect them; overwhelm me with impressions, sights, and sounds of their new worlds; enchant me with their characters; and dare me to write them.'
>
> Sherryl Jordan[7]

Voice

Read from the literature to hear the voice and tone that is present in YA novels. James Aldridge's language in *The Girl from the Sea* (2002) has a literary style and content that is possibly more suitable for adults, yet it is about young people. However, there are many YA readers who enjoy a challenging or thoughtful read.

Here are a few 'voices' to try or find your own novels to read for voice:

Bauer, M.G. (2006). *Don't Call Me Ishmael*.
Gardner, S. (2011). *The Dead I Know*.
Haddon, M. (2004). *The Curious Incident of the Dog in the Night-time*
Marchetta, M. (1992). *Looking for Alibrandi*.
Wakefield, V. (2011). *All I Ever Wanted*.
Zorn, C. (2014). *The Sky So Heavy*.

When writing YA fiction I believe it's imperative to capture the 'voice' of the narrator. I didn't start writing *Marrying Ameera* (2010) for quite a while as I couldn't hear the right voice for Ameera's first person narrative. Once that came the story followed. Jennifer Hunt, when she was editorial director of Little, Brown, stated, 'When the character has an original voice and it's coupled with a great plotline, that's what makes a book truly distinctive.'[8]

Voice is probably the single technique in writing YA fiction that you must have right or the novel won't work. Teen readers want a voice that sounds like theirs, not a voice that sounds like an author writing about them. Thus the voice of a first-person narrator must determine the story's style, content and structure. The narrator's tone of voice sets the tone for the story. The author's voice is present for those who know you well. Yet I believe it is possible to be a different sort of narrator every time. I don't think writers need to be 'stuck' in a rut writing the same old way. Try something new. I wrote *The Tales of Jahani* (2016) with a formal distance since it is a set in 1662, but *Zenna Dare* (2014) gives the impression of events happening this second. I achieved those differences with the help of the choices involving point of view, voice, tone and tense.

Browne and King agree that the writer's voice in a novel generally belongs to a character, though the writer's and character's voice are connected.[9]

Keep an appropriate language for the age level, and be consistent. If you have two alternating points of view, always check you haven't mixed their voices. Make sure they are different in some way. If you know those characters well, there will always be different quirks about them and their voices.

Determine how old your character is and stick to it. Work out first of all the types of things this character is interested in, the level of language s/he uses, the sort of humour s/he will cope with. If your voice keeps coming in over the character's, and it is an older voice or a more satirical voice, then think about whether you need to write for a different age group. Read lots of the age level you want to write for.

Tip

I found it worked to concentrate on the characters and the story, and let my voice, and style, take care of itself. An author's voice doesn't develop overnight. It can be encouraged though: while reading over a draft, check for the passages that sound good; see if they sing. Absorb the rhythm or simplicity of what you've written. This will represent your voice at its most effective for now.

Which are the passages that you don't like? What makes them different from the ones you do? Is it flat; does it have a poor use of words? Is it awkward, forced, dull? Get bite into your writing, check for 'telling' instead of 'showing'. Read it aloud. The more you know your character, the less you will drop out of her voice.

Tips from Catch Tilly, author of *Shadowalker*

Two tips on YA voice that no ordinary writing book will tell you:

- **Do not censor**

  Young adults don't have a developed frontal cortex. They don't think their words through and can be politically incorrect or absurd. Let them speak how they would to their friends, not their parents.

- **Good writing or good voice?**

  'Yeah, right.'
  'I like, really had the hots for him, you know?'
  'Sat in the chair and glared.'

  Use of adverbs, word choice, sentences without subjects, and clauses without verbs can create a strong YA voice. Be careful how you edit. Correct English rarely sounds like a teenager. NOTE: Verbless clauses and sentences beginning with a conjunction are on the Year 10 English syllabus in Australia.

Dialogue

After voice, dialogue is what publishers check when a YA manuscript comes across their desk. We need to convey the flavour of teen speech yet be careful of popular slang unless it's imperative to the story. I tend to only put it in dialogue. My editor asked me to delete too many 'heaps' I had written in *Zenna Dare* as she thought they may date the book, yet I had Joel in *The Keeper* speak as I thought he would, using Australian ockerisms and it worked for him. Slang can date. Authors like Sonya Hartnett don't use any 'teen speak'. Many writers say they shouldn't water down the YA expressions, yet others indicate the teen mind through the energy of the words rather than through particular expressions.

Be careful of dialect and languages other than English – use only a word here and there. What does this excerpt from *Marrying Ameera* show you about the characters and their language?

> Afterwards they took me on a tour of the house.
> 'This is the mejalis,' Asher said. 'It has a door to the lane and is where Abu meets with his friends. He sleeps here with Haider and me, but sometimes Zeba can sleep with Haider and me too.
> 'Where do you sleep usually?' I asked Zeba.
> She spoke to me for the first time, in Urdu. 'With Ummie ji. She has a big soft bed.'[10]

At times, as with Zeba here, I'll say a character is speaking a different language. I also eliminate contractions in a sentence that is spoken by someone whose English is rusty or they are speaking in another language. I use only a few words from the language and the first time such a word is used I show in the sentence its meaning. Ummie ji should be self-explanatory. Some publishers like to have a word list at the back and I know many younger readers enjoy these to check a 'foreign' word they may have forgotten the meaning of. I try to resist them, as well as italics for words other than English, especially in YA as the language is not foreign to the character, only to the reader. I also try to make sure that the meaning of the word is nearby, if not in the same sentence in the one after. For example: 'That's a pretty dupatta,' Meena said, watching her sister fold the scarf.

Tip

If you don't want your book to date, then keep current affairs, famous actors and current music to a minimum. Some authors make them up. Be careful of fad fashion/slang unless it is set back in time, for example, the 1960s like some of WA author Julia Lawrinson's novels.

See some other great tips on dialogue in John Dufresne's excellent book, *The Lie That Tells a Truth.* (2003).

Workout

- Write a dialogue between two teens, or one teen and an adult. One wants something from the other. Write your dialogue showing the conflict between them and try for teen diction if appropriate. Show the difference in the two voices. Do they use different words? Do they have a different emotion from each other? Does one have an older 'tone' than the other? Now

write the above piece in present tense (or past if you did it in present). Which do you like best?
- How can you show that two characters sound different from each other in their speech patterns?
- Try writing different ages again. This time your character is 13, hoping to impress his or her friend at the movies but things don't go as planned. Now try it from a 17-year-old's perspective. Are the two pieces different in some way?

Workout
Tone
There will be a tone of voice in your writing. It may be a combination of your underlying voice, that of the narrator's and your attitude towards the subject.

Write a paragraph of a favourite fairy story. Choose a certain character to tell the story. Write it with a certain tone. Choose one of these or another of your choice: satirical, humorous, upbeat, nostalgic, scary or impending doom, angry. Then rewrite it in a different tone. Does the story or character change?

Workout
Use your senses
- We tend to write description as though sight is the only sense there is. Try writing using the other senses. Imagine your friend has been colour blind from birth. How would you

describe the colour yellow to him/her? Red? Blue?
- *Tip*: think about how these colours make you feel and what you associate with them. Remember your art classes where colours were described as warm or cool.
- Has there been a death? Smell of death can depend on past experience and places. One of my friends couldn't stand the smell of jasmine for it reminded her of her father's funeral. The smell of dying could be a banana, if a loved one had died on a tropical plantation in north Queensland.

Tense

Although traditional storytelling was in past tense, much young adult literature now is written in the present tense. Present tense can give a sense of immediacy. I wrote *Zenna Dare* (2014) in present tense to capture Jenefer's teen voice. It was also a contrast to the historical story that she was unravelling, which I wrote in past tense in respect of the story being from the past. But it doesn't have to follow that historical stories need to be written in past tense. Catherine Jinx wrote her *Pagan* series set in medieval Europe in present tense. No doubt it can help readers to relate to that era. I have even read a story written in future tense. So choose which tense suits your story best.

Workout
Take a section of your story and change the tense. Which tense suits your character and his or her voice best?

Place/landscape
Characters don't float without a place. It's good to get practised in the art of looking. Think of the little details. Place is not just the setting or backdrop for our characters. Place can explain or show a lot about our characters. I've found if I can't visit a place to gain an appreciation for the atmosphere and specific details, then I need to do lots of research. I have viewed travel videos and photographs on the web to gain those little details that make a setting live. I try to know the landscape well enough to individualise the features.

Look for the details. The crow wheeling in the air. A solitary tree on a hill – the kids always meet there. What sort of flowers, rocks, birds? The character trudging up a hill – we see her in action. By watching her actions within the landscape we don't have to be told how she is feeling. We observe and translate what we see to the reader, so they believe they are there.

Since I always think of my characters as having a backstory, where the character was born and grew up will have affected them. I need to know that. Shahana wouldn't be who she is if she didn't live in a forest in the winter and survive a conflict. See the difference between the green forest of the Ents and the Orc-made desert of Mordor.

Landscape can be a metaphor, for example, the lighthouse in *Sailmaker* (2015). It can be a parallel to the characters' lives and become central to the action, even be a character in itself. In *The Messenger Bird* (2012) the house is one of the characters telling Nathaniel's story.

Think of the movie *Braveheart* (1995) set in the Scottish highlands – it is the landscape as well as his family background and politics that help shape Wallace. The sea in Moby Dick defines Ahab. Mary Lennox is changed by her secret garden; she blossoms and grows along with it. Catherine and Heathcliff are as wild as the moors they live on.

Novels work best when the landscape is real and alive. I've found, and I gleaned this idea from Eleanor Nilsson, that if the plot is flagging and nothing seems vibrant, then I change the setting. I have the characters go to an interesting place so they aren't always talking in the house. The setting can then be used in imagery or can echo mood and tension. I found the storm in *Sailmaker* helpful in defining character and moving the story forward. A road trip in *Finding Kerra* (2018) give Blake and Jaime a chance to get along better; the tough landscape echoes the way Blake has been treating his sister. I enjoyed *The Ingo* series (2005) set in Cornwall by Helen Dunmore. In these books the sea is so beautifully evoked I could smell it. I felt as though I too could breathe underwater.

Workout

Making a list can be helpful in 'seeing' a landscape and is an idea of Professor Thomas Shapcott's from my workshop days at the University of Adelaide.

- Write a list of things you'd see at the beach (or place of your character's choice). In first person write about a teen waiting for a friend to come. Change to third person and re-write.
- Did you find the list helped in seeing the landscape better?
- Which POV did you like better?
- Which tense did you use? Try a paragraph in another tense. Which one suits your character best?

Fun ways to bring words to life

Don't tell me the moon is shining, show me the glint of light on broken glass.

Anton Chekov

Try playing with the sense of words to form comparisons or images, for example, if you have a character who likes horses and visits the sea, she may think in a simile that 'the waves look like horses rolling in'. But why not let the verb do the work: 'The waves galloped in to shore'. It presents a thought more vividly to the reader's imagination. No need to overuse images as one well-placed metaphor will do more than a glut of them on the page, thus weakening their impact. Especially if they don't relate to each other or your character. Images should always serve a purpose, perhaps to make the unfamiliar more understandable, or to show a feeling.

Hyperbole

This is comic imagery, overstating. It is used a lot in young adult literature. For example: The good thing about church is seeing Nanny and Grandad ... All their friends still come too—the ones not on life support, that is.[11]

Personification

Giving personality to inanimate objects or nature. 'The waves clawed at the rocks, retreated and charged again.'[12]

Synaesthesia

I met a girl who saw sounds in colour. She had the condition, synaesthesia, where her brain processed data in the form of several senses at once. Markus Zusak is an author who presents images or ideas so that they appeal to more than one sense. See his work, especially *The Book Thief* (2005), for examples of this.

Tip

Discover new ways of writing about a person, event or place. Make sure your imagery grows from your character and your character's setting. In *The Messenger Bird*, Tamar's father is restoring their house. Tamar thinks: 'Then there was Dad, a crumbling pillar, trying to hold both of us up.'[13]

Ameera in *Marrying Ameera* has been told folktales from the Indus River. Water runs through Pakistan and through many of its stories. At first water just seemed to happen in images in the manuscript: 'Waves rippled in my stomach'; 'cologne, subtle and fresh like a beach breeze'. I realised that water had become a motif in the novel, the cleansing water that could bring new life but could also kill.

How not to create images[14]

- The ballerina rose gracefully and extended one slender leg behind her, like a dog at a fire hydrant.
- He was deeply in love. When she spoke, he thought he heard bells, as if she were a garbage truck backing up.
- Her hair glistened in the rain like a nose hair after a sneeze.

Showing not telling

The secret of being tiresome is to tell everything.
Voltaire

Show how the characters feel. It's worth repeating this yet again as I see so much of it in new student's work. See how emotion is told using an adverb here, for example, 'You can't go,' she said angrily. When used with said, 'ly' words are only explaining the character's emotion. Adverbs that can correctly be used with 'said' are softly or clearly, that is, words that refer to the verb itself and not the emotion in the sentence before.

Author Ruth Starke tells of an adverb game which she used to play with her daughters to deter them from overusing them:

> 'The central heating doesn't appear to be working,' he said frostily.
> 'Damn, I've put on two kilos round the hips,' she said thickly.
> 'Fluffy has just given birth behind the sofa,' she said cattily.[15]

These are examples of Tom Swifties. There are entire websites devoted to them.

'Look! There's a prisoner climbing out of the prison window,' said Tom condescendingly.

'The surgeon removed my left ventricle,' said Tom, half-heartedly.[16]

Try this website as a starting point to have some fun: www.fun-with-words.com

Maybe a character could have an interest in playing with words in his way.

Writing from reading

Read as much YA literature as you can. There are lists of some of my favourite titles included near the back of this book. Check what works. Pull apart the plots to see how the authors have structured their novel. What language works? Do the words make you see a situation in a fresh new way? Try using this critique sheet I prepared for *Don't Call Me Ishmael* by Michael Gerard Bauer (2006) as a help in deciding what works (or doesn't) in a novel you have read.

- Whose story is it? Does the voice and POV reach the targeted audience? Does the voice ring true?
- Do the characters react in a genuine way for the age group? Write notes on the journey of the main character – does it remind you of the hero's journey?
- What style is the text written in? What genre?
- How do dialogue and actions in the scenes contribute to character development?
- How is bullying treated? Is it realistic?
- What is/are the central theme/s?
- What worked especially well or didn't?
- What was the function of humour in the story? Did it work?
- Did the story affect you? Did it change your attitude about anything?
- What could happen next?
- Discuss the plot. Try 'deconstructing' the plot by writing notes on when things happen in the story. Is there a story arc or shape? What causes events to happen? How is the climax treated? The resolution? What do you think of the final sentence?

Verse novels to check out

Fensham, E. (2008). *Goodbye Jamie Boyd*.

Deller-Evans, K. (2016). *Copper Coast* has a Cornish theme, set in Moonta on the Yorke Peninsula, SA. Maddy emigrates from Cornwall to Moonta,

> missing her old life but discovering a new one with friendships, secrets and danger.

Wild, Margaret. (2001). *Jinx*

McCormack, P. (2006). *Sold*. This is a powerful, if confronting, verse novel showing what happens to a Nepalese girl sold to an Indian brothel.

Steven Herrick is a master verse novelist. He has many titles to check out.

Poet

A poet weeping,
Too much in the world to tell.
He writes a haiku.

Morton Benning[17]

Genres

I've included just a few titles here to kick start a search for the YA novels that you may enjoy. There are more in the reading lists later. I find it interesting how genres often mix in YA. Brian Caswell's *Double Exposure* (2005) seems to be a realistic novel and morphs into a thriller. Vikki Wakefield's *Ballad for a Mad Girl* (2017) is literary realistic fiction and yet a crime novel as well. It explores mental health, peer pressure, coming of age, friendship, family and a ghost story. It won the Sisters in Crime's 18th Davitt Awards: Young Adult Novel, 2018, and was shortlisted in four other categories.

Fantasy/Speculative/Dystopian
Cornish, D.M. (2006). *Monster Blood Tattoo*.
Goodman, A. (2008). *Eon.*
Jordan, S. (2018). *The Anger of Angels*. An exciting historical fantasy.
Kaufman, A. and Kristoff, J. (2015). *Illuminae.*
Lanagan, M. (2012). *Sea Hearts*. Retelling of the fairytale of the selkies.
Millard, G. (2009). *A Small Free Kiss in the Dark.*
Pierce, M.A. (1982). *The Dark Angel* trilogy. This is older, one of the earlier vampire titles but a beautiful read. She also wrote *The Firebringer* series reissued in 2006.
Westerfeld, S. (2009). *Leviathan*. Steampunk
Zorn, C. (2014). *The Sky So Heavy.* Dystopian

Also check out Kate Forsyth's interview with Sherryl Jordan about *The Anger of Angels* on Kate's website.[18]

Historical
Caro, J. (2015). *Only a Girl.* Story of Queen Elizabeth I as a teen.
Forsyth, K. (2013). *The Wild Girl.*
French, J. (2010). *A Waltz for Matilda.*
Jordan, S. (2000). *The Raging Quiet*. In medieval times.
Murray, K. (2003). *Bridie's Fire.*
Worthing, M. (2018). *Iscariot.* A thought-provoking portrayal of Judas Iscariot.
Yolen, J. (1992). *Briar Rose. A* powerful retelling of Sleeping Beauty set in WW2 in Nazi Germany
Zusak, M. (2006). *The Book Thief.*

Realism

This genre often deals with identity and issues. Often realistic YA is referred to as the problem novel.

Bauer, M.G. (2006). *Don't Call Me Ishmael.* Norwood, SA: Omnibus. Bullying and humour: it can be done.

Gardner, S. (2011). *The Dead I Know.* Crows Nest, NSW: Allen & Unwin.

Green, J. (2012). *The Fault in Our Stars.* Thought to be the first of what is popularly known as sick lit.

Haddon, M. (2004). *The Curious Incident of the Dog in the Night-Time.* A murder mystery told by 15-year-old Christopher who has Asperger's Syndrome.

Lomer, K. (2016). *Talk Under Water.* A gentle story of a hearing impaired girl and a hearing boy. Delightful.

Marchetta, M. (1992). *Looking for Alibrandi.* Cultural identity.

Wood, F. (2016). *Cloudwish.* This is interesting as it deals with a second-generation teenager whose family came from Vietnam in 1980. Vân Uóc does not want to be stereotyped as a smart Asian kid, when she also feels Australian. She wants to be accepted just for who she is by her parents as well as by her friends. I saw this title as the 2016 YA novel which most reflected contemporary Australian culture for teens. A few incidents will determine it to be a senior high title in some schools.

Culture/war/identity
Abdel-Fattah, R. (2016). *When Michael met Meena.* Politics, prejudice, refugees. Set in contemporary Australia.
Hawke, R. (2015). *The Truth about Peacock Blue*. Religious freedom and blasphemy, set in Pakistan.
Kwaymullina, A. (2012). *Ashala Wolf.*
Jaye, P. (2017). *Out of the Cages.* Shows what happens after a Nepalese girl is rescued from a brothel.
Thurloe, H. (2017). *Promising Azra*. Forced marriage, Pakistani culture, set totally in Australia at school and home.
Through my Eyes series, editor Lyn White portraying young people living in war zones.

Riding the Wind

Guest Author: Claire Zorn[19]
Words and Music

I shouldn't be a writer. I find writing extremely difficult. Even now, as I write this, I'm deleting, rewriting and editing these opening sentences and the process seems so fraught, so counterintuitive. I keep the certificates for awards I've won propped on my windowsill of my study, directly in my line of vision from where I sit to work. They are there for one purpose only, to remind me, to convince me, that I can do this. I am a writer.

Words don't come naturally to me. I am not confident with them, but they are the bricks I have to use to build the worlds I can see with unfailing clarity in my head. I see story visually, like a film playing and I have to scramble about to try and find the words to do it justice. I use a dictionary all the time, because no spellcheck in the world can translate the work of someone who, to this day, can't remember whether upholstery begins with an 'a' or a 'u'. My method is to spew out all the words and then re-order and rearrange them so they appear as though they were written by someone who actually knows what they are doing.

When talking with other writers I am in constant fear that I will slip up and use a word which doesn't mean what I think it means. This happened most recently in front of Michael Grant. He's a pretty successful guy. He seems like the kind of person who may well own a Learjet, or at least have a friend who does. I was to appear on a panel with him and he asked what the panel was supposed to be about. I said 'The pretense is: teenagers love fantasy and sci-fi - why is that?'

I knew a beat too late that 'pretense' was not the word I was looking for. No. I was after 'premise'. Pretense is 'an attempt to make something that is not true appear true.'

Oh, the delightful levels of irony!

I have always written stories, however for a long time they were unreadable to anyone except me. Reading my own work or anyone else's presented absolutely no trouble at all. All the reading and being read to, usually by my mum, has obviously paid off. However, I think there's something else at play which I've overlooked: music. (Please do not excuse the pun.) I like a short sharp sentence. I like a sentence with rhythm and balance. I only enjoy a select few classic novels, generally old, thick, important books are too ... wordy. I think my parents were the same, there were never any Classics in my house. There was usually a record playing, though. Neil Young, Bob Dylan, The Beatles: people who knew how to turn a phrase.

'I've seen the needle and the damage done, a little part of it in everyone' was a line I heard a lot, probably since the day I was born. What a succinct and perfect grouping of words. What a picture. One single sentence, sung to music, is more powerful to me than any book. Drug use was never something my parents had to worry about for me as a teen, probably thanks solely to Neil.

I vividly remember when my parents first bought a CD player and amp: a big, heavy boxy thing which was wired up to the speakers my dad had built as an electrical apprentice in the early seventies. The first CD played was Elton John. Daniel was leaving on a plane and Elton could see the red taillights heading for Spain.

I can still see the image those lines formed in my head so very clearly and I wonder if I learned more about writing from songs than anywhere else. Yes, I read a lot as a kid, but I listened to even more music, and when I was old enough to choose my own it was not books that I sought solace in during my horrible teenage years, it was albums.

My latest book, *One Would Think the Deep* is about a lot of things: violence, grief, surfing, family secrets. But the central thing that pulls my protagonist, Sam, along through all of this is music. He listens to music every moment that he can, it is his constant, unfailing companion through the turmoil and mess of his life. *One Would Think the Deep* is a homage of sorts to the pivotal role music has played in my life.

Vikki Wakefield says that learning to write is like learning to play an instrument and she is dead right. I'm going to stick with it because I don't know how to play anything else. Writing is supposed to be hard.

That big clunky amp is still wired to those gorgeous freestanding wood-panelled seventies speakers. Mum and Dad gave them to me and now I have to tell *my* kids not to jump near the record player. I force feed-them Beck, Radiohead, The National and, of course, Neil – the very same copy of *Harvest* that my parents used to play. I've done away with digital music almost altogether and returned to vinyl.

It just sounds better.

11
Rewriting and Editing as Writers

Writing is selection, choosing – it's what you don't write which makes your writing great.
Thomas Shapcott

It wasn't until I became part of the HarperCollins stable, and of University of Queensland Press, that I discovered what an editor is supposed to be able to do, if given the time and money. I did learn lots from my freelance editor at Lothian, but I've also enjoyed learning from subsequent editors, structural editors, senior editors, junior editors, copy editors, trained typesetters and excellent proofreaders. With UQP I can relax if they need a manuscript before I've rewritten it as many times as I'd like because I know they'll pick up details I've missed. I've learned tips even from what the editor will say to the typesetter on the manuscript. Most editing is done now in Microsoft Word with Track Changes, but a few years ago it was all on hard copy and there would often be different coloured pens: for me, for the typesetter and for the designer. I was told to do my changes in pencil. I found the edit for *Marrying Ameera* (2010) quite daunting at first with so many pencil/pen marks to follow.

An editor is an experienced and trained professional who looks at a raw manuscript and helps transform it to a polished product. Remember that the editor has a feeling for the work, the structure and for detail. The three main stages of editing in a publishing house are:
1. Structural edit

2. Copy edit
3. Proofreading

Structural editing

So let's talk about structural editing first. Most publishers will do a structural edit on your manuscript if their professional readers say it is worthy of publishing but a few things need reworking. A structural edit is different from a copy edit where details of punctuation, grammar, clarity and word usage are addressed. A structural edit looks at your manuscript as a whole and decides whether the plot, structure, character development, setting and theme are working to convey the story you have in mind. And whether the length is suitable.

If your manuscript is accepted, the senior editor or the publisher will write a structural report, though in the case of *Marrying Ameera* (2010), since I was new to the publisher, acceptance depended on me rewriting according to the structural edit. Structural edit reports always state what is working and what the editor enjoyed about the work. Then it offers some general comments. In this case the structural edit included cutting between five and eight thousand words (yes, I managed it – a bit like decluttering my office: terrifying to start with, then it becomes fun); fixing the ending as it was rushed; the folktales didn't work well and they needed to flow as part of the text; more motivation for some characters' actions.

Then more detailed points are considered from the notes the editor made on the manuscript while reading.

Questions are raised: why doesn't she want to marry Shaukat? Did she have enough relationship with Kamil (Tariq) to justify her refusal? This meant I needed to fix that in the first third of the story; more justification for Ameera's brother finally helping her when he didn't look after her in the first place. More reason why her father would organise a forced marriage, since I don't treat him as a stereotypical villain but a father trying to do his best, however misguided. This called for a new scene with Ameera and her father. And a new title: it was originally called *Stolen Bride* which the editor said made it sound like a bodice ripper not a thoughtful, if thrilling, love story dealing with forced marriage.

The *Shahana: Through My Eyes* (2013) structural edit report was 12 pages long, ranging from switching the first and second chapters to explaining more about culture practices mentioned in the story. I also learned a lot from that one, and not only to rewrite more times before I submit.

So how do we do this editing ourselves? We do the best we can, considering we are not professional editors. A well-structured manuscript needs to convey meaning, flow logically from sentence to sentence, paragraph to paragraph, chapter to chapter. I always do my own structural edit after the first or second good draft and then my own copy edit before I give the manuscript to a reader to check. They may have more ideas. I rewrite again and again until I finally submit, either due to a deadline or because I'm getting to the stage where I'm changing things and making it worse. As with this book which seems never ending, I just have to trust that the Holy Spirit has prompted me to add what needs to go in.

Tips

When structurally editing our own draft we can think of the following questions.

- Does the beginning start too early? Is the first chapter backstory? Could we cut it or insert later?
- Does the character come to life? Is there character development in each chapter?
- Does the character have a clear goal, is motivation for actions clear?
- Does the voice of the character or narrator ring true? Is it consistent?
- Have we left out any character for too long?
- Is the structure suitable for the age level intended? For example, are there long flashbacks?
- Do the chapters follow on if there is one point of view? Are some chapters in the wrong place?
- If there are two alternating points of view in different chapters or sections, do the voices sound different from each other?
- Do the chapter endings give a sense of something coming next? I don't think we need too many cliff hangers, but connections/links between chapters can make the narrative flow more smoothly.
- Are some chapters too long?

- Are all the chapters needed? Do they all advance the plot or character development? If a chapter diverts or doesn't cause the next event to happen, then it may be best to cut it.
- Have we written in scenes rather than summary?
- Do the paragraphs lead into each other? Are they linked so they flow smoothly?
- Are there parts with too much description and too little action?
- Are the episodes of excitement/fear/amusement evenly distributed?
- Does the tension rise?
- Is there a climax?
- Does the end lag on too long?
- Is the resolution satisfying?

When I finished the draft of *Shahana* I read Debra Dixon's *GMC* (1996). It inspired me to draw this table in my journal to check if I could see the elements of the plot and structure played out in the story. I wrote a note to myself in my journal: 'Put Shahana in a terrible position, where she has to make a sacrificial choice. Shorten the time frame to cause more tension.' I realised Shahana needed to be pushed further in order to save Tanveer.

Rewriting and Editing as Writers

Shahana	External	Internal
Goal/ desire What	Keep Tanveer safe Survive through the winter	Wants someone to care for her Wants peace
Motivation Why	He has weak lungs He's her only relative as Nana ji died last winter She's responsible for him They are orphans He is abducted She will rescue him and do whatever it takes	She is unhappy, stressed, traumatised, and wants to feel better herself. She's tired of the conflict She feels alone
Conflict How	Zahid Amaan Mr Nadir The weather and setting The avalanche	Can she trust Zahid? Amaan reminds her of her trauma She finds it difficult choosing what to do

I was reminded during the structural edit that if we provide strong enough motivation our reader will follow us and our characters anywhere.[1]

Copy-editing

When I first read Strunk and White's classic on style and editing, I wrote lots of tips. This chapter is a list that's grown over the years from Strunk and White to tips I've discovered or learned from all the editors I've had the joy to work with. Yes, I say joy because editors are those magical people who can suggest you change one word and the whole sentence is transformed. Maybe it will even sparkle. Most of what I know about writing comes from teaching it; I've even learned some from reading and practising writing. But I've also learned a huge amount from editors. I respect editors highly as I want my story to be the best it can be and at times I don't see how to do that because I'm either too close or I'm blinded from reading it twenty times. Some writers even proofread by reading backwards. I haven't gone that far. In short, I get very nervous if I think I know more than the editor. After 25 years of working with editors, there are only a few times I've disagreed with a junior editor and had to appeal to the senior editor if the junior one is sticking too closely to the rules in order to be safe.

Style and voice are different. Voice can change for different characters and stories, and I think style can too. Style is like your literary DNA, which we now know is not as set in stone as scientists first thought. Our writing is unique: how we use words, length of sentences and the type of words we choose. Overall, qualities for a good writing style include clarity, simplicity, elegance, vigour and variety. We can preserve our individuality by avoiding the use of stock phrases and clichés. We also need to keep in touch with our character's speaking voice.

Tips

- Clarity: Be clear, get the word order right so there is no ambiguity. I still get my word order up the creek at times. Keep it simple rather than complex. See how the meaning in the following sentence is not clear: She skipped down the path and turned in to a door. Or: Most kangaroos are killed by cars crossing the roads at night.
- Position words carefully. Take the word 'only'. I only met her at the beach. I met only her at the beach. I met her only at the beach. I met her at the only beach. Only I met her at the beach. Which one did I mean?
- Simplicity doesn't mean bland. It can be sharp and elegant.
- Elegance: Be economical, keep the narrative flowing. Listen as you write and read aloud to hear if the writing is balanced and smooth. This works for me as I can hear the clunky bits when I read aloud.
- Rhythm is the feel for words. Read aloud for rhythm too. Listen to the way the prose sounds.
- Try not to be boring. Use strong verbs for tighter, picturesque writing, and active verbs rather than passive: 'Saturday roars round fast.'[2] Remember that 'said' in a speech tag is mostly

invisible to readers so resist the urge to change 'said' to melodramatic words like groaned, moaned and sobbed. If your character does groan, which can be quite effective to show how a character is sympathetic to news he has heard, put it in a sentence of its own: 'I didn't know if it was a stray bullet or if we were being targeted,' I said. Matt groaned.[3]

- Use simpler words where appropriate, and prune unnecessary adjectives and adverbs and qualifiers: really, just, well, very. Beware of qualifier words that don't define and will weaken your text, such as: it seems, almost, sometimes, quite. Beware of adjectives which don't show your meaning like beautiful, wonderful. Be specific. Decide what you mean by the word 'sometimes', and use that detail. If nothing else will fit then you may need to keep it. But don't use it without first trying for a more fulfilling word. Also be careful of using ten words when two will do. Keep it tight.
- Vary your vocabulary, length of sentences, and paragraphs. Some repetition is fine if done for a reason, but avoid thoughtless repetition. Avoid all thoughtless words, of course. Check if you have accidentally used the same word in the same sentence or paragraph. This is easy to do. You may have chosen the repetition, however, as in this sentence from *Marrying Ameera*: 'That night Shaukat delivered his surprise. He had also

delivered a difficult baby and he was tired.'[4] I had to appeal to the senior editor to keep the first 'delivered'.
- Australian fiction style indents each new paragraph except the first one in a chapter or after a section break.

Dialogue style

Publishing houses have their own in-house style, and now most Australian publishers like single quote marks used with dialogue. If a character quotes someone's words within the dialogue, then the quotation is in double quote marks. Most US usage is around the other way: double quote marks for dialogue and single quote marks for quoting within dialogue. But this can also be a style issue, so the final arbiter is the publisher's style guide.

Remember to indent when a new or another speaker starts a new line of dialogue. A change of speaker begins a new paragraph.

When a character tells a story which lasts for a few paragraphs, use a single quote mark for the beginning of each paragraph, leave off the final quote mark at the end of each paragraph, but insert it at the end of the final paragraph of the story. Dialogue within a story being told by a character will then be in double quotes. See what happens to the dialogue punctuation when Jaime tells Kerra a story called Prince Hamid in *Finding Kerra*:

'Prince Hamid did as he was bid, sat on the carpet and immediately it lifted into the air and

Riding the Wind

flew around the city. He was overcome with joy and bade it to take him back to the shop.'

'A flying carpet,' Kerra said as if she'd seen one herself.

'"I'll take it." The prince thought what fun he and Noori would have with it. He rolled it up and slung it over his shoulder.

'A seller of strange wares showed him an ivory tube. "Look through this, sire and you'll see whatever you are thinking of." Prince Hamid was usually thinking of Princess Noori, so it was she who appeared at the end of the tube. His smile faded as he realised he was seeing her as she was right then and she wasn't happy as usual. She was tossing on her bed, moaning.

'"I need to help my sister, quickly. What can I do?"'[5]

This is not the end of the story or there'd be a closing end quote. Having a character interrupt, as Kerra does here, adds warmth to the storytelling time and eliminates large blocks of story.

Tip

Get rid of clichés on your second draft. Don't worry about them in the first. You can get away with clichés in dialogue if you have a character that habitually speaks in clichés. Try turning other clichés into new images. Finish this sentence: It was so cold that ... A high school student in one of my workshops wrote: It was so cold that the cat's whiskers froze.

Try using the opposite meaning. This is used a lot in YA writing. He walks as fast as... For example, try an opposite image to show how slow he actually is. An Australian example of this play with words (based on an American idiom) is: He's as fast as molasses in winter. Or: Her nose is as straight as a fish hook.

Using the right word

I love the Peanuts character Snoopy, especially when he is writing while sitting on his kennel. One of my favourite Snoopy cartoons shows him typing a story. He starts with 'It was a dark and stormy night.' In the next frame he writes: 'Suddenly, a shot rang out.' Editorial queen, Lucy wonders if 'suddenly' is the right word. So Snoopy writes, 'Gradually a shot rang out.'[6] There is much literary wisdom in this humorous cartoon.

Suddenly is often used as a device when a writer can't think of another way to show tension. I know I've done it myself even when I think I haven't and after the editor has pointed it out, I find there's usually another way to express surprise or tension. It pops up in children's adventures a lot but be careful of overuse. The sentence usually sounds better without it but once in a blue moon it might work, as Snoopy will probably see.

Also be careful of words that weaken the text like **somehow**, another dastardly qualifier. Think about what 'somehow' means. Take the sentence: 'Somehow he knew.' Ask how he knew. By the look on his mate's face? By the note in his hand? An instinctive feeling? Then write that. 'Somehow' can be a lazy word because it doesn't show 'how' an event happened at all. There may be a few places where it is fine, where you are trying for a cryptic atmosphere, but never overdo it and only use after considerable thought. Check if your sentence has the same meaning with the word omitted. Usually it will sound tighter. The same goes for 'something' and 'someone'. Be specific.

The word **hopefully** was often misused in my earlier manuscripts. Hopefully means with hope. Not, 'Hopefully I will leave on the next plane,' but 'I hope to leave on the next plane.'

Here it is used correctly: 'Did I hear food mentioned?' Pepper said hopefully.

The torch shone hopefully in the scrub as I crept to the long drop.

Anymore/any more. There always used to be a distinction between these words. Can you see the difference between these two sentences?

- 'Have you ever had a friend who you can't talk to anymore?' Here 'anymore' is used as an adverb, meaning any longer.
- She didn't eat any more pizza. Used as a determiner, referring to a quantity. However, it seems to have become a matter of style. Australian usage leans towards two words, 'any more', and US towards 'anymore'. Some editors say to choose one and be consistent in its use. I still like to use both, but it distresses inexperienced editors. In such cases I bow to the

publisher's in-house style. After all, they may be seeking a market in the US.

Around/round. The classic word to use for looking around is just that: around. An orange is round, one of my editors reminded me. Again, I have noticed that 'round' usually takes the place of 'around'. And often I find 'round' has better rhythm in a sentence.

All right and alright are also now interchangeable but they never used to be. The correct usage was 'all right'. I still use 'all right'. Unless a character uses 'alright' or 'orright' in his speech.

Awhile or a while: Wait awhile. She waited *for* a while. When in doubt use 'a while'.

Apart and a part. What do you think the writer intended here: 'We want to make the newcomers feel apart of our community.'

Lie, lay, laid. This is easy to mix up. I find it helpful to separate the meaning of lie and lay. Of course the tricky bit is that 'lay' is also the past tense of lie (to lie down).
1. To lie down: I can lie on the bed today. Yesterday I lay on the bed. I had lain on the bed.
2. To lay an object down: Today I lay my books on the bed. My hen laid an egg. My hen had laid an egg. 'Lay' and laid' in this meaning need an object. It helps me to remember that laid is usually for hens.

Which or that: 'that' is more definitive, that is, a particular horse: that horse.

Like before a clause that could stand as a sentence on its own is being let through the hoop now in much young adult literature because it is the way we speak. I've heard some teens use 'like' like six times in like the same sentence. Is this next sentence showing correct usage? 'I felt like I had a lion inside me.' Older and correct usage would be: 'I felt as though (or as if) I had a lion inside me.'

Correct usage of 'like' as a simile is: She looks like her mother. However, because we speak using 'like' before a clause with a verb, it has crept into our writing. I use it in dialogue but not in narrative unless my narrator is a first person teen. Some editors are nervous keeping it in in case it looks incorrect but some let my characters speak the way they need to in first person narration so that their voice sounds like a teenager's.

Tautology

Check you haven't said the same thing twice. Which words will you cut in these examples?

- The reason for this is because we have an appointment that day.
- Raze the house to the ground.
- I hope to find the original source.
- And the most famous one: Come for a free gift.

Writing about eyes

- 'She tore her eyes away from his face and cast them onto the lake.' How clever. I hope she can swim so they can be retrieved.
- 'She dropped her eyes to the floor as he came in.' Be careful with dropping eyes all over the floor. My father had a glass eye and it didn't bounce. We can drop our gaze, however. As with all comments about writing technique you may find an incidence of eye dropping that works.

Checking punctuation

Commas

This sentence came from a draft: 'It must have been a plant we did not know for by the time we had eaten Mustara began groaning.' Did they eat Mustara? Where should the comma go?

Here's another example of a need for a comma: 'We drank our juice, and then I left a note for Bob and Mike and I went for a walk.' Who went for the walk here? Any sentence where clarity is compromised needs to be rewritten.

Over-dashing

Don't be tempted to use too many dashes as we do in emails. Some editors see this as a sign that a writer doesn't know how to use a semicolon. My early manuscripts are scattered with them, but I tend to lay off the dashes now and only use them when a colon or semi colon won't work. I also use dashes in dialogue as it looks less formal. Dashes work best in pairs.

'He was much bigger than me by then – only fifteen months older – but he felt like a twin.' This is possibly one of the main times to use dashes, to highlight a phrase as brackets would. For fiction, dashes look more casual than brackets.

Colons
I found these sentences in another draft:
- 'The tears I felt in the vet's threatened to creep back, but it was a different sort – it was the red and black of the crow-like shadow that growled in my corner at night.'

    Here a colon will work instead of the dash, as we can ask, 'What sort of tears?' If you can ask a question in the first part of a sentence and can answer it in the second, then a colon is a good choice.

    'The tears I felt in the vet's threatened to creep back, but it was a different sort: it was the red and black of the crow-like shadow that growled in my corner at night.'

    The colon tightened the sentence.
- A colon can also introduce a list.
    'Tamar loved all sorts of music: Celtic, classical and blues.'

Semicolons
Semicolons are often needed to join two sentences when they run on into another one. 'Michael liked pies, he ran

to buy one.' This is actually two sentences as each part has a verb. It could be written: 'Michael liked pies and he ran to buy one', or if a tighter sentence is needed to show the movement, a semicolon can be used: 'Michael liked pies; he ran to buy one.'

I have seen this relaxed in YA narrative lately too, especially if the narrator is a first person POV teen. Run on sentences can work well in dialogue to show what kind of speaker a character may be. I think semicolons are too formal for dialogue.

'Dad went to see her every week, Mum said that was enough.' If this were dialogue this sentence would be fine as it is and, with an innovative editor, it may be fine for a first person narrator too. This is more conventional for narration: Dad went to see her every week; Mum said that was enough. And in dialogue it could be better as two sentences separated by a full stop.

Commas work better than semi-colons if a character is telling the story in a stream of consciousness style.

A semicolon can take the place of a dash too.

'To get well might mean you have to face things again – you might be treated differently too.'

'To get well might mean you have to face things again; you might be treated differently too.'

Both of these are fine, but the semicolon can take the place of 'and' or 'but' between the sentences.

Books like *The First Five Pages* (2000) by Lukeman and *Self-editing for Fiction Writers* (2001) by Browne and King give pointers on common mistakes made by writers. *Eats, Shoots and Leaves* (2003) by Lynne Truss is a hilarious help with punctuation.

Workout

When we were restoring our 160-year-old garden I kept finding pieces of crockery. I discovered I could write a history of the previous inhabitants of our house: thick blue wide striped crockery from Cornwall; old Rhine crockery from Germany; Willow from England; even 1970s made-in-Japan china. The fragments became a metaphor at first for the fragments of the story I was writing: *The Messenger Bird*. Tamar's mother began picking up crockery as I was. Then I tried piecing some together to make half a plate of Willow and I saw the image of what the mother was trying to do: to put the family back together again.

Here's an exercise from author Ursula Le Guin.[7] Write a scene showing your character finding an object from the ground. What is it? Whose was it? What does the character do? Or you can use a scene from a story that you are writing.

Go through your text and cut out the adjectives and adverbs, and underline the verbs. Change each of the verbs, except 'said', into a stronger verb. Try to eliminate an excessive use of verbs to be, such as 'was', 'is'.

Watch out for weak qualifiers, such as: very, just, sort of, really, quite.

The point is to give vivid description of a scene or an action, using only verbs, nouns, pronouns and articles. Adverbs of time may be necessary but be sparing. Le Guin says adjectives and adverbs are fattening in your prose, but 'the bakery shop of English prose is rich beyond belief and narrative prose needs more muscle than fat.'[8]

How did this cutting/pruning affect your scene? Did it change your choice of verbs or simile and metaphor? Did you find it would be better with the addition of a few adjectives or adverbs, or is it effective without?

An example of cutting

This extract is from a draft. When I showed this to my students they were extremely encouraged as they could see that they already write much better than this.

> The next morning we left – it was the twenty-fourth day of August. This time it only took an hour to round up the camels and load them. While Alec and I went to get the camels the others made sure the packs and loads were ready when we returned. The loads were heavy with the extra water. The casks were carrying twenty gallons each. The four camels we took with us west were not as rested as the others. Alec was riding Reechy, Mr Giles was on Pearl. The cow we took west called Wild Gazelle and Malik the young bull were listless. Padar told me I was to keep an eye on them.

Here is the rewrite which I submitted and which stayed as the final version. Cutting helped define my thoughts about what I was trying to convey.

> We left Ooldabinna on the twenty-fourth day of August. Wild Gazelle, the pack cow we had taken

> west, and Malik were listless after the long trek with little water. 'Watch them for fatigue,' Padar said. 'If they can't keep up we will have to stop the string to put them at the end.'[9]

Also when editing this draft, I found an overuse of the continuous present and realised it weakened my text, as the following example shows. Do you agree the second sentence is stronger?

> 3. Mr Giles strode up and down a lot more that day and was continually watching the camels even though he had ordered me to do it.
> 4. Mr Giles strode up and down a lot more that day and continually watched the camels even though he had ordered me to do it.

Workout
Try cutting this sentence to tighten it. Or maybe rewrite it for clarity.
> The green, leafy foliage mainly hid Chloe from the frightening, sinister man as she sat crouched and huddled with her trembling sister in abject fear.

Proofread with passion
Proofreading needs to be undertaken with care as we often read for word shape and miss details of the letters if they are incorrect. Surprise yourself by reading this poem by author Mark Worthing.

Srcamebld Wrods

Waht a wsate, tohoght I, wehn frsit I hread,
Tohse yuothufl yaers sepnt lnearnig persicley
The porepr palce for erevy lteter wtiihn erevy wrod –
No eorrs aollwed wehn one witres cnosicely.
Taht old shcoolmram of mnie culod not ask for mroe.

But wiat, dceclerd smoe Egnlsih epxret, tihs weke psat,
It mtatres qitue litlte how a wrod is sepleld,
So lnog as the ltetres taht cmoe fisrt and lsat
Ararnge tehmsevles as tehy're cmopelled,
In wrods so blod to vetnure fuor lteters and mroe.

Ohter lteters mihgt mnigle and dncae trhuogh the air
And stetle wtihin wrods weherver tehy palese.
Our eeys, it semes, dno't ralley crae
So lnog as ecah and evrey lteter is tehre, at esae.
Hnece a taost to seplling psat, if you palese.
a noamd evremroe[10]

Mark Worthing

Also beware of relying on computer spellcheck programs.

Riding the Wind

> ### Old Two Spell Chequer
>
> A spell chequer makes all things write;
> It leaves know mistakes, knot a single won.
> Wee May trust its work inn fading lite
> To Brighton our righting like the shinning son.
>
> Sum May say wee kin knot trust
> That witch wee can knot sea,
> But eye find know knead of cite
> To show the weigh to me.
>
> Sew eye kin right Moore perfectly
> When Spell cheque is their too cover my treks,
> An insure that eye will bee
> All weighs rite – won hundred pro cent.
>
> **Mark Worthing**[11]

Workout

This editing checklist uses elements of a structural edit as well as copy editing. Try compiling one of these checklists for yourself. Include items you specially need to remember. You may want to use different headings.

Self-editing checklist[12]
1 Structure
- Opening hook? Time, place, characters clear? Every word choice?
- Where are the tension peaks? Is the climax obvious?

- Does it resolve satisfactorily?
- Does the narrative bog down anywhere? Any superfluous scenes?
- Are the logical links clear? Does it flow from one scene to another?
- Check showing not telling – is it able to be visualised/acted?
- If I remove the emotion words, is it still evident?
- Is the ending neat, well-written? Memorable?

2 Language
- Is the tone appropriate for theme/genre? Mood/s identifiable/consistent?
- Choice of POV best? POV shifts clear?
- Choice of tenses best?
- Are all five senses used? Should something other than visual be emphasised?
- Any clichés?
- Adverbs necessary, describing verbs not emotions?
- Verbs strong where appropriate, not lazy?
- Nouns interesting, better synonyms not available?
- Use of poetic language? alliteration, rhyme/chime, assonance, rhythm, metaphor.
- Check dialogue moves plot forward/develops characters, use of colloquial or slang appropriate.
- Title catchy, indicative, clever/unusual?

3 Characters
- Are they distinctive? What characterises each?
- Lovable/likeable/fascinating?
- Names effective?
- Able to be identified with?
- Stereotyped or unique? Identifiable as an actual person? (if so, change)
- Individual speech patterns, mannerisms?
- Do they develop/learn through the story?
- Are they consistent within themselves?
- Is narrator's voice separate from characters' and the author's? Or is a character the narrator? Is this clear?

4 Setting
- Is this significant?
- Is it meant to be somewhere recognisable? Is it based on actual place?
- If fantastical, is it consistent?
- Check name doesn't exist if it's intended to be fictional
- What role does setting play? Is it used to full effect?

5 Presentation
- Is the grammar tight, appropriate exceptions in dialogue?
- Is spelling correct? Is punctuation standard except for obvious reason?

- Line spaces only for shifts in time/setting/POV?
- Double-spaced, wide margins? (adjust for specific guidelines)
- Header for title and author, footer for page numbers? (adjust for specific guidelines)
- Title page needed?
- Acknowledgements needed?

6 Impact

- Is there any unintended stereotyping? Inadvertently offensive?
- Permission needed for quotations, use of cultural/personal references?
- Does the story make the reader keep thinking or does it tie up loose ends so tightly it's easily forgotten?
- Is it a recognisable genre? Is it like someone else's work?
- Have all facts been verified by research?

archaeology

this archaeology of words
this fragile frame of structure, form,
this tension of expression –
look closer
sweep aside the soft dirt,
dig beneath the rubble,
drop a stone down into
the quiet lake,
the infinite within,
immerse yourself.
only you can find the meaning
in the symbols that sing
beneath your touch
anoint yourself in secret rhyme
time will not touch you here
dissolve the darkness
drink deeply
awaken.

Elizabeth Snow[13]

12
Reflecting On Our Writing

How do I know what I think until I see what I say?
EM Forster[1]

Firstly, before I start writing a novel I begin to reflect. Who is this character I'm meeting? How will she or he act in the story? What is her heart's desire? Then as I write the novel I also reflect. It's more than the ideas and the mind maps, though they help me formulate my thoughts about the writing, it's the writing about my writing in my journal that truly helps me understand my process and guides me to know what to write next. I'm also learning that it's a good idea to write an evaluation of the fiction that I complete, which leads me to why we do this. The purpose of reflecting on our writing is to improve our writing and to grow as writers.

Academic and author, Robert Graham, believes that 'your thinking about your work has little or no value until you have made it concrete in the form of words on the page.'[2] If you are not convinced by this statement, try writing about your writing to see what he means.

Reflecting is thinking and exploring our feelings about our work and how we have created it; the experience we went through. Reflection is good in teaching us our process. How did we achieve what we like about the story? If there are parts we don't like, what went wrong? Why? How will we make it better next time?

There are many times when we'll need to reflect on or write about our writing. You may be asked to write an author reflection either for study, a review magazine or blog which asks for your inspiration and story behind your book and how it went for you.

Author statements

It's beneficial to not only reflect on our work to see what we have done, but also to go a step further and discover how we actually write. When we've finished a project it's a good idea to ask ourselves what works, what doesn't and why. This helps not only in the editing process and but also later when we may be asked for a statement about our writing. It certainly helps with the next story we write.

Here are some excerpts from an author statement on writing a short story 'Pay Me in the Spring' by Colleen, one of my students, where she reflects on what she did and why and what literature influenced her:

> While memorabilia, artefacts, people, animals, places and photographs provide inspiration, my structural development really begins when the characters are sufficiently revealed on the page ... This story began with Jake as the narrator, but it soon became apparent that an omniscient narrator was present. So that readers could understand Emmaline's and Jake's thoughts and feelings, I felt writing from both points of view would help advance the story...
>
> I see writer's block as the autumn, and writing as the spring – an unfolding and flowering of a garden of words ... 'Pay me in the Spring' is inspired by colour, and the age of the protagonists determine an eleven to fourteen-year-old readership ... The narrator's voice is lyrical ...

> Zusak's fine use of lyric in [*The Book Thief*] shows the reader the winter skeleton of Himmel Street, and sets the tone of his narrative. As I believe that young adults understand the music of language, I chose to experiment with a lyrical opening hook ... In order to develop tension and contrast, this narrative is structured around adversity, growth and hope.[3]

Workout

When reflecting on my writing I use questions that could be pulled from the previous chapters of this book – hence reflection stitches together the inspiration, the influences and the choices I make into the process and then I reflect on what worked well and what didn't.

Answer these questions in your journal and/or create more of your own.
- What inspired you to write this story?
- What research did you do for the story?
- What influences helped in making decisions while writing?
- What choices were difficult to make and why?
- What problems occurred and how did you resolve them?
- What do you think works well in your story?
- Does anything bother you in the story that you'd like to rework?

Now write up your answers into an author statement.

Some author statements that have been published are interesting to look at to understand the writer's process. Mem Fox's talk on writing *The Green Sheep* called 'Page-ripping writer's rage: from first idea to final word in a picture book'[4] is a good example where she discusses the whole process from idea, to collaborating with the illustrator, to cutting the manuscript of 342 words to the 190 words it is in the book.

Libby Gleeson wrote a book called *Writing Hannah: On Writing for Children* (1999) in which she shares from the notebooks and diaries she kept while writing *Hannah and the Tomorrow Room*. It is an interesting study of the process of writing the novel. There is also comment on writing for children in general and references to her other novels and picture books.[5]

Rodney Martin and John Siow published *The Story of a Picture Book* (1981) about creating their picture book, *There's a Dinosaur in the Park* (1980). Although the technology is different now it is fascinating to see the process from idea to handwritten notes to manuscript and how it changed. It's also interesting to see how picture books were made in the 1980s.

Tip
Keep a record of what you read. Not only will you have information for your writing evaluations, but the books you like to read may help you know what you like to write and why.

Blogs

Often authors need to translate self-evaluations in to another form of writing, such as a blog post. When your book is published you may be asked to provide a post for a blog. My publishers usually instigate this, but you may have friends with blogs where you can provide posts for each other. Sometimes the post will take the form of interview questions, in which case your personal evaluation of your work will be helpful. Other times they may ask for an author statement and you will have a head start on that too.

A simple example of writing about writing in a blog is 'The Joy of Rewriting' which I wrote after finishing the rewrite of *Jihad* and its transformation into *The War Within*.[6]

Exploring the process of your writing, such as with the questions suggested above, could provide content for your own blog. Also see the comments from author Claire Belberg about blogging in Chapter 16.

Articles

When writing up your reflections as an article you may like to consider your inspiration; how did the story start? Do you have a background the same as the characters in the book? That is, what is your authority for what you wrote? If you wrote about tigers, have you worked in a zoo, for example? Do you have any idea where your character came from? What research did you do? Why did you write the book? How do you think your book will be helpful in schools?

An example can be seen in an article I wrote for the online journal *Writing4Children* called 'Crossing Borders in Faith and Culture: Writing *Marrying Ameera*'.[7] Included are papers from other Australian authors in this special Australasian issue.

Author Talks

As an author we will need to talk about our writing. When authors are asked why and how we write, the questioner doesn't always mean how we put the words on the page, but how we decided things, how we chose the idea, and chose content and why. If we haven't thought about these things, we will not be able to discuss it. We'll end up being the writer, who when asked about her writing, will respond with: 'Look, I just write, that's all.' I think we can do better than that. Young people as well as adults want to know how we do it and what we think about it.

I'm often asked to speak about writing historical fiction for children and YA. When writing *Taj and the Great Camel Trek* (2011) I had to reflect constantly on my writing. I wrote about my struggles in turning history into fiction and the problem I had with the concern of appropriating history and how much I could change to make the story work. Did I have any right to do that? I learned such a lot through that process, and teachers, in particular, find it interesting. I'm asked also to talk about my writing process for *The Tales of Jahani* (2016) which is historical fantasy. I had difficulties with writing history into fantasy too and, fortunately, I had to think about it continuously and write about what I was writing to try to make sense of what I was achieving, if anything. It did all come together, finally, and my journal notes helped to make an interesting author talk along with the images that inspired me as a Powerpoint presentation.

Essays

An essay for a journal or for a creative writing course is also reflecting and writing about your work. A postgraduate thesis may explore, in part, the writing process and why and how you chose techniques to use in the creation of your story, or you may compare your work to similar literature already published. Many theses are based on a question which needs to be answered. This question would arise naturally from the research behind the story or a theme that runs through the work. For example, if you have written a novel in the genre of magical realism, you might write an essay about some aspect of magical realism that hasn't yet been explored. Some essays will incorporate more than one of these suggestions. The essay I wrote to correspond with *The Messenger Bird* discussed Cornish literature in Australia and how the diaspora brought about Australian-Cornish literature, especially children's and YA literature. One chapter was a commentary of my process of writing such a novel. It's always good to refer to other literature in the field (a literature review) and show how our novel sits with this other literature, and how it has inspired our own work. We do not create in a vacuum.

We also need to think about how our novel is adding something new to contemporary fiction.

There are many examples of writers writing about their work in literary journals, especially in the online journal *TEXT*.[8]

Writing about our work always involves examining why we write and how we write. This then becomes the theory of our writing.

Broader reflection

Here are some questions to help you reflect on your writing as a whole: What kind of writer do you think you are? What sort of writer would you like to be? What do you write well? What would you like to improve? What do you intend by writing your stories – is there an overall reason for your writing? What energises you? What do you like to write about? Do you like writing plot driven stories or character driven stories?

To think about your process as a whole: How do you usually begin a story? How do you draft? What is your opinion on what works best for you in planning? What do you think about character and plot?

It took me years to formulate how I actually write. I needed to reflect on my work as a whole and so, with help from colleagues, I worked through my process and discovered that my faith has a large part in what I choose to write about, how I begin with characters and even how I structure a story and resolve them. I call my writing faith-informed because of a statement from academic, George E Marsden (1997). Faith-informed fiction highlights the idea that belief systems built around religious faiths should have equal standing in scholarship with other worldviews.[9]

'Faith-informed' is a modest term in a pluralistic setting and yet my own Christian perspective can be reflected upon as part of my identity as a writer. These thoughts grew into a paper that I presented at the School Library Association ('Addressing the Sacred through Literature and the Arts') conference held at Australian Catholic University in Sydney in 2013. A shorter version of the paper called 'Art and the Sacred' (2014) can be read in *Review: The Christian School Library Magazine*.[10] Here is the first paragraph.

> Madeleine L'Engle writes that to talk about art and the sacred is for her one and the same thing. I agree; I believe everything we do can be done to the glory of God and so there is no division between the secular and sacred in my life or therefore in my art. My writing for instance can be performed as an act of worship; when I write I feel close to God. Thus talking about how I write also means sharing the meaning of my life and my worldview. I appreciate L'Engle's image of the artist as birth giver[11] and as an obedient servant. My worldview, like L'Engle's, is Christian. By the term 'faith' I mean faith as related to the divine. My personal sense of the sacred is a belief that I write in the presence of a creator God who loves relationship.

Spiritual journals

I have mentioned the use of a daily spiritual journal. This probably tracks my spiritual and emotional growth, but it also helps me to see how spirituality and my writing mesh. Reflections from this journal feed into my writing and also help me grow as a writer. I agree with Claire Belberg when she writes:

> Writing a personal journal that tracks my spiritual and emotional journey is invaluable in my personal growth as a writer (hence my blog also) and I would like to see that encouraged – reflections not necessarily for others to know or hear about. This is more about me growing in understanding about how my writing fits into who I am and the other aspects of my life, and contributes to the world.[12]

Our writing and our communities

Another avenue of reflection is how our writing impacts where we live, our clubs, our churches, our readers' lives. How does our art affect the community? This is a topic we often need to think about when applying for a grant. Will the book you aim to write be helpful to any particular part of your community, or even further afield? Will it be beneficial to any people group, or further the acceptance of diversity, for example, in the community? Think about why and how your writing could, as Belberg puts it, contribute to the world.

Guest Author — Penny Jaye[13]

I'm often asked how I can write about such a difficult subject as *Out of the Cages* and I don't really know how to answer. I know that the writing was difficult. There were several scenes I didn't even want to write. In fact, I put off writing them as long as I could because I didn't want to have to imagine what it would have been like, I didn't want to capture in words the fear, bewilderment and betrayal of my main character. And yet I knew I needed to, to better tell her story. Because I knew that Meena's story, although completely fiction, was also utterly true. My research had proven it, and perhaps that's what drove me to keep going, to tackle those scenes I didn't want to write, because of the very truth of the story I was writing. I knew this was a story that needed telling and more than that: it needed to break my heart so it would be real in the heart of my reader.

    I believe very strongly in the power of story to motivate change, be that of attitude or action. It was always my goal in writing this novel that it wouldn't just inform or even educate, but it would allow readers to feel and move. To inch towards believing in a different world and believing we can do something to fight darkness. So although there is a lot of heartache in this story, and the subject matter is certainly challenging, I tried hard to point the gaze away from despair and towards hope. To defy, I guess, those forces that wish to keep these types of things in silence and speak instead of love, friendship, healing and freedom despite it all.

13
Writing for Children Matters

Do you like titles that have a double meaning? My editors do. So I felt chuffed when this one appeared at the top of my page. It fits the bill for an interesting title. Writing for children truly does matter, however, here we'll discuss matters we may need to consider while writing for children.

What do you think?
> 'Give us books,' say the children, 'give us wings.'
> Paul Hazard[1]

- Are children affected by what they read? Positively or negatively? To what extent?
- Think about what makes a good book for children. Maurice Saxby presents his criteria in *Books in the Life of a Child* (1997).[2] Or read some blogs, for example, *The Conversation* by Nicholas Reece.[3] This will help inform your future writing.
- 'Fairy tales ... acknowledge the reality of darkness.... This is why we do readers – even very young readers – a disservice when we sanitise and soften the violence and brutality that figure so significantly in many traditional fairy stories. In so doing, we weaken the power of the tales and rob them of their full impact.'[4] Do you agree with Ware's statement?

- Do children and teens need a 'real' depiction of their condition? Would young people rather 'cut the crap' and see an issue for what it is, or rather escape into a different world for a while?
- Do you think the fact that a book has swear words means it is immoral?
- Why is it that books which adults often don't think are suitable, young people enjoy?
- Do you think there's room for both literary and more popular texts in a child's life?

Books that stand out are those that dare to be different, in style, in content, in treatment, in ideas.
Pam MacIntyre

We've already looked at a writer's values but what about values in books? We all know that our own worldview will seep through our story and themes. The publisher who accepted *The Last Virgin in Year 10* (2006), which explores spirituality and sexuality, said she liked the values in the book. These values come, I hope, through the characters, the nature of their problems and how they solve them.

Is there so much political correctness now that books can lack heart?
Maurice Saxby[5]

Political correctness, originally designed to protect minorities or those who'd been discriminated against, does seem to be getting out of hand where ideologies are being protected rather than people. I've found the best way to handle political correctness in my writing is to be kind; to give respect and dignity to every person. Tolerance doesn't seem to be enough as I find people are tolerant until you disagree with them. However, if the whole world were kind there wouldn't be greed or wars and we'd look after the earth. Surely we can accept people without having anything in common or without agreeing with their worldview.

Having said that, here are a few matters I've had to watch in my writing: diverse characters, gender, stereotyping characters, prejudice and racism. These will overlap but let's look at diverse characters first and how we write about them.

In Mark Haddon's *The Curious Incident of the Dog in the Night-Time* (2004) the narrator has Asperger's Syndrome. He is authentic, respectfully drawn and totally wins the reader's rapport. *My Life as an Alphabet* by Barry Jonsberg (2013) also successfully portrays a protagonist with a different way of seeing the world. My book *The Keeper* (2015) has a protagonist with ADHD but it is never mentioned. However, readers who have ADHD recognise themselves and are gratified; other readers enjoy the adventure.

Watch the terms we use: if talking about characters with a disability, they are not disabled people, for example, the protagonist of Eleanor Spence's *October Child* (1967) has autism. Today he would not be referred to as an autistic boy. Folks do not like being defined by a disability or illness. In the same way, UK minister Rev Sam Allberry, who experiences same sex attraction, will not call himself a gay Christian. He says he is not defined by his sexuality but by his relationship with God.[6]

Gender diversity

Kate Walker's *Peter* (1991) was possibly the first Australian YA novel to explore same sex attraction. Lately, I've seen more gender diversity in YA and middle grade fiction where a main character identifies with a non-traditional gender. In some cases, a throw away sentence about a minor character's sexual orientation is included to show, perhaps, that the author is being inclusive. I don't have experience in writing in the LGBTQ field, but I found Will Kostakis' *The First Third* (2013) a warm and humorous look at Greek culture and a teenager's coming out. US author Emery Lord's *The Names They Gave Us* (2017) is a thought provoking and helpful YA novel about same sex attraction where Lucy helps on a camp for troubled kids and learns about her prejudice and the lives of people much different from herself. In all these examples respect and kindness for others needs to be shown.

Gender

Publishers do seem to like to see strong female characters in a leading role, and maybe even doing jobs that men may have normally done. There are female plumbers and truck drivers now, so this diversity needs to be shown in our writing if our story is set in contemporary times. However, it's good to remember that this can't be arbitrarily done. The character and story still needs to be 'obeyed'. The character's attitudes and the way they interact with each other is still more important than showing we can be diverse.

US editor, Cheryl Klein, describes in *The Magic Words* (2016) how in good books characters and the prose display some fresh personality. They have an energy or uniqueness not seen before. 'When agents and editors say we're looking for a strong voice, what we're really looking for is this unique personality, combined with the discipline of all these other virtues.'[7] The other 'virtues' that she outlines in her first chapter are principles of good writing under the umbrella of clarity and connection. It's worth reading this enlightening book.

When I had written the draft of *The Tales of Jahani* (2016) I gave it to my son Michael Hawke to read as he has a remarkable spatial capability of reading a manuscript and seeing the loopholes in characterisation and plotting. He drew a graph of the storyline on his whiteboard, took a photo and presented it to me. The main problem, he said, is that this is supposed to be Jahani's story, isn't it? I nodded. You think you have a strong female character with agency? I nodded again. Well here, he pointed to the graph, Azhar has the idea first, and over here it is Rahul. I was astounded. I thought I had given Jahani agency. It all had to be rewritten.

Yet we mustn't forget the boys. I wanted to write a boy-oriented series as well in order to encourage reluctant boy readers to read. In *The Keeper* (2015) Mei is Joel's friend. She doesn't get to make the decisions in the story but she does try to keep Joel out of trouble. That could be criticised too, as Joel gets to be the wild one and Mei has a quieter life, but this series is Joel's story.

The problem with trying not to stereotype gender is that some girls do like reading or playing with dolls. Many boys do like playing with machines. In our stories we may be just portraying life as it is. Or are we forcing gender views that in some children aren't necessary? A boy shouldn't be made to feel bad if he wants to play Barbies with his sister (probably for the time spent with his sister rather than his love of dolls) but a girl shouldn't be made to feel inferior for wanting to play with dolls either. In avoiding stereotyping characters make sure every character is interesting and has reasons for why they are who they are. Make sure the elderly aren't stereotyped; I'm a grandmother but I don't sit in a rocking chair, knitting, nor do I ride a Harley. Do research and meet people who are similar to your characters. Search your heart for prejudice. If it's there, you'll write it. If you have empathy, that will come across too.

Racism

Children's literature seems to show what a culture is like at any time. In *We of the Never Never* Indigenous people are not portrayed well. When I read the Billabong books, for instance, I'm not sure I noticed the class and racist views. As an adult I see in *Wings Above Billabong* (1935) aging stockmen calling a 12-year-old boy 'Master' and Aboriginal stockmen acting as if they don't know anything. I understand these books, like Enid Blyton's, have been 'cleaned up'. Instead of ignoring the racism or trying to re-write it, maybe we can alert young people to how people thought at the time. And learn not to do it today. I reread *Seven Little Australians* while writing Kerenza's story set in 1911. Sadly there is no mention of Indigenous people just as there had been none in all my dad's and great uncles' memoirs of pioneering in the Mallee, so I tried to put that right in *Kerenza: A New Australian* (2015).

When we lived in the UAE, we knew there was Arab privilege and we didn't have it. In Australia there is white privilege; just ask any brown person. Having white privilege doesn't mean a white person is racist, but white people do need to be careful not to perpetuate racist ideas by denying that white privilege exists. This would also deny the suffering of so many and erase their cultural history. We may not all look the same or be the same, but we can be treated with the same dignity and respect.

Melissa Lucashenko's *Killing Darcy* (1998), and works by James Maloney, Meme McDonald and Boori Pryor show a different view from the classics, and give equality to Indigenous characters. However, there was controversy over Phillip Gwynne's YA novel, *Deadly Unna* (1998). It shows the racism in a country town, yet it was based on the author's experience and he didn't feel he was being racist in writing what he saw. When the film adaptation *Australian Rules* (2002) was launched, directors Gwynne and Goldman, came under attack from Aboriginal and some white critics, accusing them of 'appropriating' an Aboriginal story, of implied racism and racist stereotyping. Gwynne stated:

> I believe what happened in Adelaide is indicative of where this country is at the moment in terms of white/black relations. It is at breaking point, and our film was just a catalyst, because feelings are so strong. Any film on the same subject could have done it. Mine just happened to be it … Aboriginal people have the right to their stories. I agree with this. But *Australian Rules* is a white boy's story. In fact, it's my story. Don't I have the right to my story?[8]

Writing other cultures

One reviewer accused my novel *Re-entry* (1995) of stereotyping a Pakistani family. The mother in my story did stay home, spoke little English and wore shalwar qameezes, but I wrote what I saw. I was telling the truth.

So why is half of my work about other cultures? I often write about Pakistan because I enjoyed living there. At first, I wrote Pakistani stories for my children as they wanted books set there. Even recently, *The Tales of Jahani* (2016) was written for my children.

Author Arundhati Roy[9] stated, 'There's really no such thing as the voiceless. There are only the deliberately silenced, or the preferably unheard.' I have written about people from other cultures to give them a voice, because I felt they were unheard. At times I want to explore what it would be like living in another culture or make sense of an issue I've heard about, for example, asylum seekers as in *Soraya the Storyteller* (2004). I also want to help people get the help they need by bringing an issue into the open: Trafficking (*Mountain Wolf*, 2012), forced marriage (*Marrying Ameera*, 2010), blasphemy laws (*The Truth about Peacock Blue* (2014) and forced labour (*Chandani and the Ghost of the Forest*, 2019). I believe that if an issue is opened to the world, the harder it is for it to be perpetuated. Many social ills like domestic violence, child labour, persecution and slavery rely on people not knowing about it; in some cases, so that powerful business men can keep making money, and escape being convicted of a crime. Social problems are often about money/greed and power. War and much religious persecution are driven by political power.

Finally, I like to build bridges – I see that many people in Australia are fearful of cultures they do not understand, or they are dismissive of them. I like the poem by Mary Lathrap, 'Judge Softly' where we need to walk a mile in another's moccasins to understand.

Some other authors write to draw people into a character's plight. Robin de Crespigny's *The People Smuggler* (2012) is a true story written in first person. YA readers may enjoy this. Deborah Ellis, with her *Parvana* series, and editor Lyn White's *Through My Eyes* series, also generate sympathy for children living in war zones. A true story on forced labour for children is *Iqbal* by Francesco D'Adamo (2001). SA author Wendy Noble's fantasy series called *Beast Speaker* (2017) is actually dealing with child soldiers even though the protagonist can mind-speak with dragons.

The distance of fantasy may better allow young people to process confronting content.

My ideas for cultural writing come from everywhere: living in Pakistan, online news, websites on persecution or trafficking; the human rights list and natural disasters. The horrific flood of 2010 in Pakistan inspired the *Kelsey* series. Or maybe a person in history wasn't heard and a writer will bring some incident to life, for example, Tommy Oldham being stolen (probably with his permission) in *Taj and the Great Camel Trek* (2011).

Ethics of writing another culture

What right do we have to write a culture other than our own? If we write about a high profile person we don't personally know, for instance, and slander him/her, then we could be sued. However, legally, we can write what is our own experience even if it involved someone else. But is being lawful enough?

Ethically we need to be respectful of a person's POV; is it right to pen their story? Will it do them harm? Can they do it themselves?

I have a third consideration: is it morally correct to write someone's story if they haven't asked you to? Will it be kind, loving and helpful to them to do so, or will it cause trouble for them?

I always ask if I can use someone's story or idea and I get it checked by a person from that culture. When I had finished writing *Soraya the Storyteller*, I asked some Afghan teenage girls to read it for breaches of culture or language. They said the culture was fine, but they suggested I change the spelling of Dari words to a more phonetic style, which I did. When I wrote *Zenna Dare* with a supporting Indigenous character, Caleb, I gave it to a descendant of the Ngadjuri people, Fred Warrior, to read. He pronounced it suitable for publication. The title of *The Messenger Bird* is used with permission by Ngarrindjeri Elder and poet, Margaret Woods.

I don't write Indigenous stories or stories with a main Indigenous character as there are people writing those stories themselves. I also don't feel I have a right to do so as I have not lived with Indigenous people nor do I have Indigenous relatives. Even author Boori Pryor, who is Indigenous, asks his aunties if he is allowed to write a certain story as a children's book.[10] If you feel drawn to write such a story, always first ask permission to use it. It can appear arrogant to want to rewrite an Indigenous story and the custodians of those stories may be nervous that it could be written incorrectly or subverted in some way. I don't appreciate it when a non-believer rewrites Biblical history by reinterpreting what they see as a myth to be pillaged.

Across the Creek (2003) includes Indigenous spirits but this information was found in *Ngadjuri* by Fred Warrior, Fran Knight et al. and I asked permission from one of the authors. Check out the protocols for Indigenous writing[11] online.

Many authors in Australia are writing their own cultural stories now so they are not 'unheard' such as the following: Boori Monty Pryor and Meme McDonald, *Njunjul the Sun* (2002); *The Interrogation of Ashala Wolf* by Ambelin Kwaymullina (2012); Will Kostakis, *The First Third* (2013); Melina Marchetta *Looking for Alibrandi* (1992); Randa Abdel-Fattah, *Ten Things I Hate about Me* (2006) and *When Michael Met Mina* (2016).

Some believe that we only have a right to write about our own culture; anything else is cultural appropriation. But if a person or group of people are not being heard, then I think we can write for them if we do it sensitively and respectfully. Do lots of research and have a person from that culture check it. An outside point of view can give fresh insight and may even be able to serve insiders who feel silenced. We can tell the truth with sympathy, balance and kindness. We can't be one-eyed, but we need to show both sides, as with Ameera and her father in *Marrying Ameera*.

One important thing I've learned is to be careful that my cultural voice doesn't override the character's voice. In a draft, Soraya says that she'll speak Arabic in heaven. It is true that Muslims believe Arabic will be spoken in heaven but they do not presume they will actually go there; the confidence of going to heaven by grace is a Christian belief. I changed the sentence to 'Arabic is the language that will be spoken in Paradise'. It's also helpful to show the character's cultural identity as a natural part of their personality, not always as an issue or problem. Fiona Woods' *Cloudwish* (2015) is a good example of this.

In case you have been asked to write a biography, here is a helpful statement on the ethics of writing another's story from biographer, May-Kuan Lim, author of *A Fish in the Well*.

> In recounting real-life stories, I try to avoid extremes. An obsession on feel-good stories can trivialise challenges, while an over-emphasis on injustice can victimise and disempower people. Ethical storytelling is about going beyond my own agenda and adopting the position of the listener-learner. I aim to use my craft to serve the people who tell me their stories. After completing a piece of work, I often ask myself: would I want myself or my children portrayed in this way? If it is a 'yes', then it passes my personal ethical storytelling test. When working with marginalised people, a good guide is that the more vulnerable the people, the greater degree of control I try to give them in directing the story and reclaiming their narrative.[12]

Research

An extra note on research since we're talking about ethics and rights. Whatever we write, we must know the world in our story: the culture, religion, history, arts, folklore, society, work, technology, government, education, hobbies, lifestyle, sport, food, fashion, landscape, transportation. It's by research we can know all this background to our novel. It would be easy to think fantasy writers don't need to do research, that they can make it all up. I suggest research will also help in the building of a world. I always look for folktales, stories or songs that will show the background and world of my characters. To me, novels which don't refer to what characters believe or think about the world seem un-researched and the characters lack authenticity. In my historical novels the research was huge. I have a thick A4 book of research for *Kerenza: A New Australian*. *Taj and the Great Camel Trek* took four years to write with much research before and during that time. I was researching *The Tales of Jahani* for ten years before I wrote them. Readers notice when we have researched or more specifically, when we haven't.

Tip
We need to be careful not to dump our fascinating research on our readers. Use it seamlessly so it is unseen yet stitching the story together.

Copyright matters
We do not need to register our copyright work in Australia. Copyright protection is automatic upon creation of your manuscript or artwork. So be wary of websites that ask for money to register and protect your copyright or to have a copyright protection plan. These are scams. Always refer to the Australian Society of Authors if ever in doubt about a legal issue. The Copyright Agency Australia[13] is the official group to approach if you have any copyright questions. They are a not-for-profit organisation that provides licensing solutions to use copyright-protected words and images in Australia. It's good to join once you have a book published as they will collect monies for you from educational institutions or magazines from copying or publishing a chapter of your book.

Language: to say or not to say

The ideal is to show beauty in our language, but some characters speak differently from ourselves. Forms of language can be a contentious issue for some, but some characters will swear. And we need to decide how 'true' we need to be to those characters. Usually we won't get away with swearing in a middle grade novel, but there seems little restriction on language in a YA novel. Since I don't swear in real life, I try to think of different ways to show that my character is swearing rather than write it out in full. So to me it is a matter of show not tell. I find swearing that's only used to show character and emotion to be lazy writing, like emotive adverbs tacked onto speech tags to tell what the character is feeling. The writing that rises above the pavement is that which evokes and shows mood, atmosphere, character and setting by the way words are used rather than what can easily spill out of the character's mouth.

There are times when we may need to use certain words. As my trusted reader said after reading the draft of *The Messenger Bird*, Gavin would not have stayed silent when he thought Tamar was drowning. 'He would have sworn three times,' she said. I think I managed the 's' word twice.

Joel, in *The Keeper*, does swear, though only once at his darkest moment do we hear it. At times he throws 'a few choice words' through his shut door. In *A Kiss in Every Wave* the grandmother with Alzheimer's disease swears once using the most famous Australian adjective. I left that one in to show how Alzheimer's changes a person's personality. Claire Zorn writes so seamlessly true to her characters that if there were swear words in *One Would Think the Deep* (2016), I don't remember. All I remember are the characters, their stories, and how it was written to transport me to the coast every time I opened the book. That novel reminded me of Tim Winton's work.

Cynthia Grant's *Uncle Vampire* (1993) also uses a swear word once which is very effective. The story is a psychological thriller; the main character, Carolyn, sixteen, has Multiple Personality Disorder. When she finally faces what has happened to her, she answers the counsellor's question of, 'What did your uncle do?' with, 'He f … me.' The shock to me as the reader made me feel the pain the character had been experiencing all through the story.

Bear in mind that swearing and some adult content in a YA novel can exclude it from school libraries. So have a thoughtful reason for everything you choose to write. But never write for sensation or titillation or use gratuitous violence.

What do you think of toilet humour? Many boys like it so much they'll read it when they didn't like reading before. I heard Andy Griffiths say that he was rounding up some boys who were late to class and on the walls in the boys' toilet he found toilet humour. Many of the boys in his class didn't like reading and so he wrote some stories for them with toilet humour included. By the end of the year the boys' reading levels had soared like rockets. That's how his career in writing began, I understand.

I haven't managed to finish *The Day My Bum Went Psycho* (2001), sorry Andy, but academic Suzanne Eggins says it is a clever, well-sustained parody of the epic male heroic quest typified by Tolkien's *The Lord of the Rings*.[14] So there you are, as my mother would say.

Here is YA author and journalist Scott Monk's take on language and content in novels for boys:

> I try to tear down the stereotypes of young men as 'hormonally-charged cretins' normally presented in movies. They can be creative, intelligent and respectful individuals, not just bodies. Any topic can be dealt with – even the Bible doesn't present a whitewashed humanity – but do so with wisdom, trying not to sensationalise obscenity.[15]

Subversion and censorship

I have worn many hats: teacher, mother, information studies student, author, lecturer and, although I understand parents' concerns about what their children read, my teacher/librarian/writer hat is on the firmest. Quite often books are criticised or banned when people haven't even read them. Imagine my shock when Dame Jane Lomax-Smith launched *Soraya the Storyteller,* and she said it was subversive. I had always thought subversive meant defying the authority of the government or some equally dire deed that could get you tortured in prison. Alison Lurie in 1990[16] argued that all children's literature was subversive. She takes subversive to mean where characters challenge authority. Perhaps that is why *Soraya* then ended up on an anarchy blog list of fifty Australian novels of all time with overt political content. Six were children's or YA. Yikes.

However, to be subversive shouldn't there be something that is subverted? Screenwriter Brian Godawa sees a deeper meaning for us as writers: 'In subversion, the narrative, images and symbols of one system are discreetly redefined or altered in the new system.'[17] With this definition I can see how *Soraya* could be subversive. The novel can change readers' perspectives on asylum seekers by showing a human face to the issue. I can see too how some novels about history or Bible figures can be slightly changed to give a different view such as Geraldine Brooks' novel about King David, *The Secret Chord* (2015). Some children's books that are challenged or banned are maybe just subversive or controversial, having challenging content or language.

Censorship is a can of worms and will take more space that I have here, so here are a few things to think about. Is the written word processed differently than visual movies? My kids thought a book was less confronting than images on a screen, or language on a screen. 'I can skip bits in a book,' my eldest daughter said.

Even though we don't mention it, most children's authors self-censor and make selections of what they will or will not write about. I know I do. Books have been banned or not selected for diverse reasons: language, racism, witchcraft or sexism (gender roles). Dr Seuss' *The Lorax* was challenged because of the environmental issues which people didn't want to face in 1971. I have a copy of Enid Blyton's 1944 edition of *The Three Gollywogs*. Here is the first paragraph:

> There were once three golliwogs who were most unhappy in the nursery cupboard. None of the other toys liked them, because their little mistress, Angela, didn't like their black faces.

Unfortunately one of them is called N-g--r which is an extremely offensive word in Australia today. Only recently there were gollywogs entered in a competition at the Royal Adelaide Show. Many people protested so that the convenors had to remove the gollywogs. Then others protested that they should be put back as they were works of art. Censorship never pleases everyone.

Enid Blyton has also been caught out with racist remarks about the Cornish. In *Five Go Down to the Sea*, where the five are on holiday from England, the Cornish are seen as 'other'. The boy Yan cannot talk properly; the fisherman the children stay with only utters syllables and is shown to be dark and swarthy like a Spaniard. The Spanish don't fare any better. Did this prejudice sail over my head at the age of 8? Or does an attitude like this seep into our souls? I devoured her books, especially the mysteries, but now I see it as a reminder to be careful, kind and humble when writing.

Fantasy concerns

Any book on witches is automatically taken from the shelves. What then are we do to with the witch of Endor and Samuel's ghost? Must we remove the Bible from the shelves because it contains not only ghosts and witches but incest and murder and lust and rape? We human beings tend to distort and misuse, if not abuse, the original goodness of creation, but that does not make the original good less good.

Madeleine l'Engle[18]

US author, Katherine Paterson, received criticism about a character dying in *A Bridge to Terrabithia* (1977). I received criticism about *The Keeper* being an evil book from a mother who hadn't even read it. So I felt sorry for JK Rowling when her witch hunt began. It happened because some readers didn't understand the difference between fantasy and Biblical magic and witchcraft. A few such people still ban CS Lewis' *The Lion, the Witch and the Wardrobe* due to the witch in it. They don't seem to make a distinction that the witch is portrayed as an evil character.

Author and pastor, Andrew Lansdown[19], states that in the Bible, witchcraft and magic is the idea of superhuman power gained and exercised by occult means. Real magic involves evil spirits. It involves a person discovering extraordinary things with the aid of a spirit. It's the spirit not the person who performs the magic.

In *Harry Potter* there is no alliance between humans and spirits. Magic is not supernatural but natural, and happens because people are born with magical abilities and also because objects possess extraordinary properties. These are elements of fantasy. The closest the novels come to Biblical witchcraft is in the character of Voldemort but Rowling condemns him, presenting him as murderous, treacherous and ugly. She encourages her readers to see him as evil too.

Finally, there needs to be a balance: the chief end of reading is not just to produce a desirable sense of virtues, nor only to entertain. We know there is power in literature to enrich lives. The heart needs to be touched as well as the mind. But how is a parent expected to know which books do that? I encourage families to find out together. Go on a mystery tour. Read together. I did this with my kids up to senior high, though I didn't want to read the stuff my son was into at 16. Through discussion and being exposed to different types of books, children will learn to discern which books are good ones so that when they are older they can decide what they like and what they don't. Children will often stop reading if a book makes them feel 'weird or unsafe'.

When I found my 12-year-old neighbour, Sam, reading Phillip Pullman's *The Northern Lights* (1995) I said, 'See if you can work out what the author's worldview is.' When he'd finished all three books, he said to me, 'He's a great writer but he sure doesn't believe in God.' That's true; Pullman doesn't, but Sam enjoyed the novels and he learned to be discerning about what he was reading.

Parents need to look beyond Christian versus non-Christian as a selection tool. By only buying 'safe', and probably not the best written, books from a Christian bookshop, we are cheating our children of much beautiful literature and the chance to learn to be discerning about what is not.

Journalist and author, Scott Monk, makes an interesting statement about censorship and faith.

> Thousands of secular YA books are produced worldwide annually, with no mention of faith ... a closed shop approach to religion devalues the intelligence of teenage readers. They are smart enough to make their own decisions. It would be better if they were presented with a much more balanced view of religion – and not be the victims of secular censorship.[20]

Monk also believes Christianity has a role in mainstream fiction. We can't ignore our beliefs when shaping a story; we write with our own value system that's built from our worldview.

A good way to finish this chapter is with some thoughts from academic, Maurice Saxby. He says the books that endure do so because they illuminate the human spirit. They reach down to the core of what it is to be human. He cites favourites like *Sarah, Plain and Tall*; *Storm Boy* and *Charlotte's Web* as profound expressions of the human spirit. 'For the searching and attuned reader they provide, as James Joyce has it, an epiphany – an enlightenment, a showing forth.' Saxby had a student who shared how as a child *The Last Battle* by Lewis had aroused in her such a sense of the mystery and wonder of life, she was able to apprehend the amazing concept of redemption. Saxby asks, 'Can any literature achieve more than this?'[21] Literature not only entertains and challenges but also it nourishes the imagination.

Writers shape human experience so perceptive readers are able, as Katherine Paterson says, 'to find not only order but meaning in story' and 'make sense of their own lives and reach out toward people whose lives are quite different from their own.'[22]

> ### Guest Author — Dr James Cooper[23]
> ### Reading Challenging Literature
>
> In everyday life we constantly come into contact with worldviews that depart from what we believe as Christians. Understanding the differences, and being able to empathise, evaluate, dialogue with and navigate different worldviews, is essential if we are to live in the world but not of it (and also to write for a world in need of the Gospel). Reading complex and challenging literature can be a useful training ground for developing those skills, while in our writing we ought never to shrink from dealing openly and fairly with the highs and lows of human experience.
>
> For some writers of faith, engaging with more worldly literature can pose a challenge. It's essential to remember, however, that when writers depict language or behaviour that is deplorable, they are not necessarily advocating that way of behaving; nor does this necessarily amount to the writer behaving badly *in the exact same way* as the character being portrayed.
>
> Clearly, Jesus enjoins us to live pure lives, to be perfect as our Father in Heaven is perfect (Matt 5:48), and

St Paul rightly urges us to cultivate the habit of virtue by attending to whatever is true, noble, admirable and pure, etc. (Phil 4:8). Certainly, spending prolonged periods feeding our imagination with ungodly images and ideas is fraught with spiritual danger, and is best avoided. At the same time, one of the reasons we ought to feed the imagination with all that's good and pure, etc., is to enhance our spiritual vision, so that we may see more readily when and how things can go wrong. Good literature – like all good art – serves to enhance our vision in this sense. Further, this can legitimately involve presenting a negative image in order to define the positive, so to speak.

We recognise salvation, holiness and the light of truth most poignantly in contrast to the facts of sin, vice and falsehood in our lives. The Bible, don't forget, contains vivid accounts of some horribly depraved actions. Why? Not in order to commend or trivialise those actions, or simply to entertain, but because of what they have to teach and remind us about our human condition and our proper dependency on God's love, grace, forgiveness and moral law, etc.

Every artist has an obligation to try to see the world honestly, and to share a vision of life that is just – i.e. accurate, realistic, true to life in all its texture. This includes the inescapable facts of sin and suffering on the one hand, and yet the possibility of redemption and a real cause for hope on the other. It so happens that the writer who is a Christian has the best possible grounds for adopting this 'stereoscopic' perspective.

14
Preparing to Publish

Preparing to submit a manuscript is still the same as it always was: that is, it needs to be developed to the best of your ability, rewritten as many times as you have time for, leaving gaps of time between the later rewrites so we don't start changing the good bits to bad. It's the process of sending that has changed. Most publishers now want submissions via email or a portal on their website and only at certain times. It's extremely important to check each publisher's submission guidelines. The cover email (which I think is good manners) needs to be precise, perhaps a pitch sentence about your book, including target age of audience and genre, a sentence about yourself and any story awards or experience you've had in publishing, that is, your bio, and your other contact details.

Workout
It takes a lot of practice to write a bio about yourself and a few pitch sentences describing your book well enough to grab a publisher's attention. To get yourself over the hurdle of writing about yourself, try these:
- Write five things about yourself.
- Write a paragraph about you from the perspective of a person who only knows you professionally.
- Write a paragraph about you from a person close to you.

What did you notice about your responses? Did they grow more positive? In your bio you need to be positive. Don't say you know little about writing but have thrown this together and what do you think? We all know little about writing, especially when emerging, but there's no need to remind the publisher.

The bio

We write different bios for different functions, for example, for an academic journal we would include academic qualifications, published titles, and no mention of our cats and goats.

For a children's magazine, online chat room or a children's book festival, we would include more about our interests, where we write and our quirky pet that we based our latest book on. For speaking at a Children's Book Council conference we would include more publishing information, maybe themes in our recent book, and awards.

Look at some author bios on the back of children's books. Make your bio 50-100 words, unless otherwise specified. Follow instructions from the publisher or online blog who is asking for it. Start with your name and write an objective paragraph about yourself in the third person. Third person helps to distance yourself when writing a bio. Include details about you to match your story. If you are a vet and are writing about rare spiders, say you are a vet in your bio.

The pitch

A pitch tells a publisher why they should read your story. A synopsis tells the story. You can give them a synopsis if they are interested after your pitch. At times, writers' centres, festivals and conferences offer pitch sessions with publishers and agents. These sessions are usually five minutes. So it's good to prepare a two-minute spiel about your book and leave the rest for their questions. It's very difficult to write only a sentence or two about a novel so start with writing a paragraph of your story. This could suit a cover email. Time yourself and see how much you can say in two minutes – it's probably a page. This could suit a pitch at a writer's centre.

What to include

Start with a hook – an interesting statement relating to the subject matter of your novel. For example: What if your dad arranged your marriage without you knowing? Introduce your character, setting and what the character needs to do. Keep your language tight. Be specific when stating the genre. Don't waffle: 'Oh I think it's a bit of this and a bit of that.' The publisher will turn off. State the title rather than referring to it as 'my novel'.

Choosing who to pitch to: Have you researched who publishes the style of book you have written?

Answering questions: Know who your audience is. What's unique about your book? Where does it fit on the shelves and what titles would a reader need to like to pick up yours? Why did you write it? Are you qualified to write the content in your book? Is your book finished? I'd finish it before pitching it in case a miracle happens and the publisher wants to read it on the plane. Just kidding. Usually they'd ask for it to come the normal way via email, however, they may want it soon. They may have only this window of a few weeks to read manuscripts.

Workout

Write two sentences or 50 words about your story. This could become your pitch sentence/s when answering the question 'What is your book about?' Or you could use it for to begin a cover or query email. Remember your story/plot will have some basic elements you need to mention: the character, the situation that the character is in, what the character wants to do about it, what's stopping your character, the climax or darkest moment.

Example: Ameera is sent to attend her cousin's wedding in Azad Kashmir and discovers the wedding is her own; she doesn't know the groom and wants to go home. She tries to leave but is beaten, her passport taken, and she has to face a forced marriage to a stranger.

Synopsis
What a synopsis is not
A synopsis is not a blurb. This is the catchy piece on the back which leaves you dangling and wanting to buy the book. This does not work on an editor. They want the whole story, even the resolution. Also, it is not a plot or

chapter outline. The synopsis must be written as continuous prose.

Workout
Write a synopsis of your book
- Include the title of the book, genre and target audience.
- Use an interesting 'hook' to grab attention.
- Say who the story is about and what. Use the character's name early on.
- Give motivation, the reasons for the action.
- Don't add subplots and minor detail.
- Write the plot in a logical progression, tell the action.
- Include important plot turning points and climax.
- A synopsis is the whole storyline so include the resolution.
- Use a similar writing style as in the novel but write in present tense, third person as when writing about a book you've read.
- No dialogue or cute stuff.
- It's not a blurb so don't leave the editor hanging on a question at the end. They need to see if it will work or not.
- The synopsis must be written well; keep the sentences tight.
- I try to use one page for a children's novel. Maybe spill over onto a second page for longer YA novels. Even though I use Times New

Roman 12 font and 1.5 spacing for manuscripts, I single space a synopsis to fit it on one or two pages; this is allowable. Don't use fancy fonts or formatting as publishers prefer a professional submission.

Synopsis check

Is the story affected if you leave certain events out of the synopsis? Be economical yet tell all the story.

It's scary but at times a book is sold on the basis of the synopsis, as not everyone in a large publishing house has time to read a manuscript when the editor submits it for consideration. Maybe only she and a professional reader has read it, so she gives everyone a synopsis and the reader's report. One publisher would ask me for a half page synopsis just before she would take my manuscript to the acquisitions meeting. Probably they had a lot of books to think about and a half page would at least mean the sales people had some idea of the book. If they don't like it from that, it gets rejected. So practise writing good synopses.

What an editor looks for in the first instance

Let's say you've sent the first three chapters of your children's novel and a synopsis and the submissions editor is deciding whether to ask for the rest of the manuscript. She will look for:

- Your ability to write, so don't make any mistakes in the cover email or synopsis, or it

may deter the submissions editor from reading your first chapter.
- Clean appearance of the manuscript; don't leave any Track Changes from drafting.
- Engaging character and innovative story.
- Authentic voice of the narrator.
- Arresting title. This can be difficult so at least aim for interesting.
- Thought-provoking beginning.
- Colourful descriptions and images.
- Tight writing.
- Satisfying ending, though at this stage the editor will only see the ending in the synopsis.
- Whether the writing style and content fits the target age level.
- Whether it fits her list.

Query email

You may not need to send a query email as most publishers now have all information and guidelines on their websites. However, you may need to find out if a publishing house is taking on projects like yours if it is slightly different from the information on their website. The following is only if a publisher hasn't the information you need on their website.

Let's imagine a publisher doesn't have any fantasy titles on their picture book list and they haven't stated that they are accepting them either. Your query email might look like this:

Dear (find out the submission editor's name or use the title they suggest on their website)

I have written a story called *Nat's Cat* which could suit your picture book list. It's a warm and engaging story about Nat and his alien cat saving the moon. Would you like to see the manuscript?

I have six children's short stories published. Two have been included in the X anthology, and four in *School Magazine*.

Thank you.

Blurb

This is where you can end on a question and not give away the resolution.

A good beginning hook is essential – check out some blurbs on books. Your pitch sentence and your pitch paragraph should help here. Just don't include the climax.

Do your marketing research

- Sit in the library or take baskets of books home. Discover who publishes books that are in the same category as the project you are writing. Bookshops help in this regard too as they have all the latest books.
- Check the publishers' websites. Read carefully, as I got caught out in the early days and sent a manuscript to a Western Australian publisher only to have the manuscript returned with the note: Sorry, we only publish authors from WA. I'm sure that wasn't written in the *Writers' Marketplace*.

- Join a writers' group, as often publishing tips are passed on. Join up to an e-zine journal like *Pass it On*.[1]
- Join the Writers' Centre in your state, as publishing tips and competition details are posted on their websites.

In the end it boils down to whether the submissions editor connects to your character and your story. If she's intrigued enough it is sent to a professional reader. On the basis of the reader's report your story may then be read in-house. Agent Dyan Blacklock, when she was the publisher at Omnibus Books, always read her own slush pile. That way she discovered many talented writers like Markus Zusak, Michael Gerard Bauer, DM Cornish and Tamsin Janu. Not all publishing houses do this, so polish that submission.

By all means, do a writing course to hone your skills, employ a professional editor or use a manuscript assessment service to improve your manuscript, but do not expect a publishing house to take notice of these things. Attaching a letter from a manuscript assessment agency or from a lecturer of a writing course will not move your novel up the slush pile. I have heard these things are disregarded in publishing houses, and your story is read for its own merit. However, a course, an editor or assessment will help you improve your writing so that it has the best chance of being read.

Guest Author — Susan J Bruce[2]
Writing for the Mainstream

A few years ago I told a Christian friend that I wanted to write novels. She said, 'Great. We need more people writing books that are safe.' This comment made me squirm at the time and it still does now. I don't want to write safe books – the Bible isn't safe – but I do want to honour God and the call he's placed on my life. I've thought a lot about this over the last few years. Is it possible to write books that are meaningful in the light of my Christian world view, that entertain and inspire people who would never buy novels from the local Christian bookstore or from the faith section of the Amazon website? If so, what do these books look like? Sex, violence, death and destruction are all part of the human experience (and very present in the Bible). Should a Christian write about these things? To what level? Can I mention faith in a novel in a way that won't exclude it from the general market? I still don't have all the answers to these (and many more) questions but the best advice I've read comes from philosopher, Jacques Maritain: 'If you want to make a Christian work, then be Christian, and simply try to make a beautiful work, into which your heart will pass; do not try to "make Christian."' I think if we can do that – if *I* can do that – then we will soon crawl out of our Christian ghettos and start impacting the world with our craft.

15
A Publishing Story

The question I'm asked a lot at conferences and seminars is how I became published and how has publishing changed throughout my career. There is never time to say what the questioner really wants to know, the whole journey, so I'll include that history here for those who are interested. The lessons I learned about being a writer throughout this time are included in Chapter 16.

1 The beginning
I began writing seriously in Pakistan while we were aid workers there. During that time I did a correspondence Christian Journalism course with Ken Packer and read a lot of classics, and anything else I could find in Pakistan, learning how authors treated characters and plot. MM Kaye's *Far Pavilions* (1978) was probably my favourite, *The Source* by James Michener (1965) was amazing, *Pride and Prejudice* (1813), and AJ Cronin's *The Lady with Carnations* (1976). After reading this one I can remember thinking that my own character development was very poor indeed and rewrote my novel. It was my daughter who gave me the impetus to get my work published. So when we returned to Australia in mid-1991 I began sending work out. I had written a few novels, adventures set in Pakistan and Afghanistan – also a dog in the bazaar story that my youngest daughter wanted. That one ended up as a serial in a Baptist magazine that went out to missionary kids.

A Publishing Story

The novels were like boomerangs. I had a current copy of *Australian Writer's Marketplace* and I poured over it, highlighting possible homes for my books. I often sent three at a time. But don't do that to an agent or to publisher who expressly warns against it. The only guides we had then were the imprint pages of books and the yearly *Australian Writer's Marketplace*. Often an address or a list requirement would have changed before the new edition was released.

In the meantime, I became involved in the SA Writers' Centre, attended the Workers' Education Association (WEA) workshops, learning, learning, learning. And kept reading everything in my preferred age level.

I wrote articles and got one into *Christian Woman*. I wrote plays, devotionals for teens and a few short stories. One story went into a YA magazine by Pearson, *Pursuit*, which sadly is non-existent now; one of the changes in publishing is the limited print opportunities for sending short pieces. At least we still have *The School Magazine*.

By 1993 my manuscripts *Woven Secrets* and *The Lonely Dancer* had received many rejections. Some publishers didn't think they could sell a book set in Afghanistan. One even said their readership wouldn't know where Afghanistan was. They didn't state the real reason: that the novels weren't written well. One publisher said *Woven Secrets* would be too hard to place in the market, but they thought it was exciting, though the characters weren't lifelike enough, but if I ever wrote a book set in Australia, they would like to see it. I knew that this was a 'foot in the door'.

So I began writing *Re-entry* about a teenage girl brought up in Pakistan who returned to Australia for senior high school. It had more depth than what I'd written before as it had at its emotional core my own experiences of culture shock and displacement. I sent the first few chapters in February 1994 to check if it was what they liked. They did. They said to send the rest. I hadn't written the rest yet. So I wrote like crazy. It was a subject I found I could write quickly as it was inspired by my own experience of displacement as well as our own children's feelings of being 'third culture kids'[1] in returning to Australia.

Finally, I posted it at the beginning of June 1994. Manuscripts had to be single sided, double spaced (though I soon reverted to 1.5 to save on postage and no one seemed to mind), inserted loose in a folder, with no ribbons or staples. It cost $15 or so each time. I went through so much postage and paper money for years with no return. To pay for all this and my children's schooling, I relief taught and had three mornings a week at Tyndale Christian School helping ESL high school students to write essays, and running gifted and talented sessions in creative writing.

On the 4th of July, a month later, I received a phone call. 'Yes, we like *Re-entry*. We want to publish.' After I put the phone down, I cried. In 1995 I became a published author of a YA novel. In 1996 it was a Notable Book in the CBCA awards. I was given a lot of encouragement from Max Fatchen and Pegi Williams who were like patrons for local writers. Teachers at Tyndale were supportive as well as the writers in the children's book writers group in Adelaide called eKidnas.

After *Re-entry* was accepted, I decided to re-work material I already had, so I rewrote *Woven Secrets* which had been rejected so often, and put Jaime from *Re-entry* in it. It became a different story except that the adventure was still there. Jaime brought the depth it needed. Journalist Ken Packer had also looked at it and told me the POV was up the creek, so he gave me information on that. Most of the problem was moving from a third person narrative to a first person. I submitted. The publisher said they would do it in 1996 since it now acted as a sequel. Unfortunately, I was disappointed with that publication: editing mistakes, change of title because two words wouldn't fit with the artwork. It didn't take me long to realise we had published a draft. Another author told me I should get a new publisher – you won't learn anything with them, she said. Yeah, right, I thought. Easier said than done.

That publisher said they would not publish the next manuscript I'd written – too many Pakistan stories – there wouldn't be a market for it. 'Write another one set in Australia.' So I wrote *Cameleer*, in which. Jaime (from the published books) is doing work experience in the far north. It was a family mystery. But before it could be contracted, the publishing house folded.

However, I was thankful for the beginning chance this small publisher gave me. It got me off the worst slush pile. By this time I knew writing was what I was born to do. It felt like a call similar to the one we received when we went to Pakistan. This 'call' on my career kept me persistent and resilient during the usual challenges the writer or artist faces.

2 The roller-coaster ride

I kept writing. I received a grant from ARTSA to write a novel called *Zucchini Soup,* about Jessie and her Nanny with Alzheimer's. I renamed it *Babe,* then *Granddaughter from Hell* when the cute pig movie was released. It was rejected by twelve publishers. I also wrote a snow leopard picture book, *Yardil*, which scored twenty rejections. Usually the reasons given were: how can we market it, set in South Asia? Who will be interested in endangered snow leopards and these Kalasha people living in a forgotten Pakistani mountain kingdom? Now, the Australian National Curriculum has Asian studies as one of its three big topics to cover, as well as Indigenous issues and sustainability, so my cultural stories are more easily accepted.

Scripture Union in London paid me to write devotions and skits for YA. I wrote a nativity play in five acts and sections for a Year 8 teacher in Tyndale Christian School, Mrs Wildman, which she proceeded to stage for the end of year arts night. Scripture Union published that in a special Christmas edition. I kept writing unpublishable picture books. The *Cameleer* manuscript travelled all over the country.

Then in 1997 I was sworn at by a 6-year-old while relief teaching in a northern school. In the same week I was helping a 14-year-old Greek boy with his English essays. What if I wrote a book for 14-year-old boys who were reluctant readers with interesting content like bikers, Harleys, fishing, boats, deep sea diving and sharks? So I wrote *The Keeper* (2000) about a boy called Joel who is hyperactive with no sense of danger. I sent it first to Omnibus, which I always did, but they didn't care for Joel as a character. I sent it to Lothian, also on my list. It was 1998 when they accepted it. It had been four years since my previous novel and I wasn't 'sleeping on the streets' anymore – I was in a publishing house again!

Lothian went on to publish ten more of my books, including *Soraya, the Storyteller* and *A Kiss in Every Wave* (2001). Lothian had seen this and rejected it under the name of *Zucchini Soup*. No one remembered or had a record of it as the title had changed. In these digital days I doubt we'd get away with that. In the meantime a little obscure publisher (husband and wife) called Benchmark Books accepted twenty-times-rejected *Yardil* (2003). Never give up. Sadly that publisher died and his list was taken over by Windy Hollow Books, who later published a book that my daughter and I collaborated on, *The Wish Giver* (2008).

I realised later that Lothian didn't have the money to give structural edits. They sent my work to a wonderful freelance editor who was only given time and money to do a copy edit. Once or twice she'd say such and such a character hasn't been in the story for a while, can you put her in this scene, or similar, but there wasn't time for full structural rewrites. When I wrote *Zenna Dare* (2002) which had attracted a grant and kept me writing, I hoped it was worth having a fresh critical eye read it. It was more complex than my former works with two points of view, so I asked gifted English teacher and dramaturge, Janet Fletcher, to read it. She wrote on it in red pen like a Year 12 essay and it was so much better for it. Reviewer Katharine England pointed out in her *Zenna Dare* review[2] that I'd had a rather public apprenticeship as a writer, but had finally got it right, five stars. Librarians chose it in their Clayton awards. Thank you, Janet Fletcher. But *Zenna Dare* missed being entered in the CBCA awards. I had to learn a lesson regarding pride of achievement.

During this time I was advised by Peter Bishop at Varuna House to have an agent. I was finding the contracts difficult to negotiate. He gave me a name to try. When that agency said they were full I asked who they would suggest. The next time I was successful. My agent then took over submitting my work, negotiating offers and contracts. What a relief.

3 Complications

Lothian was taken over by Hachette in 2006. We authors were told that we would still be Lothian authors as Lothian would be an imprint, but each time I, and others, sent a manuscript and the Lothian publisher would like it, the new sales people wouldn't. They only kept authors whose books sold well. Publishing is a business after all.

My agent kept sending work around without immediate success. In 2006 I won an Asialink Fellowship to Pakistan to research *Daughter of Nomads*.

A Publishing Story

The Asialink program offers a range of opportunities for writers and the broader community in Australia and Asia to experience each other's cultures and written expression. Do keep applying for grants and fellowships. In Pakistan I had so many new ideas that I returned to rewrite *Taj and the Great Camel Trek* (which had been rejected locally) and wrote *Marrying Ameera*. HarperCollins accepted it after I completed their structural edit and it was published four years after my last Lothian novel, *The Last Virgin in Year 10*. Then HarperCollins didn't need an explorer story on their list but the University of Queensland Press (UQP) took *Taj and the Great Camel Trek*. UQP have been publishing most of my novels ever since. I was asked to write a novel for a series about children in war zones which Allen & Unwin published, *Shahana: Through My Eyes*. That was when I discovered I could write a book in less than a year.

HarperCollins said the short story called 'Only a School Girl' which I wrote for their UNICEF anthology[3] would make a good novel, but when it was finished their sales people said no probably because the sales figures for the trafficking novel *Mountain Wolf* weren't high enough. The publisher was very disappointed but, fortunately for me, Allen & Unwin said yes and it became *The Truth About Peacock Blue*.

Lately it's been a joy to finally have a novel with Omnibus (*Kerenza*). Another joy has been to be able to rewrite my early novels with Rhiza Edge and see *Liana's Dance* finally find a home. Having Robert

Ingpen and DM Cornish illustrate my books has been a dream come true.

4 Agents

I've found my agent extremely helpful. Agents act as a quality control gatekeeper and in the beginning mine, having worked as an editor with a major publisher, did her own structural edits for me to rewrite before submitting my work. Agents give advice, if asked, check contracts, look after finance, legal issues, getting rights back from publishers, and suggesting what to write in sticky circumstances.

Plus agents meet regularly with publishers and other agents at festivals and other events and often know who wants what when it's not on their websites yet. The call for proposals of series, for example, often come through the agents. They also can help with distributing PLR/ELR and copyright payments. The publishing industry changes so quickly that I find it easier now to have an agent who keeps abreast of copyright law as well as general industry practices and trends.

5 Fellowships and grants

These have helped me tremendously. My first Fellowship (2000) at Varuna, NSW, where I rewrote *Zenna Dare* and wrote the draft of *Sailmaker*, changed the way I thought about my writing life. I was beginning to see there was more I could learn and it became the impetus for getting an agent and doing extra study. A May Gibbs Fellowship gave me time away in Canberra to finish the draft of *The Last Virgin in Year 10*. The effect of the Asialink Fellowship in 2006 pushed me back into the publishing world with *Marrying Ameera* and many more ideas for future novels.

Grants from ARTSA have encouraged me and spurred me on, besides being helpful financially. The first grant allowed me to stop relief teaching for a semester to write *A Kiss in Every Wave*. The grant for *Zenna Dare* kept me writing as, since publishing had hit a low for me, I had undertaken an Information Studies Graduate Diploma to become a librarian. But, if I got the grant, I thought, I wouldn't pursue a library job; I'd keep writing. Country Arts were helpful in getting me to Cornwall to speak at the Cornish Studies Centre and to visit schools. *Marrying Ameera* (under the title of *Stolen Bride)* attracted a grant and the Carclew Fellowship. Never give up on the grants even if you don't succeed at first. Feedback can be given; I was told after my first *Stolen Bride* submission was rejected for a grant that there just wasn't enough money and to try again on the next round. I'm always thankful for these blessings.

6 Then and now

I'm often asked about differences in publishing and technology over my career.

I have a folder that shows the change from hard copy, even handwritten letters, to digital. After a manuscript was accepted, it was edited on hard copy; it was returned to me by mail and I would make changes on that hard copy and return it. Self-addressed and stamped envelopes were included. These were called SASE. The publisher would ask for the disk (three and a half inch floppy) so the text didn't need to be keyed in, but even after typesetting, the proofreading was also done on hard copy. One of my publishers, UQP, still send a hard copy of the first (typeset) pages to make proof changes on in pencil – it's much easier to find mistakes. They will also send a hard copy of the Track Changes when doing an edit. It's helpful to be able to refer to that when all the different Track colours on screen are making me cross-eyed.

I'm grateful for what others call success – books published – but it has been a bumpy ride with much resilience needed, and I know it could end at any time. My writing, ideas or themes could become outdated; the interest in Asian, immigrant experience, multicultural issues and Cornish themes could change. But I'm told by readers if I write more historical fantasy like *The Tales of Jahani* I should be fine for a while.

7 Highlights

This is another question I am asked. The highlights of my writing career include comments from readers, for example a Year 10 reviewer wrote that her view had changed after reading *Soraya the Storyteller*. Others say they want to be an author and that I've inspired them. (Every author is told that one.) A few high school girls told me recently to never stop writing. I'm used to telling others that but to have some teenagers tell me truly touched me. Readers saying they want a boyfriend like my boy characters are also encouraging. One mother told me *Zenna Dare* got her daughter off drugs. A 15-year-old girl told me that when she was depressed, she read the picture book *Yardil* and she felt better. Also encouraging, are emails from girls who have read my books, their questions and requests for sequels. After reading *The Keeper*, a boy I didn't know asked me how I knew so much about him. Boys who are reluctant readers running to the school library after an author visit and the teacher emailing me, 'Remember that boy who didn't like reading? Can't keep up with him now.'

These are the true successes and awards.

16
Being an Author

This chapter contains some of the information I have picked up along the way which would have been helpful to know sooner. I'll deal with them in the order you may encounter them.

Early on I realised that I needed to join the Writers' Centre in my state. This is important to do as from this first port of call we find out about workshops, writers' groups and competitions. I also attended WEA (Workers' Education Association) workshops which is where I learned how to format a picture book from local illustrator, Sally Heinrich.

There are also lots of opportunities of sharing with other writers on the web. So search for groups that are meeting online with the same interests as yourself and join in. Social media also has writing groups where you can ask questions, share how excited you are that your first book has been accepted, and where you may find a critiquing group.

A word of caution: some authors, after writing one book, will offer themselves on the web as an expert on writing and editing and charge to look at your manuscript. These people may be on the level and hold an editing or writing degree or have worked with publishing houses and have decided to freelance, but be wise in such circumstances. Check if they are recommended and ask for their credentials if they are not displayed. Australia has groups for accredited editors such as Freelance Editors Group or Editors

South Australia, Editors Queensland. I'm sure each state will have one. Check these groups for the name of the person or ask with which group they are affiliated. Also be wary of 'publishing houses' who charge to read your work or who ask you to 'partner' in the printing costs. Also be discerning when self-publishing. I won't deal with that topic here in detail but self-publishing is becoming a more achievable and accessible option now and many good books are emerging, like the early novels of Cecily Paterson.

One **Tip** though: if you are self-publishing and you are not an editor, please invest in the services of an accredited editor. They may cost $40 an hour and, depending on how long your manuscript is, it may cost a few thousand. So start saving.

Publishing may be quite different in a few years. Young people still like print books, though many are getting into audio books. But as technology changes further so will our publishing scene. Authors may need to be more creative to gain readers.

ASA

The Australian Society of Authors[1] is like a union for authors. They are an advocacy group, offering support and advice to writers. Besides campaigning at industry and government level for writers' and illustrators' rights in copyright, contracts and fair pay, they provide training and mentorships and run awards. They even assist writers in need with a benevolent fund. I have found ASA very helpful with contracts and legal issues, especially before I had an agent. You can join as a full member if you have one book published, but if you are not published you can join as an associate member.

Critique
This has been discussed in Chapter 1 but here it may be helpful to mention that even as an author, our writing is regularly critiqued. It just doesn't happen before we are published. If we belong to a writer's group, we critique each other's work or ideas. After submission professional readers and the editor will make comments about our work. After publication there will be reviewers and readers to critique our work. May I suggest you be careful of defensiveness? We can't control what a reader or editor will say about our work, but we can control our response. As already mentioned defensiveness can keep us from the truth about our writing and can perpetuates self-doubt. Constructive criticism can be liberating. Pride keeps us on the defensive. Some people believe their gift means they shouldn't change a word. We need to be open to the truth without justifying our work, to grow as writers and work towards excellence, which is *our* personal best, not *the* best.

Social media/reader platform
Some publishers expect that you will already have a reader base growing from your social media platform, including a blog where you may be posting poems and short stories. You can still get published without this, but many feel it is helpful for publicity and for getting your book known. It is good to have some form of web

presence similar to a website, a blog that may be attached to it, your favourite form of social media whether it be Facebook, Twitter, Instagram or any of the many others.

There is much information online or at the local library on how to set up social media and a blog. I have a webpage which I paid a fair bit of money for, but my son and many others make their own websites from free sites online. My blog is called 'A Writer's Journal'. I try to write about works in progress (when I'm not working on the works in progress). However, I don't spend enough time to get traffic to the blog and am not sure if it is worth the effort.

A few publishers, usually the larger ones who have paid PR persons, will say to concentrate on your writing, unless of course you're extremely good at social media and it doesn't seem to take up much of your time. It takes me ages to write a blog post or work out how to set up the blog site for a start. I still can't get Instagram to work. Publisher Julie Straus-Gabel states social media only works well when it is genuine to who you are.[2]

Publishers may also ask for a marketing plan when you submit. This is mainly so they can see how much publicity you have access to, your media contacts and whether you are keen to tour or hold events to publicise your book. The author needs to help with publicity. I must admit I'm not so good at selling books, I'd rather write them, but a certain amount of self-promotion is expected. I have business cards printed – I do mine with a recent book cover on the back and the address details that I don't mind a teacher or librarian knowing. I sometimes make postcards to give away at conferences or school visits but, as friend and author Grant Lock says, there must be information about the book, author and website on the back, not left blank for readers to use (or to throw away). Make sure the card is not flimsy. He also uses a portable (roll up) banner so that when he is speaking at a function the banner stands outside the door guiding people in. At the moment I have the cover of my latest book on the back of my iPhone under a clear casing. When I take photos of people, they comment on it.

Guest Author — Claire Belberg[3]
Blogging to find an audience

I blog. Millions do it but still I imagine I can add something unique to the welter of personal material the internet teems with.

I started blogging because it's the cheapest way to promote yourself as an author. I read dozens of 'how to build a platform' blogs and learned very little that I could apply. Part of my challenge is that I don't want to invest my writing time into building an audience; I'd rather spend it on building worlds that an audience wants to enter through my fiction and poetry.

To keep the blog from eating into my creative space, I write monthly. This is a big no-no (is that why my blog doesn't have millions of followers? I doubt it!)

but it works for my life as a writer. And I made a discovery: I like blogging. It gives me an opportunity to share different sorts of thoughts. It's a new space, and I chose to focus it on two things that matter to me: writing and personal growth.

When I named it *The Character Forge*, I didn't realise there was something else called that. It's a gaming feature and it gets most of the first few pages of a Google search. Sigh. But it sums up nicely what I'm striving to achieve with the blog. I want a place where readers and writers connect and explore common human experiences in the struggle to become who we are. Each post ends with a question that seeks to link the reader's experience to what I've just written, although their context might be quite different.

I have learned that the best way to gain traffic to my blog is to visit others and leave comments. Isn't that life? It's the Golden Rule: do to others what you'd like them to do for you. Or as Jesus put it, love your neighbour – be interested in and willing to engage with those who cross your path, for their good as well as your own. As a writer, I want to engage with readers. I'd love them to engage with my published work but even if it only goes as far as commenting on the blog, it's connection.

Some writing teachers suggest that you, the writer, are the most important audience. In one way I agree. If your own writing doesn't engage your inner self, if it doesn't satisfy something by the doing of it, it's not very likely to capture others. But I write for an

> audience of more than myself. I shape what I'm trying to say to that imagined audience, and I long to see if and how it hits the spot. I write to bring hope, to suggest other ways of seeing and experiencing the world, to increase understanding of self and others. None of that will be fully satisfied without a wider audience, preferably in dialogue with me so that I learn from their experience too, and grow in my craft and my humanity.
>
> Does blogging give me the audience I'm seeking? Not entirely, but it does give me another writing opportunity I enjoy.

Rejections

I have a folder full of rejection slips and letters from publishers, as do most authors. Some very famous books had many rejections, such as *Harry Potter*. This is what I've learned about rejections. Firstly, don't fear them. They are part of the journey and when you get your first one, celebrate. Now you are a real writer; you have joined the ranks of all other writers and are one step closer to your goal. Choose to learn from the comments, if any. I read my rejection letters carefully and often there was a sentence stating if ever I rewrote it or write something else, they'll look at it. This sentence is often couched between the comments you are reeling from, if the submissions editor had the time to write about your work at all.

Since publishers and editors are time poor, if they do write about your work it can mean you have an opportunity to rework your manuscript and try again. One of my students received a rejection letter with a carefully worded sentence like this, but all he saw was the 'sorry we can't publish'. He didn't realise from their comments that he could try again. When a publisher rejected one of my manuscripts and wrote, 'We think your characterisation could improve but we liked the story and how you write. If you write something set in Australia, we would be happy to look at it' I realised I had an invitation to send them a solicited manuscript. I wrote a book set in Australia and that book was accepted. But not before I had lots of rejections for my other stories. It doesn't stop either. Throughout our careers we will still receive rejections when a book doesn't suit a list. Even the sales department of our own publishers will reject a book if they don't think this one will sell well, or if the last one didn't. That's how we can end up with multiple publishers.

It's important to nurture a positive frame of mind about rejections or 'returns' as author, Janeen Brian, calls them. Yes, it's disappointing, but after a while go back and read it for what you can learn. After each rejection I rewrote the manuscript. If didn't receive feedback I gave it to another writer or friend to read and then rewrote it. The only time I didn't totally rewrite after a publisher's comments was when they suggested I change the theme and genre of the story. It would have meant writing an entirely new novel. Fortunately another publishing house appreciated the existing theme and genre. Keep close to God in the difficult times and our courage will ride the wind.

> People are often unreasonable, irrational and self-centred. Forgive them anyway. If you are kind, people may accuse you of selfish, ulterior motives. Be kind anyway. If you are successful you will win some unfaithful friends and some genuine enemies. Succeed anyway. If you are honest and sincere, people may cheat you. Be honest and sincere anyway. What you spend years creating, others could destroy overnight. Create anyway. If you find serenity and happiness, people may be jealous. Be happy anyway. The good you do today will often be forgotten. Do good anyway. Give the best you have and it will never be enough. Give your best anyway. In the final analysis, it is between you and God. It was never between you and them anyway.
>
> Mother Teresa[4]

Reviews

I chose to do the same thing with reviews. One in the beginning mentioned poor editing, which was a shame. Even that made me want to send a better manuscript to the publisher next time. Often the reviews were encouraging, not brilliant. I longed for the day when someone would say the writing was beautiful or the book well-crafted and, when I least expected it, it happened. Things like reviews, encouragements, grants and awards are a little like gifts of the Spirit – it's best to seek and yearn for God, not his gifts, and then one day when you are favoured, it doesn't matter so much as you already have what's most important: the passionate love and support of an omniscient Father.

Working with publishers, editors and other writers or illustrators

My perspective on working in the industry is that, on a spiritual and emotional level, I need to have respect and care for those I work with, and to have joy and passion in my work; to stay peaceful when a story has been sent, and have patience when waiting to hear from publishers or agents. Nothing usually happens quickly with publishing, so I wait on the Lord. I have seen new writers get an agent, which is a remarkable feat, but then they find waiting for the agent to achieve a sale too difficult and start sending it out themselves. Agents will not tolerate what they see as a lack of trust. They may have already sent the MS to a publisher saying they are the only ones to view it. Both the agent's and the writer's credibility will be damaged. Either have an agent and get on with your next project or don't have one if you'd rather do it yourself.

Grumbling and being critical destroys us. So it's best to be kind when dealing with editors and proofreaders. Editors usually know more than I do so I respect them and learn from them. Integrity as a writer, I believe, as in all walks of life, is simply doing what God thinks is right. I try to have positive and respectful values and so don't consciously plagiarise, or use others' stories and ideas without permission. I try to be faithful in my work ethic: if I have a deadline, to stick to it as far as is possible. To deliver what is expected. Be gentle and think of others' needs; be accepting when it comes to an illustrator illustrating my text – it is their turn to be creative and to tell their side of the story. To have self-control in being disciplined and persistent with my work, and not to lose self-control if something doesn't go my way. I have seen an author of adult nonfiction lose it at a festival when she found her books weren't on the book table. It was not pretty.

Publishing houses like dealing with people who are delightful to work with just as everyone does. In the publishing world I use the basic rule of 'Do to others as you would like it done to you.' Our attitude makes a difference in how God can work in our lives. It certainly makes a difference in how we become a respected member of the team, or stable, of a publishing house.

In the same way I think of my agents as my friends, the good guys, going to bat for me if anything does go wrong. Take contracts. I don't understand them well so before I had an agent, I sent a contract for assessment to the ASA (the Australian Society of Authors). Join as soon as you can as an associate member if you are serious about a career in writing. The literary lawyer at ASA suggested a few percentages that should be changed. When I suggested these changes to the finance department of a publishing house I was asked if I wanted my book published or not. At that time there was a compromise and later I got an agent. I didn't know then that the publishing house was going through a hard time and didn't have the money to raise my percentages. ASA are lately taking steps to ensure their advice is workable with what publishers can handle.

For this reason I find an agent is very helpful, not only to deal with contracts and finances, but also to field any legal problems which may arise. Some authors handle their affairs very well without an agent, but for me and my personality the agent's fees are worth it. The ASA or your state writers' centre is the first port of call for finding an agent. While we're discussing finances, when your first book is released, apply for Educational Lending Rights (ELR) and Public Lending Rights (PLR). These are Australian Government programs that compensate Australian creators and publishers in recognition of income lost through library lending or school class sets of books. Information on this can be found on the web or your publisher will forward you the forms.

Launches and signings

One of my memorable launches was for *The Keeper* at Adelaide Writers Week. I asked Mac Hayes, the leader of the Longriders Motorcycle Club, to launch the book since the supporting character is a biker. The Writers' Week convenors were worried as they didn't want a whole biker club descending on the Pioneer Gardens. There's enough noise from car races and jet fighters overhead. They said he could launch the book but not to bring his bike. Now Mac may be a Christian guy, a social worker in his community, but he is also a biker. Like Aslan, he is not tame. How would he get there if he didn't bring his bike? Nor did he want to launch the book without it. The convenors finally agreed he could bring his bike, but not the whole club and he couldn't start up his bike. Mac turned up in his usual attire – black vest showing all his tats. Of course all the kids there wanted to hear what that bike sounded like – it was sort of hidden from view and there were also bikers in the crowd, maybe not the whole club. It was a lot of fun and Mac did a brilliant job. I hope it did a lot to challenge a stereotype. I even heard people say, 'You wouldn't expect a biker to speak like that.' Mac is a writer himself.

Launches have worked better for me than signings. And I think physical launches get better results than online ones. Some publishers don't like launches and would rather spend the money on bookmarks, posters or other PR, but I've found that people will come to a launch when there is entertainment, food, wine and people they can network with. Writers will do the rounds of launches to support each other, but launches do seem to pick up a fan base. It makes me do the promotion work so people know about the book whether or not they can come. My most successful launch in terms of numbers and books sold was the first one as it was a novelty for everyone.

After the Writers' Week excitement, the next was *Marrying Ameera* in Kapunda because I had booked Bollywood dancers. Even people I didn't know came to that one. I find people will come when a person launching the book is someone they want to meet or if there is music. *The Messenger Bird* proved that, as we held a Celtic concert and filled the Soldiers' Memorial Hall in Kapunda. Fiddler Jeri Foreman wrote a song for the book called 'Nathaniel's Waltz.' When Phil Cummings launched his picture book *Feathers* in 2017, he sang a song he had written for the book with music by Glyn Lehmann. Afterwards a Powerpoint showed the pages of the book with Phil's voice reading the story. My husband thought that was the best launch he'd ever attended.

Other ideas include involving children from a local school. All the parents will also come. I try to have food that matches the book like Cornish pasties for *Kerenza*. Three camels came from a local camel farm for *Taj and the Great Camel Trek*. For a younger children's book it's good to have activity stations with crafts or messy things to do and then get together to read the story. Having the pages on Powerpoint is helpful for the parents to also see the story.

Where? I've held them in bookshops, art galleries, libraries, schools, university, conferences and Adelaide Writers' Week. If the book is set at a beach, why not have the celebration on the beach or jetty? One launch of Katrina Germein's was held in a restaurant. You can let your publisher know, if they don't already, that they can tender or ask for a grant to have your book launched at a conference.

Here is an example of a running sheet: I usually put approximate times when I think each part will start. But it is usually played by ear.

1 A person who acts as an MC, usually the librarian if held at a library, welcomes everyone and tells people

where to meet if there is a bushfire and where the toilets are. I think it is respectful to acknowledge the original custodians of the land.

2 The MC will introduce the 'entertainment' whether it's music, children doing a play or the author doing magic tricks. If you decide to have someone launch the book, then the MC can introduce that person, or why not have an interview between the author and the launcher where the launcher asks the questions and declares the book launched at the end of the interview? This will eliminate the author and launcher having to do a speech, which children don't appreciate unless they are funny. And choose carefully: some authors are funny on paper but not necessarily when they give speeches.

3 The author responds and says thank you and reads from the book. People do like hearing the author read from their book. So that could come last.

4 The MC will encourage all to eat, drink, be happy and buy lots of books and get them signed.

Tips

Don't presume, and always check, that you and the librarian, for example, know who is doing what. Once I turned up at a library for a launch and the library had understood that all they were doing was to offer the room. I, on the other hand, thought that all head librarians, as host, would be the MC at an event in their library. I thought wrong and had to pull an MC out of the audience. Think out of the box. If there are bikers in your book, ask some nice bikers along. The Longriders

Motorcycle Club came again to the launch of *Killer Ute* in Kapunda. We're used to bikers roaring into town on their rides north.

Some bookshops don't like food and children together in their shop, so choose the venue well; ask questions. Keep advertising the event online and emails, the local paper, posters, even postcards to give out. Don't expect the venue to do all the advertising even if they do say, 'I'll put this on our mailout'. They may forget or their contact list may not be your best audience.

Finally, treat the book launch as a celebration even though it is also for publicity. It can be stressful but it's worth it.

Grants/awards

As I've observed before, grants are very helpful for the emerging writer and later on as well. They give time off from work to get a draft written. They also help validate and give support to your career. Check out your state Writers' Centre webpage to research grants. The Australian Council of the Arts has grant opportunities as well as each state Arts body. Australian Society of Authors will also have information. Country Arts also gives grants. Follow guidelines carefully and if at first you don't succeed, try again, as often it is because the money is short, not that your submission was unsatisfactory.

Finances

Get an Australian Business Number (ABN) so the government knows that writing books is a business for you, not a hobby, even though most of us don't hit the threshold. It's free, easy and helps when schools or the publisher needs to pay you. I go to a tax accountant – he's become used to me over the years asking for the oddest things for tax deductions such as travel for research or objects that saved my plot that I need to show in school. At first, he wouldn't deduct items regarded by me as research until that particular book was published and there was income to deduct it from. Now he accepts my deductions. I find it is good to have him do this for me as he knows the percentages to use for mileage when I visit schools or do a talk, anything for a launch that the publisher hasn't covered, a new fountain pen, new technical equipment, the depreciation of said technical equipment and the deductions required for working at home with electricity costs. Even a load of wood for my office combustion heater. My postgraduate supervisor had once been an accountant and he took off expenses in going to movies and reading the latest novels as these things were either inspiration or aids to his writing. Basically anything that I spend in the name of research to get a novel written is a genuine tax deduction.

There is also the artist's allowance which my tax accountant applies, depending on my spouse's wage. I wouldn't have known all this by myself. This week I received a bonus for having a low wage. Sigh. Another thing I learned is that award money is deemed income, so when I finally won an award that had money attached to it, I was bumped up into pay-as-you-go quarterly payments, which were a pain for financially-challenged me. No amount of me explaining that this wasn't my normal income moved me off those until they finally realised that for almost half the year I made no money. Our 'wages' are seasonal: another thing to get used to.

Author visits to schools, booking agents

Some of my best author visits have been with teachers who had been in my Children's Literature class or librarians who are part of CBCA or just passionate librarians and teachers who love books and kids. What a great combination.

A booking agent for school visits is a special person who books my school visits and liaisons with schools on my behalf. This is so helpful for me as at times it's hard to be firm about the rates for author visits when you know the teacher. The Australian Society of Authors stipulates the recommended rates to charge for a visit.[5] The fee (at the moment $750 a day) may sound a lot but this is an artistic fee; the author receives no sick pay, holiday pay, or superannuation, and very few royalties. The average writers' annual wage is $5000–$10,000. The school is paying for your expertise.

If the visit is for one day, there will be four sessions at forty-five minutes each or three sessions at one hour each or any combination that works for the school. For example, recently I worked two days at a school that wanted their kindy, Foundation or Stage One, plus children with special needs to also meet an author and hear a story, so some sessions were for half an hour. ASA guidelines for author visits stipulate that the sessions mustn't exceed 180 minutes in a school day, and this may spread across the timetable. Even that much can be tiring as a performer. I try to fit in with the school as they are the ones paying and it's helpful when children are within their comfort zone. I refer the school to my booking agent if they ask for nine sessions to fill each lesson slot. They may ask for half a day, which will be two forty-five minute sessions or a master class of one and a half or two hours. Fortunately, the booking agent is the one who does the maths, not me.

If I'm asked for a workshop, I ascertain what teachers really mean. Some want the whole class, or even two classes, in the workshop. This is fine except it won't be what I call a workshop. A session on writing with a whole class or two becomes a talk about my writing process which I try to make as interactive as I can with Powerpoint, whiteboard and the students trying some techniques, depending on the amount of time. But children will not all get a chance to try exercises or read out work with so many in the group. I see a writing workshop as a concentrated time of writing and trying techniques with around fifteen young writers who need to be extended and really want to be there. A master class is definitely a workshop with good writers who 'want more' and these sessions are usually longer with a break in the middle. Master classes often have fewer students, but I have done them in high schools with twenty plus students. Schools can choose from the agent's list of some workshops I have done but it can be according to what units the students have been studying. I tailor sessions for schools based on their curriculum needs unless they give me a free rein to say what I'd like, especially if a new book has recently been released.

In all my visits I hope to support the literacy and reading program in schools. When I say how many times I rewrite my work, for example, students are horrified but the teachers look validated. So many times a teacher will say, I'm so glad you mentioned 'X', I've been telling them that all year. Another great effect of school visits is that, for many younger children, meeting an author makes reading click for them. Once I told a Year 2 class how I became an author by my daughter asking me to write her a book, and in question time a boy asked, 'Do you mean to say you're just someone's mother?' 'Yes,' I said. 'And you can become an author too.' How I wished I knew that when I was seven.

Facilitating workshops and conference speaking

Just a few comments here from what I've picked up. Do use technology and/or props if you have a child audience. Adults also like to see notes on a Powerpoint to make a point stick. Adults as well as children like interesting props/objects images (on Powerpoint) to prompt writing tasks. Be careful not to always look back at the screen as you lose eye contact with children (not recommended) and your voice moves away from the microphone. Buy a clicker to move slides along so you can move around. I have been caught out when speaking to large groups of high school students where the computer is at the back or even in a side room. I had to call out to have a slide moved on.

If you don't have a laptop in front of you to show what is coming up (conference centres usually have this set up even if you bring your own laptop) then print out the slides.

Always check regarding the technology as it can mean different things to some people. I email to check if I need to bring a laptop or, in the case of clubs, I ask them to bring a cord to make my laptop speak to their data projector.

Do share your writing process, as every writer does it differently. Some parts of the process may appear similar, for example, some writers will say they don't plan, others say they outline everything before they start. But there are many shades between those two statements and if you do outline, how exactly do you do that? Or if you don't, what do you do instead? You will get asked these questions so make sure you know what your process is. It sounds daunting but all it means is: how did you write your book? Attendees at a workshop feel cheated when an author will say, I didn't do anything special, I just sat at the computer and kept writing and then I was done. Children, for example, will expect more detail, like, how do you choose the words? How do you know what will happen in the middle? How do you get past the first sentence? I suspect adults' question will be similar.

Mentoring others/volunteering

As an author we are asked to look at manuscripts. After a while some well-known authors have to say no due to time restrictions and deadlines. One year I read twelve manuscripts for either editorial comment, or for a comment for a tagline or blurb, for a publisher, launches, or to encourage a writer where to send their manuscript (or not to yet). I don't edit as there are others who are trained editors who need the work and I know how much editing gets done on my own work. I do mentor others either through the institution I work at or through high school programs. We all need to do some volunteer work. This year I am a Premier's Reading Challenge ambassador, which is a volunteer job. It is good for me to remember how I didn't know anyone who was writing when I was starting and would have appreciated the help.

A note on humility

I heard a person win an award once and in the acceptance speech said, 'I've done it all by myself.' He didn't have anyone to thank except the judges. It sounded strange to me and yet I understood. When my first book was released, I didn't think of having an acknowledgement page. The more I know about writing the longer my acknowledgement pages have become. We must always be thankful. We don't write books on our own. Even if people say we have a gift, it is still given to us by God; we are just developing it. If we place our confidence in God, humility will be more natural. If a fan says great things about your writing just say thank you. True humility is not putting ourselves down, but putting our confidence in God: He does it through us. We are the channel.

We finish with a blessing for all of us from author and chaplain, Jenny Glazebrook.[6]

A Blessing
by Jenny Glazebrook[6]

May each of us follow God's purpose in our writing. May He be our inspiration, our creativity, our wisdom, our insight, our vision. And when our eyes are blurred with tears because a dream has died, may we lift those eyes to Him and see it all from His perspective. May we wait upon Him, may our strength be renewed as we rise up on winds like eagles, seeing it all from His point of view, no longer limited to our human condition. May our vision be filled with Him.

Writer's Prayer
by Jade Wyatt[7]

Lord, you are the Word
        the Source of Life
                the Author and Creator...

You have placed within my heart
        a seed
                a word...

a breath from the same Mouth
which
        breathed
                the
                      stars...

this seed is so small
yet its weight renders me still
I cannot carry it without you

Lord, hold my hand
lift my head
and as I write the words within me,
help them grow

that this seed may become
a great tree

Being an Author

extending far beyond
my fragile skin

bringing shade and
fruit and
a place to rest and
a place to dream

where, at Your call,
more seeds will stir
and launch themselves out
across borders of every kind

and somewhere,
the words will nestle themselves
within someone's heart

and they will begin to write
and they will surrender
       to
              the
                    Word.

Reading Lists

Books mentioned here are of interest either for their innovation, controversy or great writing. Some are my favourites. See more fiction to read in the CBCA Notable lists at https://cbca.org.au

Short Story Collections
Dubosarsky, U. and Brooks, R. (2002). *Special Days with Honey and Bear*. Camberwell, VIC: Puffin.
Gaiman, N. (2008). *M is for Magic*. London: Bloomsbury.
Kennedy, M. (ed). (2013). *Reaching Out: Messages of Hope.* Sydney: HarperCollins.
Morpurgo, M. (2006). *Singing for Mrs Pettigrew: A Story-maker's Journey.* London: Walker Books.
Murray, K., Dhar, P., Roy, A. (eds). (2015). *Eat the Sky, Drink the Ocean*. Crows Nest, NSW: Allen & Unwin.
Peet, M. & Graham, E. (2011). *Painting Out the Stars*. Walker Books.

Picture Books
Ballie, A. and Tanner, J. (1991). *Drac and the Gremlin*. Camberwell, VIC: Puffin.
Becker, A. (2014). *Quest.* London: Walker Books.
Brian, J. and King, S. M. (2001). *Where Does Thursday Go?* Hunter's Hill, NSW: Margaret Hamilton.
Brian, J. and James, A. (2015). *I'm a Hungry Dinosaur* Camberwell, VIC: Penguin.
Cummings, P. and Devries, S. (2017). *Boy.* Sydney: Scholastic.
Cummings, P. and Devries, S. (2015). *Ride, Ricardo, Ride*. Parkside, SA: Omnibus Books.
Fatchen, M. and Johns, C. (2004). *Meet the Monsters.* Norwood, SA: Omnibus Books.
Fox, M. and Ghosh, R. (2017). *I'm Australian Too*. Lindfield, NSW: Scholastic.
Fox, M. and Argent, K. (1995). *Wombat Divine*. Norwood, SA: Omnibus Books.
Fox, M. and Lofts, P. (1988). *Koala Lou*. Melbourne: Puffin.

Reading Lists

Gleeson, L. and Blackwood, F. (2013). *Banjo and Ruby Red*. Richmond, VIC: Hardie Grant Egmont.
Gleeson, L. and Greder, A. (1991). *Big Dog*. Sydney: Scholastic.
Graham, A. (1987). *Educating Arthur*. Adelaide: Era.
Heffernan, J. and McLean, A. (2001). *My Dog*. Sydney: Scholastic.
Jeffers, O. (2005). *Lost and Found*. London: HarperCollins.
Jolly, J. and Heinrich, S. (2015). *One Step at a Time*. Rundle Mall, SA: MidnightSun.
Marsden, J. and Tan, S. (1998). *The Rabbits*. Port Melbourne: Lothian.
Starke, R. and Hannaford, R. (2015). *My Gallipoli*. Adelaide: Working Title Press.
Tan, S. (2006). *The Arrival*. Sydney: Hachette.
Tan, S. (2001). *The Red Tree*. South Melbourne: Lothian.
Tan, S. (2001). *The Red Tree*. South Melbourne: Lothian.
Thompson, C. and Lissiat, A. (2005). *The Short and Incredibly Happy Life of Riley*. Sydney: Lothian.
Wagner, J. and Brooks, R. (1997). *John Brown, Rose and the Midnight Cat*. Camberwell, VIC: Penguin.
Wheatley, N. and Rawlins, D. (1987). *My Place*. South Melbourne: Longman.
Wild, M. and Brooks, R. (2000). *Fox*. St Leonards, NSW: Allen & Unwin.

Chapter Books
Blacklock, D. and Smith, C. (1997). *I Want Earrings*. Norwood, SA: Omnibus Books.
Brian, J. and Stewart, C. (2005). *Rock and Roll Ducks*. Camberwell, VIC: Penguin.
Cummings, P. and Holfeld, G. (2009). *Chook Shed Snake*. Malvern, SA: Omnibus Books.
Dawe, B. and McLean, A. (2002). *No Cat and That's That!* Camberwell, VIC: Penguin.
Dubosarsky, U. and Vane, M. (2001). *Fairy Bread*. Camberwell, VIC: Penguin.
Fienberg, A., Fienberg, B. and Gambol, K. (2007). *Tashi*. Crows Nest, NSW: Allen & Unwin.

Hartnett, S. and James, A. (2008). *Sadie and Ratz*. Camberwell, VIC: Penguin.

Novels, Middle Grade
Almond, D. (1998). *Skellig*. London: Hodder.
Apel, K. (2014). *Bully on the Bus*. St Lucia, QLD: University of Queensland Press.
Balla, T. (2016). *Rockhopping*. Crows Nest, NSW: Allen & Unwin.
Bancks, T. (2014). *Two Wolves*. Ringwood, VIC: Penguin.
Bateson, C. (2002). *Rain May and Captain Daniel*. St Lucia, QLD: University of Queensland Press.
Carnavas, P. (2017). *The Elephant*. St Lucia, QLD: University of Queensland Press.
Clinton, C. (2002). *A Stone in My Hand*. Cambridge, MA: Candlewick Press.
Constable, K. (2011). *Crow Country*. Crows Nest, NSW: Allen & Unwin.
Cummings, P. (2007). *Danny Allen Was Here*. Sydney: Pan Macmillan.
DiCamillo, K. (2000). *Because of Winn-Dixie*. Somerville, MA: Candlewick Press.
Disher, G. (1992). *The Bamboo Flute*. Sydney: Angus & Robertson.
Dubosarsky, U. (2008). *Abyssinia*. Camberwell, VIC: Penguin.
Fensham, E. (2005). *Helicopter Man*. London: Bloomsbury.
Forrestal, E. (1996). *Someone Like Me*. Ringwood, VIC: Penguin.
Foxlee, K. (2016). *A Most Magical Girl*. Crows Nest, NSW: Allen & Unwin.
Fraillon, Z. (2016). *The Bone Sparrow*. Sydney: Lothian/Hachette.
Gleitzman, M. (2009). *Grace*. Ringwood, VIC: Penguin.
Gleitzman, M. (2005). *Once*. Ringwood, VIC: Penguin.
Golds, C. (2010). *The Three Loves of Persimmon*. Camberwell, VIC: Penguin.
Hamilton, A. (2016). *Daystar: The Days Are Numbered*. Capalaba, QLD: Wombat Books.

Reading Lists

Harris, C. (2008). *Audrey of the Outback*. Surry Hills, NSW: Little Hare.
Harris, C. (2001). *Jamil's Shadow*. Ringwood, VIC: Penguin.
Hartnett, S. (2004). *The Silver Donkey*. Camberwell, VIC: Penguin.
Heffernan, J. (2014). *Naveed: Through My Eyes*. Crows Nest, NSW: Allen & Unwin.
Hill, A. (1996). *Spindrift*. Ringwood, VIC: Puffin.
Janu, T. (2014). *Figgy in the World*. Parkside, SA: Omnibus Books.
Jinks, C. (1999). *The Stinking Great Lie*. Ringwood, VIC: Puffin.
MacDibble, B. (2017). *How to Bee*. Crows Nest, NSW: Allen & Unwin.
MacLachlan, P. (1997). *Sarah, Plain and Tall*. London: Walker Books.
McDonald, M. and Pryor, B.M. (2002). *Njunjul the Sun*. Crows Nest, NSW: Allen & Unwin.
Marwood, L. (2009). *Star Jumps*. Newtown, NSW: Walker Books.
Marwood, L. (2018). *Leave Taking*. St Lucia, QLD: University of Queensland Press.
Millard, G. (2003). *The Naming of Tishkin Silk*. Sydney: ABC Books.
Murray, K. (2013). *The Four Seasons of Lucy McKenzie*. Crows Nest, NSW: Allen & Unwin.
Murray, M. (2017). *Henrietta and the Perfect Night*. Crows Nest, NSW: Allen & Unwin
Murray, M. (2002). *The Slightly True Story of Cedar B. Hartley*. Crows Nest, NSW: Allen & Unwin.
Musgrove, M. (2016*). Frieda: A New Australian*. Melbourne: Omnibus Books.
Ness, P. (2011). *A Monster Calls*. Illus: Jim Kay. London: Walker.
Orr, W. (2016). *Dragonfly Song*. Crows Nest, NSW: Allen & Unwin.
Park, R. (1982). *Playing Beatie Bow*. Ringwood, VIC: Puffin.
Paterson, K. (1977). *Bridge to Terabithia*. New York: Thomas Y Crowell.
Pitcher, A. (2011). *My Sister Lives on the Mantelpiece*. London: Orion Children's Books.

Rodda, E. (2004). *Rowan of Rin: the Journey.* Adelaide: Omnibus Books.
Shanahan, L. (2017). *The Grand, Genius Summer of Henry Hoobler.* Crows Nest, NSW: Allen & Unwin.
Shepherd, M. and Pinfold, L. (2016). *The Secret Horses of Briar Hill.* London: Walker Books.
Starke, R. (2008). *Noodle Pie.* Adelaide: Omnibus Books.
Stewart, B. (2007). *Kumiko and the Dragon.* St. Lucia, QLD: University of Queensland Press.
Townsend, J. (2017). *Nevermoor: The Trials of Morrigan Crow.* Sydney: Lothian.
Wheeler, S. (2018). *Everything I've Never Said.* St. Lucia, QLD: University of Queensland
Wilkinson, C. (2003). *The Dragonkeeper.* Fitzroy, VIC: Black Dog Books.

Novels, Young Adult
Abdel-Fattah, R. (2008). *Where the Streets Had a Name.* Sydney: Pan Macmillan.
Abdel-Fattah, R. (2016). *When Michael Met Mina.* Sydney: Pan Macmillan.
Bauer, M. G. (2004). *The Running Man.* Malvern, SA: Omnibus Books.
Bone, I. (2004). *Sleep Rough Tonight.* Camberwell, VIC: Penguin.
Bone, I. (2002). *The Song of an Innocent Bystander.* Camberwell, VIC: Penguin.
Caro, J. (2011). *Just a Girl.* St Lucia, QLD: University of Queensland.
Caswell, B. (2005). *Double Exposure.* St Lucia, QLD: University of Queensland.
Constable, K. (2009). *Winter of Grace.* Crows Nest, NSW: Allen & Unwin.
Crowley, C. (2010). *Graffiti Moon.* Sydney: Pan Macmillan.
Deller-Evans, K. (2016). *Copper Coast.* Adelaide: MOG Writers' Collective.
Dubosarsky, U. (2011). *The Golden Day.* Crows Nest, NSW: Allen & Unwin.

Reading Lists

Fensham, E. (2008). *Goodbye Jamie Boyd*. St Lucia, QLD: University of Queensland Press.
Forsyth, K. (2013). *The Wild Girl*. Sydney: Random House.
French, J. (2015). *Ophelia: Queen of Denmark*. Sydney: HarperCollins.
Gardner, S. (2011). *The Dead I Know*. Crows Nest, NSW: Allen & Unwin.
Green, J. (2012). *The Fault in Our Stars*. New York: Dutton Juvenile.
Haddon. M. (2003). *The Curious Incident of the Dog in the Night-Time*. London: Jonathan Cape.
Hartnett, S. (2010). *The Midnight Zoo*. Camberwell, VIC: Penguin.
Herrick, S. (2000). *The Simple Gift*. St Lucia, QLD: University of Queensland Press.
Jaye, P. (2018). *Out of the Cages*. Capalaba, QLD: Rhiza Edge.
Jonsberg, B. (2004). *The Whole Business with Kiffo and the Pitbull*. Crows Nest, NSW: Allen & Unwin.
Jordan, S. (2018). *The Anger of Angels*. Newtown, NSW: Walker Books.
Kaufman, A. and Kristoff, J. (2015). *Illuminae*. Crows Nest, NSW: Allen & Unwin.
Kernot, S. (2018). *The Art of Taxidermy*. Melbourne: Text.
Kostakis, W. (2013). *The First Third*. Camberwell, VIC: Penguin.
Kwaymullina, A. (2012). *The Interrogation of Ashala Wolf*. Newtown, NSW: Walker Books.
Lanagan, M. (2012). *Sea Hearts*. Crows Nest, NSW: Allen & Unwin.
Larkin, J. (2015). *The Pause*. North Sydney: Random House.
Lomer, K. (2015). *Talk Under Water*. St Lucia, QLD: University of Queensland Press.
MacLeod, D. (2010). *The Life of a Teenage Body-snatcher*. Camberwell, VIC: Penguin.
Marchetta, M. (1992). *Looking for Alibrandi*. Ringwood, VIC: Penguin.
Marsden, J. (1993). *Tomorrow When the War Began*. Chippendale, NSW: Pan Macmillan.

McKinlay, M. (2015). *A Single Stone*. Newtown, NSW: Walker Books.
Metzenthen, D. (2009). *Jarvis 24*. Hawthorn, VIC: Penguin.
Millard, G. (2009). *A Small Free Kiss in the Dark*. Crows Nest, NSW: Allen & Unwin.
Monk, S. (1998). *Raw*. Milsons Point, NSW: Random House.
Nowra, L. (2015). *Prince of Afghanistan*. Sydney: Allen & Unwin.
Pascoe, B. (2012). *Fog a Dox*. Broome, WA: Magabala Books.
Pullman, P. (1995). *The Northern Lights*. London: Scholastic.
Raynes, C. (2016). *First Person Shooter*. Rundle Mall, SA: MidnightSun.
Rosoff M. (2004). *How I Live Now*. Camberwell, VIC: Penguin.
Roy, J. and Zihabamwe, R. (2016). *One Thousand Hills*. Sydney: Omnibus/Scholastic.
Sachar, L. (1998). *Holes*. New York: Farrar, Straus and Giroux.
Tan, S. (2008). *Tales of Outer Suburbia*. Crows Nest, NSW: Allen & Unwin.
Wakefield, V. (2017). *Ballad for a Mad Girl*. Melbourne: Text.
Wakefield, V. (2011). *All I Ever Wanted*. Melbourne: Text.
Westerfeld, S. (2009). *Leviathan*. New York: Simon Pulse.
Wood, F. (2015). *Cloudwish*. Sydney: Pan Macmillan.
Zorn, C. (2016). *One Would think the Deep*. St Lucia, QLD: University of Queensland Press.
Zorn, C. (2013). *The Sky So Heavy*. St Lucia, QLD: University of Queensland Press.
Zusak, M. (2005). *The Book Thief*. Sydney: Picador.

Critical Reading
Aristotle. (1996). Trans: Malcolm Heath. *Poetics*. London: Penguin Classics.
Baig, B. (2010). *How to Be a Writer: Building Your Creative Skills Through Practice and Play*. Cincinnati, OH: Writer's Digest Books.
Brooks, R. (2014). *Writing Great Books for Young Adults*. Naperville, Ill: Sourcebooks.
Browne, R. and King, D. (2001). *Self-editing for Fiction Writers*. New York: Quill.

Reading Lists

Cowley, J. (2010). *Writing from the Heart.* Honesdale, PN: Boyds Mills Press.
Crook, M. (2016). *Writing for Children and Young Adults* (3rd edn). North Vancouver, BC: Self-Counsel Press.
Dixon, D. (1996). *GMC: Goal, Motivation and Conflict.* Memphis, TN: Gryphon Books for Writers.
Dufresne, J. (2003) *The Lie That Tells a Truth: A Guide to Writing Fiction.* New York: Norton.
Edwards, H. and Alexander, G. (1998). *The Business of Writing for Young People.* Alexandria, NSW: Hale & Iremonger.
Elsheimer, J. (2001). *The Creative Call.* Colorado Springs, CO: Shaw.
Elwood, M. (1942, 1987). *Characters Make Your Story.* Boston: The Writer, Inc.
Forster, E.M. (1962). *Aspects of the Novel.* Middlesex, England: Penguin.
Frey J. (2000). *The Key: How to Write Damn Good Fiction Using the Power of Myth,* New York: St Martin's Griffin.
Gardner, J. (1991). *The Art of Fiction.* New York: Random House.
Gleeson, L. (1999). *Writing Hannah: On Writing for Children.* Sydney: Hale & Iremonger.
Gleeson, L. (2003). *Making Picture Books.* Lindfield, NSW: Scholastic.
Godawa, B. (2009). *Word Pictures: Knowing God Through Story and Imagination.* Downers Grove, Ill: IVP Books.
Graham, R. (2007). *How To Write Fiction (And Think About It).* New York: Palgrave Macmillan.
Hodgins, J. (1993). *A Passion for Narrative.* Toronto, ON: McClelland & Stewart.
Hunt, G. (1978). *Honey for a Child's Heart.* 3rd edn. Grand Rapids, MO: Zondervan.
Klein, C.B. (2016). *The Magic Words: Writing Great Books for Children and Young Adults.* New York: W.W. Norton.
L'Engle, M. (1980). *Walking on Water: Reflections on Faith and Art.* Wheaton, IL: Harold Shaw.
Lamott, A. (2008). *Bird by Bird.* Carlton North, VIC: Scribe.

Le Guin, U. (1998), *Steering the Craft*. Portland, OR: Eighth Mountain Press.
Leaf, C. (2007). *Switch On Your Brain: the Key to Peak Happiness*. Ada, Missouri: Baker Academic.
Lewis, C. S. (1982). Ed W. Hooper. *Of This and Other Worlds*. London: Collins.
Lukeman, N. (2000). *The First Five Pages*. New York: Simon and Schuster.
Lyon, E. (2008). *Manuscript Makeover*. New York: Penguin.
Marsden, G. (1997). *The Outrageous Idea of Christian Scholarship*. Oxford: Oxford University Press.
Marsden, J. (1993). *Everything I Know About Writing*. Sydney: Pan Macmillan.
Melrose, A. (2002). *Write for Children*. London: Routledge Falmer.
Morpurgo, M. (2006). *Singing for Mrs Pettigrew: A Story-maker's Journey*. London: Walker Books.
Nilsson, E. (1992). *Writing for Children*. Ringwood, Vic: Penguin.
Noland, R. (1999). *The Heart of the Artist*. Grand Rapids, MO: Zondervan.
O'Connor, F. (1969). *Mystery and Manners*. New York: Farrar, Straus & Giroux.
Paterson, K. (1988). *A Sense of Wonder*. New York: Penguin.
Prose, F. (2006). *Reading Like a Writer: A Guide for People Who Love Books and for Those Who Want to Write Them*. New York: HarperCollins.
Ryken, L. (2002). *The Christian Imagination*. Colorado Springs, CO: Shaw.
Schaeffer, F. (1973). *Art and the Bible*. Downers Grove, Ill: IVP.
Seuling, B. (2005). 3rd Edn. *How to Write a Children's Book and Get it Published*. Hoboken, NJ: John Wiley.
Strunk, W. Jr. and White, E. B. (1959). *Elements of Style*. New York: Macmillan.
Suen, A. (2003). *Picture Writing*. Cincinnati, OH: Writers' Digest.
Tolkien, J.R.R. (1947). 'On Fairy Stories' in *Essays Presented to Charles Williams*. Oxford: Oxford University Press.
Tredinnick, M. (2006). *The Little Red Writing Book*. Sydney: University of New South Wales Press.

Reading Lists

Truss, L. (2003). *Eats, Shoots and Leaves*. London: Profile Books.
Ware, J. (2003). *God of the Fairy Tale*. Colorado Springs, CO: Shaw.
Vogler, C. (1992). *The Writer's Journey*. London: Pan Books.
Yolen, J. (2006). *Take Joy: A Writer's Guide to Loving the Craft*. Cincinnati, OH: Writers Digest.
Zinsser, W. (1998). *Worlds of Childhood: the Art and Craft of Writing for Children*. New York: Houghton Mifflin.

Journals
Magpies – Talking about books for children and YA.
 https://www.magpies.net.au
Reading Time – The Children's Book Council Journal
 http://readingtime.com.au
The Literature Base https://www.magpies.net.au/the-literature-base
Pass It On – Australia's premier children's book industry e-zine
 https://jackiehoskingpio.wordpress.com
The School Magazine, a literary magazine for children.
 http://theschoolmagazine.com.au
The Book Curator: The Librarian's Guide to Books for Kids & Teens. https://www.bookcurator.com.au

Websites
Fox, M. 'Tips for writing picture books.'
 http://memfox.com/category/for-writers
Lowe, V. Information about writing picture books:
 http://createakidsbook.alphalink.com.au
Buzz Words at www.buzzwordsmagazone.com
Hosking, J. See www.pass-it-on-blog.blogspot.com for publishing and poetry resources.
Jill McDougall has an e-book: *Become a Children's Writer.*
 www.jillmcdougall.com.au
McAlister, M. www.writing4success.com (Marg generously sends tip sheets.)
Sampson, A. https://theideaofhome.blogspot.com.au/

Reviews
www.childrensbooksdaily.com
www.kids-bookreview.com
Visit publishers' and authors' sites.

Especially for YA
Australian Centre for Youth Literature:
    http://www.slv.vic.gov.au/learn/centre-youth-literature
Australian Young Adult Literature sites and information
    http://www.squidoo.com/australian_ya_fiction
Inside a Dog: www.insideadog.com.au
Loveozya: http://loveozya.com.au/
YA reviews and interviews with authors: http://www.yarr-a.com

Chapter Notes

Chapter 1 A Writing Life
[1] L'Engle, M. (1980). *Walking on Water: Reflections on Faith & Art*. Wheaton, IL: Harold Shaw, p. 18.
[2] Ueland, B. (1938, 1987). *If you Want to Write*. Saint Paul, MN: Graywolf Press, p. 4.
[3] Buzan, T. (1993). *The Mind Map Book*. London: BBC Books.
[4] Klauser, H.A. (1987). *Writing on Both Sides of the Brain*. New York: HarperCollins.
[5] Hawke, R. (2005). *Jack & Jen in Oz and the Genesis of Glanville Park*, unpublished PhD thesis. [Krauss, R. (1994). *The Originality of the Avant-Garde and Other Modernist Myths*. Cambridge, MA: MIT Press, p. 167.]
[6] 'Interview with Sherryl Jordan.' URL: https://www.bookcouncil.org.nz/writer/jordan-sherryl/
[7] Sampson, A. (2013). 'Prayer as the Birthplace of Creativity' in *Zadok*, 118, Autumn, p. 2.
[8] L'Engle, M. (1980). *Walking on Water: Reflections on Faith & Art*. Wheaton, IL: Harold Shaw, p. 75.
[9] Elsheimer, J. (2001). *The Creative Call*. Colorado Springs, CO: Waterbrook Press, p. 5.
[10] PH Court (2018) Personal correspondence, 27 April. Used with permission. Court is an academic and author of *Sub Urban Tales*.
[11] Noland, R. (1999). *The Heart of the Artist*. Grand Rapids, MI: Zondervan.
[12] Shanahan, L. Facebook, March 28, 2018, 12 p.m. Used with permission @lisashanahan
[13] Laube, S. https://www.writefromthedeep.com/success-conversation-steve-laube/
[14] Lamott, A. (2008). *Bird by Bird.* Carlton North, VIC: Scribe, p. 178.
[15] Prose, F. (2006). *Reading like a Writer*. New York: HarperCollins, p. 4.
[16] Lamott, A. (2008). *Bird by Bird.* Carlton North, VIC: Scribe, p. 121.

[17] Zorn, C. (2018). 'Booktopia Ten Terrifying Questions.' Personal Correspondence, 11 Dec. Used with permission of the author.

[18] Snow, E. (2018). *Then there was You*. Edinburgh, SA: Elephant House Press, p. 8.

Chapter 2 Children's Literature

[1] Hunt, P. (1994). *An Introduction to Children's Literature*. Oxford: Oxford University Press, p. 3.

[2] Fensham, E. (2013). Personal correspondence, 28 June. Used with permission.

[3] In Goldberg, N. (1986). *Writing Down the Bones*. Boston: Shambhala, p. 113.

[4] Saxby, M. (1997). *Books in the Life of a Child*. South Yarra, VIC: Macmillan, p. 19.

[5] Dahl, D. (1982). *The Peerless Roald Dahl discusses his Work and Loves, on Pebble Mill at One*. BBC Archive. Accessed at URL:https://www.facebook.com/BBCArchive/videos/474625489577153

[6] In Zinsser, W. (1998). *Worlds of Childhood*. Boston: Houghton Mifflin, p. 14.

[7] Veith, G.E. (1990). *Reading between the Lines: a Christian Guide to Literature*. Wheaton, IL: Crossway, p. 28.

[8] Hooper, W. (ed). (1982). *CS Lewis: Of this and other Worlds*. London: HarperCollins*Religious*, p. 43.

[9] Nilsson, E. (1992). *Writing for Children*. Ringwood, VIC: Penguin, p. 2.

[10] Quoted in Ricketson, M. (2000). *Paul Jennings*. Ringwood, VIC: Penguin, p. 130.

[11] Marwood, L. (2012). Personal correspondence, 5 March. Used with permission. www.lorrainemarwood.com

Chapter 3 Keeping Fit: Writing and Storytelling

[1] Godawa, B. (2002). 'Redemption in the Movies' in *The Christian Imagination,* (ed.). L. Ryken.

Chapter Notes

[2] Lambert, R., Rilstone, A., & Wallis, J. (2015). Artwork by Omar Rayyan. John Nephew, Atlas Games: www.atlas-games.com
[3] Zorn, C. (2018). Personal correspondence, 10 Dec. Used with permission.

Chapter 4 Characters can write your Story
[1] Elwood, M. (1942, 1987). *Characters Make Your Story*. Boston, USA: The Writer, Inc., p. 1.
[2] Buzan, T. (1993). *The Mind Map Book*. London: BBC Books. www.buzan.com.au
[3] John Marsden speaking at Adelaide Writers Week Festival, 2004.
[4] Cornish, D.M. (2013). Personal correspondence, 16 July. Used with permission.
[5] Dixon, D. (1996). *GMC: Goal, Motivation and Conflict*. Memphis, TN: Gryphon Books for Writers, p. 10.
[6] Snow, E. (2018). *Then there was You*. Edinburgh, SA: Elephant House Press, p. 32. Used with permission.
[7] Shanahan, L. (2018). Personal correspondence, 14 April. Used with permission. www.lisashanahan.com www.facebook.com/lisashanahanbooks

Chapter 5 Characters and Plot
[1] Dufresne, J. (2003). *The Lie that Tells a Truth.* New York: Norton, p. 160.
[2] Forster writes about this in his book *Aspects of the Novel* on p 38 and also in his chapter on plot.
[3] Aristotle. (1996). Trans: Malcolm Heath. *Poetics*. London: Penguin Classics, p. 13.
[4] Hodgins, J. (1993). *A Passion for Narrative.* Toronto: McClelland & Stewart, p. 126.
[5] Forster E.M. (1962). *Aspects of the Novel*. Middlesex, England: Penguin, p. 33.
[6] Gardner, J. (1991). *The Art of Fiction.* New York: Random House, p. 56.
[7] Yolen, J. (2006). *Take Joy*. Cincinnati, OH: Writers Digest, p. 146.

[8] Hodgins, J. (1993). *A Passion for Narrative.* Toronto: McClelland & Stewart, p. 127.

[9] Dixon, D. (1996). *GMC: Goal, Motivation and Conflict.* Memphis, TN: Gryphon Books for Writers.

[10] L'Engle, M. (1980). *Walking on Water: Reflections on Faith and Art.* Wheaton, IL: Harold Shaw, p. 22.

[11] Campbell. J. (1968). 2nd ed. *The Hero with a Thousand Faces.* Princeton, NJ: Princeton University Press, p. 3.

[12] Vogler, C. (1999). *The Writer's Journey.* (2nd edn). London: Pan Macmillan, p. 1.

[13] Yolen, J. (2006). *Take Joy*. Cincinnati, OH: Writers Digest, p. 147.

[14] Hodgins, J. (1993). *A Passion for Narrative.* Toronto: McClelland & Stewart, p. 142.

[15] Aristotle. (1996). Trs: Malcolm Heath. *Poetics*. London: Penguin Classics, p. 17.

[16] Snow, E. (2018). 'write'. *Then there was You.* Edinburgh, SA: Elephant House Press, p. 65. Used with permission.

Chapter 6 Writing Short Stories

[1] Melrose, A. (2004). *Write for Children*. London: RoutledgeFalmer, p. x

[2] French, J. (2018). 'Don't call us Nice'. *The Australian Author 1969-2018*, Vol 50, No 2, p. 129.

[3] Dixon, S. (2015). *Countdown, School Magazine.* October, Vol. 100, No 9, p. 7. Used with permission of the author.

Chapter 7 Writing Picture Books

[1] Fox, M. 'The Gossip behind *The Green Sheep.* https://memfox.com/gossip-behind-mems- books/where-is-the-green-sheep-illustrated-by-judy-horacek/

[2] Zinsser, W. (1998). *Worlds of Childhood.* Boston: Houghton Mifflin, p.14.

[3] Nilsson, E. (1992). *Writing for Children.* Ringwood, VIC: Penguin, p. 2.

[4] Nilsson, E. (1992). *Writing for Children.* Ringwood, VIC: Penguin, p. 4.

Chapter Notes

[5] L'Engle, M. (1980). *Walking on Water: Reflections on Faith and Art.* Wheaton, IL: Harold Shaw, p. 18.

[6] Gable, J. (Director). (2005). 'Interview'. *Keith Urban Livin' Right Now*. Nashville: Guitar Monkey Entertainment.

[7] Nilsson, E. (1992). *Writing for Children.* Ringwood, VIC: Penguin, p. 39.

[8] Hosking, J. https://jackiehoskingblog.wordpress.com/jackies-editing-service/

[9] Hosking, J. *Rhyme like the Experts* available at: https://jackiehoskingblog.wordpress.com/jackies-editing-service/

[10] Nilsson, E. (1992). *Writing for Children.* Ringwood, VIC: Penguin, p. 52.

[11] Cummings, P. & Swan, O. (2015). *Newspaper Hats*. Lindfield, NSW: Scholastic, pp. 4-5.

[12] Fox, M. 'Tips for Writing Picture books.' http://memfox.com/category/for-writers

[13] Brian, J. (2013). *Countdown, School Magazine*, August, issue No. 7, p. 33.

[14] Brian, J. (2013). *Touchdown, School Magazine*, May, Issue No. 4, p. 11.

[15] Brian, J. (2018). *Touchdown, School Magazine*, April, Issue No. 3, p. 26.

[16] Brian, J. (2009). *Touchdown, School Magazine,* June, Issue No 5, p. 21.

[17] Booth, C. (2012). Personal correspondence, 28 March. Used with Permission. https://www.christinabooth.com/

Chapter 8 Chapter Books for Early Readers

[1] Hawke, R. (2004). *The Collector.* South Melbourne: Lothian.

[2] Cowley, J. (2010). *Writing from the Heart: How to Write for Children*. Honesdale, PA: Boyds Mills Press, p. 41.

[3] Brian, J. (2005). *Rock and Roll Ducks.* Camberwell, VIC: Penguin, pp. 1-3.

[4] Brian, J. (2005). *Rock and Roll Ducks.* Camberwell, VIC: Penguin, pp. 15-16.

[5] Brian, J. (2005). *Rock and Roll Ducks.* Camberwell, VIC: Penguin, p. 1

[6] Nilsson, E. (1992). *Writing for Children*. Ringwood, VIC: Penguin, p. 60.

[7] Cowley, J. (2010). *Writing from the Heart: How to Write for Children*. Honesdale, PA: Boyds Mills Press, p. 41.

[8] Nilsson, E. (1992). *Writing for Children*. Ringwood, VIC: Penguin, p. 58.

[9] Cowley, J. (2010). *Writing from the Heart: How to Write for Children*. Honesdale, PA: Boyds Mills Press, p. 34.

[10] Cowley, J. (2010). *Writing from the Heart: How to Write for Children*. Honesdale, PA: Boyds Mills Press, p. 40.

[11] Apel, K. (2018). Personal correspondence, 6 July. Used with Permission. https://katswhiskers.wordpress.com

Chapter 9 Writing Novels for Middle Grade

[1] Browne, R. and King, D. (2001). *Self-editing for Fiction Writers*. New York: Quill/Harper Resource, p. 99.

[2] Dufresne, J. (2003). *The Lie That Tells a Truth: A Guide to Writing Fiction*. New York: Norton, p. 197.

[3] Millard, G. (2003). *The Naming of Tishkin Silk*. Sydney: ABC Books, p.11. Printed with permission of the author.

[4] Hawke R. (2013). *Sailmaker*. St Lucia, QLD: Queensland University Press, p. 44.

[5] Cummings, P. (2007). *Danny Allen was here*. Sydney: Pan Macmillan, p. 105.

[6] Cummings, P. (2007). *Danny Allen was here*. Sydney: Pan Macmillan, p. 105.

[7] Ryken, L. (1989). *The Liberated Imagination*. Eugene, OR: Wipf & Stock, p. 120.

[8] Hawke, R. (2013). *Sailmaker*. St Lucia, QLD: University of Queensland Press, p. 2.

[9] Hawke, R. (2013). *Sailmaker*. St Lucia, QLD: University of Queensland Press, p. 40.

[10] Hawke, R. (2013). *Sailmaker*. St Lucia, QLD: University of Queensland Press, p. 66.

[11] Hawke, R. (2013). *Sailmaker*. St Lucia, QLD: University of Queensland Press, p. 124.

Chapter Notes

[12] Godden, R. http://www.powell-pressburger.org/Obits/Godden/Telegraph.html
[13] O'Connor, F. (1984). *Mystery and Manners Occasional Prose.* London: Faber, p. 101-102.
[14] Hawke, R. (2017). *Across the Creek.* Northcote, VIC: Stone Table Books, p. 7.
[15] Daley, M. *Children's Books Daily*. URL: childrensbooksdaily.com
[16] Deller-Evans, K. (2011). 'Out of the Drought: Australia's Junior Verse novels.' *Write4Children*, Vol 3, Issue 1, p. 68-75. URL: https://vanessaharbour.wixsite.com/write4children
[17] CBCA Judges Report 2018. URL: https://cbcacloud.blob.core.windows.net/documents/National/BookOfTheYear/2018/Judges_Report_2018.pdf
[18] Hooper, W. (1982). Ed. *CS Lewis: Of this and Other Worlds*. London: HarperCollins*Religious*, p. 58.
[19] Ann Greer's thesis on magical realism can be read at the library of Tabor Adelaide.
[20] Lloyd, A. (2019). Personal correspondence, 15 Feb. Used with permission. www.alisonlloyd.com.au

Chapter 10 Novels for Middle School & YA

[1] Tolkien J.R. (2014). *On Fairy Stories.* Eds Anderson, D.A. & V. Flieger. Sydney: HarperCollins.
[2] Mordue, M. (2003). 'The Secret Life of us.' *Australian Author*. Sydney: Australian Society of Authors, Vol 35, No. 1, April.
[3] Gurdon, M.C. (2011). 'Darkness too Visible'. WSJ. URL: https://www.wsj.com/articles/SB10001424052702304314404576411581289319732
[4] Brooks, R. (2009). *Writing great Books for Young Adults.* Naperville, IL: Sourcebooks, Chapter 1.
[5] Mordue, M. (2003). 'The Secret Life of us.' *Australian Author*. Sydney: Australian Society of Authors, Vol 35, No. 1, April, p.14.

[6] Hawke, R. (2015). *The Keeper*. St Lucia, QLD: University of Queensland Press, p. 28.
[7] Jordan, S. URL: https://www.encyclopedia.com/arts/educational-magazines/jordan-sherryl-1949-sherryl-brogden
[8] Hunt, J. in Brooks, R. (2009). *Writing Great Books for Young Adults*. Naperville, IL: Sourcebooks, p. 26.
[9] Browne, R. and King, D. (1993). *Self-editing for Fiction Writers*. New York: HarperCollins, p. 174.
[10] Hawke, R. (2010). *Marrying Ameera*. Sydney: HarperCollins, p. 81.
[11] Hawke, R. (2006). *The Last Virgin in Year 10*. South Melbourne: Lothian, p. 27.
[12] Hawke, R. (2017). *Wolfchild: A Year and a Day*. Northcote, VIC: Stone Table Books, p. 9.
[13] Hawke, R. (2012). *The Messenger Bird*. St Lucia, QLD: University of Queensland Press, p. 3.
[14] Fictitious Year 12 exam responses available online.
[15] Starke, R. in *Pass It On*. (2007). https://jackiehoskingpio.wordpress.com 11th June.
[16] Starke, R. in *Pass It On*. (2007). https://jackiehoskingpio.wordpress.com 18th June.
[17] Benning, M. (2015). 'Poet'. E Calder et al (eds.). *Tales from the Upper Room*. Hackham, SA: Immortalise, p. 83. Used with permission.
[18] Forsyth, K. 'Interview with Sherryl Jordan'. URL: http://www.kateforsyth.com.au/kates-blog/interview-sherryl-jordan
[19] Zorn, C. (2018). Personal Correspondence, 11 Dec. Used with permission. https://clairezorn.com

Chapter 11 Re-writing and Editing as Writers
[1] Dixon, S. (1996). *Goal, Motivation and Conflict*. Memphis, TN: Gryphon Books for Writers. p. 36.
[2] Hawke, R. (2013). *Sailmaker*. St Lucia, QLD: University of Queensland Press, p. 10.
[3] Hawke, R. (2018). *Finding Kerra*. Capabala, QLD: Rhiza Edge, p.75.

Chapter Notes

[4] Hawke, R. (2010). *Marrying Ameera*. Sydney: HarperCollins, p. 235.
[5] Hawke, R. (2018). *Finding Kerra.* Capabala, QLD: Rhiza Edge, p 43.
[6] Conrad, B. & Schultz, M. (2002). *Snoopy's Guide to the Writing Life*. Cincinnati, OH: Writer's Digest Books, p.169.
[7] Le Guin, U. (1998). *Steering the Craft.* Portland, OR: Eighth Mountain Press, p. 63.
[8] Le Guin, U. (1998). *Steering the Craft.* Portland, OR: Eighth Mountain Press, p. 62.
[9] Hawke, R. (2011). *Taj and the Great Camel Trek.* St Lucia, QLD: University of Queensland Press, p. 125.
[10] Worthing, M.W. (n.d.). *The Poetic Circle*. Unpublished manuscript, used with permission by the author.
[11] Worthing, M.W. (n.d.). *The Poetic Circle*. Unpublished manuscript, used with permission by the author.
[12] Belberg, C. (2006). This checklist compiled by Claire Bell (now writing as Claire Belberg) from lectures and practice. Used with permission.
[13] Snow, E. (2018). 'archaeology'. *Then There Was You*. Edinburgh, SA: Elephant House Press, p. 67.

Chapter 12 Reflecting On Our Writing
[1] Forster, E.M. (1962). *Aspects of the Novel.* Middlesex, England: Penguin, p. 108-109. This is often attributed to Forster but he is actually quoting from the 1925 novel *Les Faux Monnayeurs* (*The Counterfeiters*) by Andre Gide.
[2] Graham, R. (2007). *How To Write Fiction (And Think About It).* New York: Palgrave Macmillan, p. 105.
[3] Tuovinen, C. *Author Statement*. Unpublished document. Used with permission.
[4] Fox, M. 'Page-ripping writer's rage: from first idea to final word in a picture book.' https://memfox.com/ gossip-behind-mems-books/where-is-the-green-sheep-illustrated-by-judy-horacek/
[5] Gleeson, L. (1999). *Writing Hannah: on Writing for Children*. Sydney: Hale & Iremonger.

[6] Hawke, R. (2017). 'The Joy of Rewriting *The War Within'*. https://rosannehawke.wordpress.com/ 2016/10/15/the-joy-of-rewriting
[7] Hawke, R. (2011). 'Crossing Borders in Faith and Culture: Writing *Marrying Ameera*'. *Write4Children*. Vol 3, Issue 1, p. 44-55. URL: https://vanessaharbour.wixsite.com/write4children
[8] *Text Journal.* www.textjournal.com.au/
[9] Marsden, G.E. (1997). *The Outrageous Idea of Christian Scholarship*. Oxford: Oxford University Press, p. 10.
[10] Hawke, R. (2014). 'Art and the Sacred'. *Review: The Christian School Library Magazine*, February, p. 4. Introduction by Rowena Beresford.
[11] L'Engle, M. (1980). *Walking on Water: Reflections on Faith and Art.* Wheaton, IL: Harold Shaw, p. 16.
[12] Belberg, C. (2019). Personal correspondence, 13 Feb. Used with permission.
[13] Jaye, P. (2018). Personal correspondence, 23 Nov. Used with permission. https://www.pennyjaye.com

Chapter 13 Writing for Children Matters
[1] Hazard, P. in Saxby, M. (1997). *Books in the Life of a Child*. South Yarra, VIC: MacMillan, p. 41.
[2] Saxby, M. (1997). *Books in the Life of a Child*. South Yarra, VIC: MacMillan, p. 41.
[3] Reece, N. (2012). 'Worth a Thousand Words: the Top Ten Best Australian Picture Books.' *The Conversation.* URL: https://theconversation.com/worth-a-thousand-words-the-top-ten-best-australian-childrens-picture-books-11359
[4] Ware, J. (2003). *God of the Fairy Tale*. Colorado Springs, CO: Shaw, p. 8.
[5] Saxby, M. (1997). *Books in the Life of a Child*. South Yarra, VIC: MacMillan, p. 264, paraphrased.
[6] Allberry, S. https://www.thegospelcoalition.org/profile/sam-allberry
[7] Klein, C. B. (2016). *The Magic Words: Writing Great Books for Children and Young Adults*. New York: Norton, p. 7.

Chapter Notes

[8] Gwynne, P. (2002). *The Sydney Morning Herald*, 9 April.

[9] Arundhati Roy is an Indian writer who is also an activist who focuses on issues related to social justice and economic inequality. She won the Booker Prize in 1997 for her novel, *The God of Small Things*.

[10] Boori Monty Pryor said this in 2012 at his Children's Literature Laureate speech in Carclew House, North Adelaide.

[11] (2002).*Writing Cultures: protocols for producing Indigenous Australian Literature.* Commonwealth of Australia, Sydney. URL: http://www.australiacouncil.gov.au/workspace/uploads/files/writing-protocols-for-indigeno-5b4bfc67dd037.pdf

[12] Lim, May-Kuan. (2018). Personal correspondence, 3 Dec. Used with Permission.

[13] 'The Copyright Agency Australia'. URL: https://www.copyright.com.au/

[14] Eggins, S. (2005). 'More than just a Laugh'. *Good Reading.* March.

[15] Monk, S. (2008). 'The Word and the Wordsmith'. *CASE*. No 16, p. 19. Used with permission.

[16] Lurie, A. (1990). *Don't tell the Grown Ups: Subversive Children's Literature*. Boston: Little, Brown. Oona Eisenstadt discusses this subject on her blog URL: https://oonae.wordpress.com/2008/07/29/subversive-childrens-literature/

[17] Godawa, B. (2009). *Word Pictures: Knowing God through Story and Imagination.* Downers Grove, Illinois: IVP Books, p. 136.

[18] L'Engle, M. (1985). *Trailing Clouds of Glory: Spiritual Values in Children's Books.* Philadelphia, PN: The Westminster Press, p. 62.

[19] Lansdown, A. (2002). *Harry Potter: Witchcraft or Story-craft?* Nollamara, WA: Life Ministries.

[20] Monk, S. (2008). 'The Word and the Wordsmith'. *CASE*. No 16, p. 21.

[21] Saxby, M. (1997). *Books in the Life of a Child*. South Yarra, VIC: MacMillan, p. 12.

[22] Paterson, K. (1995). *A Sense of Wonder: On Reading and Writing Books for Children*. New York: Penguin, p. 182, 301.
[23] Cooper, J. (2018). Personal correspondence, 17 Sept. Used with permission. Dr Cooper is the coordinator of the creative writing program at Tabor Adelaide.

Chapter 14 Preparing for Publication
[1] *Pass It On* – Australia's premier children's book industry e-zine https://jackiehoskingpio.wordpress.com
[2] Susan J Bruce is the editor of *If They Could Talk* (2018). Personal correspondence. Used with Permission.

Chapter 15 A Publishing Story
[1] TCK: Third culture kids, children who are brought up in a culture different from their parent's culture.
[2] England, K. (2002). 'Review of *Zenna Dare*' in *The Advertiser*. Sept 14, p. 11.
[3] Kennedy, M. (ed). (2013). *Reaching Out: Messages of Hope*. Sydney: HarperCollins.

Chapter 16 Being an Author
[1] Australian Society of Authors URL: https://www.asauthors.org
[2] Julia Straus-Gabel is an editor and publisher of Dutton Books, US and spoke at the SCBWI LA conference and said this. She works with writers like John Green.
[3] Claire Belberg is the author of *The Golden Hour* (2017) and blogs at *The Character Forge*: clairebelberg.wordpress.com Personal correspondence. Used with permission.
[4] Purportedly written on Mother Teresa's room in Calcutta and seems to be based on a version by Dr Kent M. Keith. Available widely online, but this version is said to be accredited to Mother Teresa. URL:http://prayerfoundation.org/mother_teresa_do_it_anyway.htm
[5] Australian Society of Authors. URL:https://www.asauthors.org/https://www.asauthors.org

Chapter Notes

/findananswer/rates-of-pay#SCHOOL%20APPEARANCES

[6] Glazebrook, J. (2018). Christian Writers Downunder Blogspot. URL:https://christianwritersdownunder.blogspot.com/2018/12/when-ive-lost-my-vision.html?fbclid=IwAR0rCUrP4CPcXVSERW-OduxyGByjp3MbwrggZoO2-2TaDy7dqPoXso3fUYw Dec 20th. Used with permission.

[7] Wyatt, J. (2015). 'Writer's Prayer.' E Calder, et al (eds.). *Tales from the Upper Room.* Hackham West, SA: Immortalise. Used with permission.

Also by Rosanne Hawke

Picture Books
Chandani and the Ghost of the Forest with L Penner, L Cooper (illus)
The Wish Giver with L Penner, M Macintosh (illus)
Mustara, R Ingpen (illus)
Yardil, E Stanley (illus)

Chapter Book
The Collector

Middle Grade Novels
Jehan and the Quest of the Lost Dog
Wolfchild
Across the Creek
The Leopard Princess
Daughter of Nomads
Kelsey and the Quest of the Porcelain Doll
Kerenza: A new Australian
Shahana: Through My Eyes
Killer Ute
Sailmaker
The Keeper
Taj and the Great Camel Trek
Soraya, the Storyteller

YA Novels
Finding Kerra
Liana's Dance
The War Within
Dear Pakistan
The Truth about Peacock Blue
Zenna Dare
Mountain Wolf
The Messenger Bird
Marrying Ameera
The Last Virgin in Year 10
Borderland
A Kiss in Every Wave

www.ingramcontent.com/pod-product-compliance
Lightning Source LLC
Chambersburg PA
CBHW072039160426
43197CB00014B/2549